RELATIVE DEPRIVATION AND WORKING WOMEN

RELATIVE DEPRIVATION AND WORKING WOMEN

FAYE J. CROSBY

YALE UNIVERSITY

New York   Oxford
OXFORD UNIVERSITY PRESS
1982

Copyright © 1982 by Oxford University Press, Inc.

Library of Congress Cataloging in Publication Data
Crosby, Faye, 1947–
Relative deprivation and working women.

Bibliography: p.
Includes index.
1. Women—Employment.   2. Job satisfaction.
3. Deprivation (Psychology)   I. Title.
HD6053.C8   158.7′088′042   81-22527
ISBN 0-19-503146-6   AACR2
ISBN 0-19-503147-4 (pbk.)

Printing (last digit): 9 8 7 6 5 4 3 2 1

Printed in the United States of America

To Toad, Tim, and Travis

Preface

It is sometimes true that the better off one is, the worse off one feels; and it is almost never true that one's feelings of satisfaction grow or diminish as rapidly and constantly as do one's actual fortunes. The relationship between objective and subjective well-being, in short, is far from isomorphic. Feelings of grievance depend less on one's outcomes in an absolute sense than on one's situation relative to some psychological standard. The nature of that standard and of the processes by which one comes to feel dissatisfaction have been the subject of relative deprivation research during the last four decades. One aim of this book is to enhance our understanding of the dynamics of deprivation. It contributes most directly to the research on relative deprivation by submitting various formulations of relative deprivation and cognate theories to validational testing.

Another aim is to describe the reactions of women and men to their job situations, their home situations, and the job situations of women generally. Rapid changes in sex-role stereotypes, in women's labor force participation, and in the prevalence of dual-worker families all invite an examination of issues currently surrounding the topic of women and work. Our examination is aided by—and indeed, to some degree, guided by—the theory of relative deprivation. Our attempt represents one of the first efforts to bring an established social science theory to bear on the question of working women.

To meet both the theoretical and the descriptive aims, we use data from a survey funded by the National Institute of Mental Health. In many ways this book tells the story of the research process itself. Convinced that a researcher's conclusions depend in part on his or her research strategies, I have tried to be explicit about the assumptions with which I began the research, the methods I used for collecting information, and the means by which I have analyzed the information.

Some aspects of this book will have special appeal for scholars in the behavioral sciences. There is also much here of general interest. My wish to reach both the specialist and the general reader has influenced the style and the organization of the book. Most chapters begin by indicating the flow of the argument and end by summarizing the major findings. Detailed information supporting the argument is reserved for the center portion of the chapters and is often contained in tables and figures. Chapter 8, in which we test relative deprivation theory, is more technical than the descriptive chapters that precede it. Even in the descriptive chapters, statistical procedures are used to determine the reliability of apparent effects. Analyses of variance (ANOVAs) are used, for example, to establish attitudinal differences among employed women, employed men, and housewives. Appendix I describes the logic of ANOVAs. It is intended to make accessible to the general reader the intricacies of my argument. Readers who are not conversant with inferential statistics but who wish to follow the complex details of my descriptive findings are urged to consult Appendix I. Also in the interest of the general reader, I have omitted F-values and p-values from the text. The advanced reader should assume that any specific findings I report are statistically significant unless otherwise indicated.

A few other points about terminology and word usage deserve comment. The term "working women" means here "women with paid employment." This is not intended to denigrate housework. The phrase is a matter of style and not of ideology. The same applies to the occasional use of the generic "he." In contrast, my use of the pronoun "we" throughout the book is not determined simply by stylistic preferences. It is also used to acknowledge that the research upon which the book is based has been, from first to last, a collaborative effort.

This brings me to the offering of thanks. They go first to Abigail Stewart. It was with Abby that the research began. In the initial attempt to study the effects of employment on women, Abby and I were coinvestigators. I am also extremely grateful to Donald Kinder. His concrete suggestions and his general support have been invaluable at critical points in the research enterprise. Without Abby and Don the research would not have been done.

Many individuals gave me guidance, encouragement, and advice before the project started. Thomas Cook, Susan Eckstein, Phoebe Ellsworth, Daniel Friedman, Robin Jones, Joyce Lazar, Pamela Porter, Gary Rosen, and Patricia Salt helped in the early research days. Robert Abelson, Guy Orcutt, Carolyn Sheriff, and Robert Zajonc each made suggestions that might have seemed inconsequential to them but that proved important to the research. Once the study was under way, Morty Bernstein, Beverly Deric, Miren Gonzalez, Laurie Rhodebeck, and Ira Roseman all contributed, as did John Goldin and Charles Reichardt. Ira kindly allowed the Roseman Mood List to be used in the survey. Larry Kerpelman, with the help of Linda deSimone, both of Abt Associates, Inc., directed the survey itself. Lindsay Evans and Elise Parker managed the New Haven operations. Susan Proctor, Sonia Meaddough, Pam Costas, and Madeline Cohen typed major segments of the work. Roxianne Bertolini, Bea Mills, and Andrée and Bob Newman helped in several ways. To all of these people, I say thank you.

I am also indebted to my editor, Marcus Boggs, to Betty Gatewood and to several colleagues who reacted to various versions of the book. In addition to Don and Abby, Philip Brickman, Elisabeth Croll, Travis Crosby, Robert Folger, Ronnie Janoff Bulman, David Kenny, Louise Kidder, Chaya Piotrkowski, Laurie Rhodebeck, Janice Steil, Janet Weiss, and Mark Zanna all have earned my thanks for their thoughtful comments on earlier drafts of the book.

I am glad to acknowledge the generous support of the National Institute of Mental Health. Grant R01-MH31595 covered the costs of the research from September 1978 through August 1981. To Yale University I am grateful for a Junior Faculty Fellowship during the academic year 1980–81. The manuscript was written during the Fellowship year. The residents of Newton have earned my thanks many times over. The survey hinged on their cooperation. Finally, the love and support of my family have helped fill my work with joy.

New Haven   F.J.C.
January 1982

Contents

RELATIVE DEPRIVATION AND WORKING WOMEN

1

Introduction

The working woman is no longer an oddity in America. Since World War II, female participation in the labor market has increased steadily. The percentage of women who work rose from 33.9 in 1950 to 44.7 in 1973 (Hayghe, 1976). By 1980 there were 44 million women in the paid economy (U.S. Department of Labor, 1980b). The Department of Labor estimates that women aged twenty-five to forty will account for approximately half of the total labor force growth in the last quarter of the twentieth century (Fullerton & Flaim, 1976). Recent statistics show "steep annual increases in the number and proportion of working wives" (U.S. Department of Labor, 1979b; Waite, 1976). The sharpest rise is in the number of workers who are mothers of young children (Johnson & Hayghe, 1977). In 1968 the paid labor force included about 25 percent of American women with children under age three; a decade later, the figure was 40 percent (U.S. Department of Labor, 1979a). From figures such as these, the government concludes that the "increase in women's labor force activity" throughout the 1970s has been "extraordinary" (U.S. Department of Labor, 1980a).

The literature on working women has also increased rapidly in the last few years (Astin, Suniewick, & Dweck, 1971; Een & Rosenberg-Dishman, 1978; Huber, 1973; Kahne, 1975, 1978; Kahne & Hybels 1978). Many studies are sponsored by the Department of Labor and appear regularly in the *Monthly Labor Review*. Although primarily concerned with tracking female participation in the labor market, the Department of Labor reports periodically on sex differentiation and sex discrimination.

According to one report, only four in ten working women in 1977 had avoided the ranks of clerical, service, or retail sales workers (U.S. Department of Labor, 1978b). Among year-round full-time workers in May 1978, the median weekly earnings were $279 for white males; $218 for black males; $167 for white females; and $158 for black females (U.S. Department of Labor, 1978a). In other words, white women earned on average only 60 percent of what white males earned and less than 80 percent of what black males earned. For black women the statistics were, of course, even more grim.

Academic studies confirm the observation that women face considerable disadvantages throughout their working lives (Darling, 1975; Epstein, 1970; Kahne, 1975; Kreps, 1971; Lloyd, 1975; Madden, 1973; White, 1967; Wolf & Fligstein, 1979). Women are crowded into the low-status, poorly rewarded jobs (Mennerick, 1975; Reagan & Blaxall, 1976). Sex differentiation appears to be decreasing in new fields such as computer science, but it persists in more traditional segments of the economy (Gross, 1968; Williams, 1976).

Simple analyses of the sex composition of various occupations constitute only part of the evidence of sex discrimination. Blatant differences in earnings also speak loudly of discrimination (Vetter, 1981). Using sophisticated statistical procedures, economists and sociologists find that female workers earn much less than comparable male workers (Featherman & Hauser, 1976; McClendon, 1976; McLaughlin, 1978; Treiman & Terrell, 1975). Typical is an analysis by Suter and Miller (1973) of unpublished census data for men and women aged thirty to forty-four. They note that the women in 1967 earned 39 percent of what men earned. They then adjust the female salary to compensate for sex differences in education, job level, amount worked in a year, and years of experience. The sizes of the adjustments are determined by the importance of each factor for predicting male salaries. After all adjustments are made, a gap of approximately $3,000 remains; the female worker is paid only 62 percent of what she would earn as a male.

A series of unobtrusive experiments have yielded further evidence of sex discrimination. In the experiments, men and women are usually requested to react to stimuli such as the job résumé of a supposed job applicant. Generally, the experimental stimuli differ in terms of sex, but are otherwise identical.

Stereotyping, prejudice, and discrimination are found again and again among samples of potential employers (Fiedel, 1970; Haefner, 1977a; Levinson, 1975), managers (Cecil, Paul, & Olins, 1973; Rosen & Jerdee, 1974; Rosen, Jerdee, & Prestwich, 1975; Schein, 1975), recruiters (Cohen & Bunker, 1975), interviewers (Dipboye, Fromkin, & Wiback, 1975), and workers (Haefner, 1977b; Quadagno, 1976). Only college students seem to be relatively free of sex prejudice (Frank & Drucker, 1977; Hall & Hall, 1976; Hesselbart, 1977a, 1977b; Peck, 1978; Spence & Helmreich, 1972; Terborg & Ilgen, 1975).

Despite persistent and often blatant sex discrimination, women express no more dissatisfaction with their jobs than do men (Burke & Weir, 1976; Deaux, 1979; Ebeling, King, & Rogers, 1977; Glenn, Taylor, & Weaver, 1977; Haavio-Mannila, 1971; Hunt & Saul, 1975; Jacobson, 1974; Kuhlen, 1963; Laurence, 1961; Liss, 1975; Miller, Labovitz, & Fry, 1975; Schreiber, 1979; Walker, 1961; Weaver, 1978b). While they may see that women in general are disadvantaged (Ferber & Loeb, 1973), most working women deny that they themselves have been the object of sex discrimination (DeLamater & Fidell, 1971; Kresge, 1970; Linn, 1971; Parrish, 1965; Simon, Clark, & Tifft, 1966). Only in a handful of studies (Epstein, 1971b; Widom & Burke, 1978; Young, MacKenzie, & Sherif, 1980) do women admit that they have encountered sex prejudice or that they are inadequately compensated. Nor are working women aggrieved about poor working conditions. Notman and Nadelson (1973), for example, interviewed female residents and interns. In the face of overt pressures, the fledgling physicians experienced little resentment. Indeed, they seemed to "feel guilty about making *any* demands on a profession that has been 'generous' enough to accept them" (p. 1127). Awareness of discrimination does not necessarily come with experience. During the course of in-depth interviews with seasoned female physicians, Walsh (1977; Walsh & Stewart, 1976) heard some harrowing accounts of prejudice and discrimination. The vast majority of the physicians nonetheless claimed that they had not encountered discrimination

in their careers. Denial seemed especially marked in the older
women. The younger women, who had had relatively fewer
hurdles to leap, seemed somewhat less willing to ignore evidence of sex discrimination than were the older women.

Blue-collar women workers are no more cognizant of sex
discrimination than are professional women (Levitin, Quinn, &
Staines, 1971). Langer (1972) conducted a participant observation study of low-status female employees in the telephone industry. After several months of research, she concluded that
the women around her were generally satisfied with their working conditions because they did not envision any possibility of
change. Even those women who felt "oppressed" evaluated their
predicament as a personal problem and remained oblivious to
the possibility of collective remedial action.

The perception of personal discrimination does not seem to
vary consistently as a function of job level. In other words, the
women who are toward the bottom of the occupational heap
are not necessarily the ones most aware of sex discrimination
(Ginzberg, 1966; Liss, 1975; Tinker, 1971; Young et al., 1980).
Concerning the job situation of women generally, as opposed
to one's own personal situation, it also seems that better-off
women are as aware and as aggrieved as are less well-off women.
Female lawyers, for example, express as much bitterness about
women's working conditions as do female legal secretaries.
Lawyers are as likely as secretaries to perceive that women do
not receive the pay and benefits they deserve (Crosby, 1978).

In sum, scrutiny of the scholarly literature on women and
work reveals some paradoxes. First, at all job levels, women express no more dissatisfaction with their jobs than do men, even
though women earn less and receive fewer fringe benefits. Second, despite discrimination women rarely perceive themselves
as victims of discrimination. Third, perceptions of discrimination and feelings of grievance are equally prevalent among high-
status women workers as among low-status workers. Finally, it
has been in recent years—when job opportunities appear to have
been expanding—that women have expressed more vocifer-
ously than ever before their resentment about sex discrimination.

One promising approach to these paradoxes is the theory

of relative deprivation. Using the theory, Pettigrew (1964, 1967) and others (e.g., Abeles, 1976; Caplan & Paige, 1968; Geschwender & Singer, 1970; Sears & McConahay, 1973) have explained how "actual gains" resulted in "psychological losses" for black Americans in the 1960s. Given the similarities between the position of blacks and the position of women in American society (Hacker, 1951; Myrdal, 1944), it seems probable that the theory might also prove useful for understanding the paradox of the contented woman worker.

Relative deprivation theory centers on the proposition that felt grievances are not simply a function of one's objective situation. Rather, felt deprivation depends on a variety of cognitive-emotional factors. Different models disagree about the specific set of factors that produces resentment, grievance, or deprivation. (We consider these three words as synonyms.) Combining the models, we would say that people who lack some object or opportunity (X) feel deprived of X to the degree that they:

1. want X
2. see that some other or others have X
3. feel entitled to X
4. thought (in the past) that X was attainable
5. think that X will not (in the future) be attainable
6. refrain from blaming themselves for their failure to possess X currently.

One theorist (Crosby, 1976) has labeled the factors "preconditions" of felt deprivation. Potentially, then, the six preconditions of grievance are: (1) wanting; (2) comparison other; (3) deserving; (4) past expectations; (5) future expectations; and (6) no self-blame.

Applying the theory of relative deprivation to the situation of working women suggests that women have been content with their objectively unsatisfactory situation because, for working women, the hypothesized preconditions of deprivation have not been met. It may be, for instance, that women are happy with "dead-end jobs" because they do not want the responsibility, visibility, or inconvenience that are thought to accompany career advancement. Perhaps women do not mind sex differences in pay because they do not especially want money. Maybe women express little discontent because the physical segregation into pink-collar ghettos (Darley, 1976; Howe, 1977) and the social isolation of female bosses (Kanter, 1977a) keep women unaware of the extent of male advantage. Or it may be that women think they deserve fewer rewards than men (Jasso & Rossi, 1977). Certainly, females generally suffer from an atrophied sense of deserving (Deaux, 1976). Women may be complacent about their situation because they never expected better (Hoffman & Reed, 1981), or optimism might be at the root of their complacency. One final explanation for the lack of resentment among working women is the well-known tendency of females to blame themselves when things go wrong (Crandall, Katkovsky, & Crandall, 1965; Dweck & Reppucci, 1973; Hoffman, 1975; Nicholls, 1975).

While any one or all of these explanations may be correct, it is unlikely that they are equally important. One wonders which of the six potential preconditions do, in reality, influence feelings of grievance among working women. Solving this puzzle was the original aim of the research reported here.

As so often happens in the course of inquiry, the search for one set of answers has led to a new set of questions. Marriage and motherhood still shape the lives—including the working lives—of American womankind (Bane, 1976; Bernard, 1973, 1975; Blood, 1965; Kanter, 1977b; Russo, 1976). Ginzberg (1966) reports that his initial efforts to look at women's reactions to employment were foiled by the untidy connections between a woman's work and other aspects of her life. Our interest in women's attitudes toward their labor outside the home, similarly, soon led to a consideration of their labor inside the home. Comparing women's and men's attitudes toward their own jobs, their own home lives, and the job situation of women followed naturally. In this way, what began as a straightforward investigation of discontent has become a much more complicated study of grievances and gratifications. From a narrow concern with the job attitudes of women has emerged a broader inquiry into the feelings of women and men about aspects of their lives at home as well as at work and about the predicament of women.

Two questions are at the heart of our research. First, how do different groups compare with one another in terms of felt deprivations and related factors? To answer this question is the essential descriptive objective of our research. Second, which of the six hypothesized preconditions of deprivation actually do predict resentments felt about one's job, the job situation of women, and one's home life? To answer this question is the essential theoretical aim of the research.

Answers to the two basic questions come from information obtained in interviews with more than 400 employed women, employed men, and housewives. Contrasts between the employed women and the employed men tell us about the role of sex in attitudes. Contrasts between the employed women and the housewives enhance our appreciation of the effects of paid employment on women.

The samples of men and women in the survey have been classified according to job level on the basis of their own occupations or, in the case of housewives, on the basis of their husbands' occupations. Half are in the high-prestige category, half in the low. Many of the sex differences reported in earlier studies are difficult to interpret because the studies confuse sex and job level, with females being overrepresented in low-prestige jobs (Brief & Aldag, 1975; Brief & Oliver, 1976; Brief, Rose, & Aldag, 1977; Gurin, 1977; Kanter, 1976; Rosenbach, Dailey, & Morgan, 1979; Taveggia & Ziemba, 1978). The present study untangles sex and job level. Because we have approximately equal numbers of women and men with high-prestige jobs and approximately equal numbers with low-prestige jobs, we can be certain that apparent sex differences are genuine and that they are not simply the hidden effects of job level. Similarly, by looking at sex and at job level independently of each other, we can gauge the importance of sex relative to job level in determining attitudes. Perhaps the differences between men and women are not spurious but yet are small in comparison with the differences between high- and low-prestige groups.

Finally, we have classified the employed women and men in terms of their family status. Since World War II, women have often had to choose between a family and a job. For women, furthermore, there has been a negative association between job level and family status. That is, the better a woman's job, the less likely she has been to marry or, if married, to have children (Fogarty, Allen, Allen, & Walters, 1971; Havens, 1973). The opposite has been true for men. Perhaps differences in attitudes that in earlier studies appeared to have been due to gender were actually the result of different family situations. The apparently high value that female workers give to interpersonal relations and the apparently high value that male workers give to money and status, for example, may have less to do with female and male motives than with the needs of single people and of parents (Cartwright, 1972; Manhardt, 1972; Reif, Newstrom, & St. Louis, 1976; Saleh & Lalljee, 1969; Schmitt, Coyle, White, & Rauschenberger, 1978; Widom & Burke, 1978). The best way to find out is to look at sex and family status separately. The four groups of employed people (high-prestige males, high-prestige females, low-prestige males, low-prestige females) in the study are each further divided into three approximately equal units of single people, married (but childless) people, and parents.[1]

Group differences are at the crux of our descriptions, but they are irrelevant to our theoretical aim. To test relative deprivation theory and, in particular, to test five different models of relative deprivation, we look at the relationships between the various preconditions and the extent of deprivation. Each model proposes a unique set of preconditions of felt deprivation. Davis (1959), for example, sees wanting, comparison other, and deserving as the essential preconditions of deprivation; but in Gurr's (1970) model, the essential preconditions are wanting, deserving, and low future expectations. The validity of Davis's model rests on showing that wanting, comparison other, and deserving statistically predict the degree of grievance experienced about one's own job, the job situation of women, or one's home life. Similarly, the validity of Gurr's model can be demonstrated if the degree of grievance depends on wanting, deserving, and low future expectations.

Although the information comes from a cross-sectional survey, we can conceive of the factors in the study as independent and dependent variables. In the descriptions concerning one's job, the job situation of women, and one's home life, we ex-

Table 1.1 Variables in the Study

Analyses	Independent variables	Dependent variables
Description of attitudes toward own job (chapter 4)	sex job level	nature of gratifications [b] nature of grievances [b]
attitudes toward job situation of women (chapter 5) attitudes toward own home life (chapter 6)	family status employment group [a]	extent of deprivation extent of dissatisfaction hypothesized preconditions
Theory testing (chapter 8)	demographic characteristics (e.g., sex) hypothesized preconditions	extent of deprivation

[a] Employment group is not considered in Chapter 4.
[b] Nature of gratifications and grievances are not included in Chapter 5.

amine attitudes as a function of various demographic characteristics. We treat sex, job level, family status, and employment group as independent variables and treat the extent of deprivation and discontent, the six hypothesized preconditions of deprivation, and the nature of job and home gratifications and grievances as dependent variables. The theoretical analyses examine the extent of deprivation, in each of the three attitude domains, as a function of the hypothesized preconditions and sometimes as a function of demographic characteristics as well. Table 1.1 depicts the divisions into independent and dependent variables.

Plan

The book takes its shape from the two purposes of the research it reports. We start with theory and we end with theory. In the interval, we describe people's reactions to their own jobs (Chapter 4), the job situation of women (Chapter 5), and their home situations (Chapter 6). The relation between theory and empirical data—to borrow an image from Bateson (1973)—resembles the relation between a river and its banks: "The river molds the banks and the banks guide the river" (p. 57).

Chapter 2 presents the theory of relative deprivation. It outlines five models of relative deprivation, two models of equity, and the frustration-aggression hypothesis in fairly great detail, but not because the theories as they now stand will adequately account for what we discover about women, work, and home life. Indeed, given the differences and disagreements between various models, it would be quite surprising if any one model could provide a satisfactory explanation of the paradox of the contented female worker. Nor are the theoretical niceties presented because they are used to interpret the specific descriptive findings at the core of the book. Rather, we devote attention to the various models and propositions at the outset because they have all contributed to our strategy for examining grievance and gratification among employed women, employed men, and housewives. In addition to outlining different permutations of relative deprivation theory, Chapter 2 sets the theory within the context of the social sciences. Looking at some literatures that bear upon but are distinct from relative deprivation research is important because some of these literatures will ultimately prove helpful in understanding the lack of discontent among working women.

A flavor of previous empirical work on relative deprivation may be had from Chapter 2. In Chapter 3 we explain our own empirical methods. The next three chapters recount the major descriptive findings. Overall, we see that people feel contented with their jobs and with their home lives. They feel less happy about the situation of working women. Among the people in our study, then, there is little sense of personal grievance; but grievance about sex discrimination is unexpectedly pervasive if not intense.

Against the backdrop of personal contentment and group discontent, group differences emerge. The group differences are at the crux of the study. In Chapter 4 we find that feelings about work depend on family status. Single people are most resentful about and least satisfied with their jobs. Despite objective sex discrimination, job attitudes do not depend on sex. The employed women and men in our sample are virtually indistinguishable concerning their feelings toward their own jobs. It is concerning the position of women, we see in Chapter 5, that employed women feel more aggrieved, generally, than do employed men or housewives. High-prestige individuals—women and men—resent the treatment of women workers more than do low-prestige women and men.

Chapter 6 documents reactions to domestic arrangements. Parents, generally, and housewives, specifically, experience the most resentment at home concerning the division of domestic labor. Concerning their marriages, all groups express great satisfaction. How work and home environments compare is the topic of Chapter 7. Feelings about work and home show many similarities. The major difference revolves around comparison processes. People tend to use others as points of comparison in assessing their own jobs, but they tend to avoid comparisons in the domestic sphere.

From the descriptive findings of Chapters 4 through 7 arise three general observations. First, the people in our study, like American citizens in other, more politically oriented studies (e.g., Kinder & Sears, 1981), tend to "morselize" (Lane, 1962) their lives. Neither the extent nor the nature of grievance at work predicts much about grievance at home. More to the point, working women's reactions to their own individual situations are largely unrelated to their perceptions of the situation of working women in general. Employed women seem unable or unwilling to draw any inferences from what they know about sex discrimination in general as to how it might relate to their own personal situations. It is as if each woman considers herself to be the exception to the rule of discrimination.

Second, we observe that multiple roles appear to offer protection against discontent with any one role. Employed women and men express more contentment with home life than do housewives for whom the home role may be all-consuming. Similarly, married people and parents are more positive about their jobs than are single people. Our observation about the protective function of multiple roles reinforces our observation about how people "morselize" their lives. The separateness of different segments in a person's life—popular commentary and traditional role theory (Biddle & Thomas, 1966) notwithstanding—probably augments their protective powers. Home offers a better refuge from the woes of work and work offers a better haven from the cares of home if each segment is self-contained than if the two segments are closely connected.

The final observation to arise from the descriptions of Chapters 4 through 7 is that subjective discontent bears no simple relation to objective conditions. Thus, for example, the women in our study earn less than men with comparable qualifications, but they feel no sense of outrage at the discrepancy and, indeed, often seem unaware of it. In making this observation, we must avoid the temptation to conclude that subjective reality, measured in this case by a set of attitude scales, bears no relation to objective reality. If there were no connection or only a set of highly idiosyncratic connections, we would not, for example, be able to predict a person's job satisfaction from his or her family status or to predict a person's satisfaction with the situation of working women from his or her job level. But while attitudes are reliably associated with characteristics such as sex, job level, and family status, the associations are not always direct. Nor are they consistent with the notion that we can estimate people's levels of satisfaction with their outcomes just by knowing what their outcomes are.

The third observation and many of the specific findings in Chapters 4 through 7 are consistent with the concept of relative deprivation. But while the descriptive findings corroborate the theory, they do not constitute proof of the validity of any specific model of relative deprivation, equity theory, or the frustration-aggression hypothesis. The various models undergo validational testing in Chapter 8. Two models are disconfirmed; no model is consistently confirmed by the tests, but the general theory receives support. We tentatively propose a revised model. The revised model claims that people feel aggrieved when wants go unfulfilled and entitlements appear violated. Making comparisons between ourselves and others, or between one group and another, helps determine what is desirable and what is deserved; but, in the revised model, there is no direct link between comparisons to better-off others, on the one hand, and feelings of resentment, on the other. Nor do expectations or self-blame influence grievance, according to the revised model.

This means that the revised model is more streamlined than previous conceptualizations.

After a brief recapitulation of the major findings of the study, the final chapter comes full circle to the paradox of the contented female worker. Our failure in Chapter 8 to validate unambiguously any one model of relative deprivation or equity theory makes it difficult to resolve the paradox in terms of the theories. But if the theory of relative deprivation fails to provide a quick and easy solution to the puzzle, we nonetheless find ourselves asking a different set of questions at the end of our endeavor than at the beginning. The questions are more pointed and, perhaps, more productive. The theoretical conclusions of Chapter 8 and the earlier descriptive findings lead us to ask in Chapter 9 why our sample of employed women feel that they are justly treated when, as a group, they receive less pay than comparable males and when they are aware of and aggrieved about sex discrimination in general. What, in other words, prevents the working woman from recognizing herself as the victim of an injustice that she knows to exist? To answer the question, we contrast women who express both group and personal discontent with women who express only group discontent. The results of the comparison, coupled with some observations from other research on justice, bring us to a better, if still imperfect, understanding of the dynamics of grievance among employed women and, by implication, among all people.

Note

1. The design is further explicated in Chapter 3. Table 3.3 illustrates the sampling design.

2

The Theory of
Relative Deprivation

Relative deprivation theory has its basis in common sense. For centuries, social observers have noted that people's subjective discontents are not simply a matter of their objective conditions. According to Aristotle, we could predict one individual's satisfaction from an assessment of his neighbor's conditions; Karl Marx has described how a house becomes a hovel when a palace is constructed next door; and every parent knows that a cookie seems a crumb if the child had expected an entire cake. Common sense and ancient wisdom agree: felt deprivations are relative and not absolute.

Ultimately common sense proves inadequate. If, for instance, the existence of some better-off neighbor were, in and of itself, sufficient to produce feelings of resentment or deprivation, then almost all people would feel resentful almost all of the time. Yet we know both from introspection and from systematically collected survey data (Runciman, 1966) that resentments are rare. Common sense may tell us that felt deprivations are relative, furthermore, but it leaves us asking: relative to what? to what others have? to what has been expected? to what is expected for the future? to what one feels one deserves? Nor do we know from common sense how the factors interact. When, for example, are a person's feelings determined by his neighbor's conditions, when are they determined by his own prior conditions, and how do his own prior conditions shape whom he considers a neighbor?

During the last few decades social scientists interested in these and related questions have sought to supplement the wisdom of common sense with formal research. At first, the concept of relative deprivation served as a convenient label for a series of unexpected findings. In a massive study of Army life during World War II, Samuel Stouffer and his colleagues discovered that military policemen were more satisfied with the promotional system in the Army than were men in the Air Corps (Stouffer, Suchman, DeVinney, Star, & Williams, 1949). This finding surprised many, not least of all Stouffer himself, because promotions were notoriously slow in the military police and rapid in the Air Corps. In accounting for the findings, Stouffer and his coworkers invented the term "relative deprivation."

The concept enjoyed increasing popularity after the war. Part of its popularity came from its linkage to the concept of reference groups, which was then in vogue. Indeed, Robert Merton's concern with the social bases of identity and reality did much to make relative deprivation a household phrase among sociologists and social psychologists (Merton & Rossi, 1957).

Research on relative deprivation has been both extensive and varied in the twenty-five years since Merton and Rossi's paper appeared. The purpose of this chapter is to review that research. We look first at the theory of relative deprivation in its various specifications. After explicating five distinct models, we briefly outline the empirical work on relative deprivation. We also place the theory in a wider context, emphasizing especially its connection to equity theory. We enter into a detailed discussion of relative deprivation and cognate theories in this chapter because the theory has provided the very terms of our descriptions of attitudes among employed women, employed men, and housewives. The chapter serves in some ways, then, as an oceanographic chart so that we may see how the waters of our theory have molded the empirical banks of the Newton study.

The concept and the theory

Over the years, the term "relative deprivation" has acquired many meanings. Often quoted is Aberle's (1962) definition of relative deprivation as "a negative discrepancy between legitimate expectations and actuality" (p. 209). Morrison (1971) writes, "The basic notion is that feelings of deprivation, of discontent over one's situation, depend on what one *wants* to have; that is, deprivation occurs in relation to desired points of reference, often 'reference groups', rather than in relation to how little one has" (p. 675). Like Aberle, Morrison also stipulates that desires must be legitimate and blocked for deprivation to be felt. To Anderson and Zelditch (1964) relative deprivation is synonymous with rank inequilibrium. According to them, one person feels deprived if he sees that another is similar to himself on one rank (e.g., education) but different on another (e.g., salary). Past expectations are critical for Snyder and Kelly (1976) while future expectations are crucial for Seeman (1977). The former call relative deprivation "the gap between expected and achieved welfare" (p. 133) and the latter considers that people are relatively deprived if they endorse the view that the lot of the common man is worsening.

Among the variegated usages of the phrase, two basic meanings of relative deprivation may be discerned. First, relative deprivation sometimes refers to a feeling. Hopper and Weyman (1975), for example, define relative deprivation as "anxious feelings of discontent" (p. 66). Second, relative deprivation is sometimes used in connection with a more formal statement—sometimes labeled a theory, sometimes labeled a model—about the relationship between objective and subjective reality. In its general form, the theory states that feelings of deprivation, discontent, or dissatisfaction are relative and not absolute. Specific versions of the theory make explicit statements about the antecedents, concomitants, and consequences of felt deprivation. Psychologists and sociologists concentrate on the antecedents while political scientists focus more on the political consequences of the experience of deprivation, including social unrest.

At least five separate models of relative deprivation now exist. The first is Davis's (1959) statement. Davis distinguishes between comparisons one makes with others within one's own reference group (in-group comparisons) and comparisons one makes to others outside one's own group (out-group comparisons). Within each group, there are 'haves' and 'have-nots.'

When a 'have-not' compares his lot with that of a 'have' in his own group, he experiences deprivation; and when a 'have' makes an in-group comparison with a 'have-not,' he experiences gratification. Davis implies that people feel entitled to possess what others in their own group possess. Not so, however, for comparisons across groups. Out-group comparisons between 'haves' and 'have-nots' result in feelings of social distance. If a 'have-not' compares his lot with that of a 'have' from a different group, he experiences social inferiority. If a 'have' looks to a 'have-not' of a different group, he feels socially superior. Implicit in Davis's theory is the idea that comparisons within one's own group lead to evaluations of one's outcomes while comparisons across groups lead to evaluations of oneself. Davis derives a number of propositions from his central theorem. The most important states that the extent of sub-group formation and, by inference, disequilibrium in any group is a curvilinear function of the distribution of outcomes, with disequilibrium being most prevalent when the number of 'haves' equals the number of 'have-nots.'

Seven years after the appearance of Davis's article, Runciman's *Relative Deprivation and Social Justice* appeared. The book opens by noting that valued outcomes are unevenly distributed in every society and that the uneven distribution is usually considered just by the disadvantaged as well as by the advantaged. Runciman then describes twentieth-century English attitudes toward inequality and seeks to account for working-class Toryism. The Tory or Conservative Party has traditionally been supported by a sizable minority of the English working classes. The riddle for Runciman is to explain why people who are objectively underprivileged support a party that endorses a system of privilege from which they themselves are excluded. One answer to the riddle is provided by the concepts of relative deprivation. As Runciman says,

A strict definition is difficult. But we can roughly say that A is relatively deprived of X when (1) he does not have X, (2) he sees some other person or persons . . . as having X . . ., (3) he wants X, and (4) he sees it as feasible that he should have X. (1966, p. 11)

Runciman also distinguishes between egoistical and fraternal deprivation. Egoistical deprivation occurs when an individual feels disadvantaged relative to others in his own group; fraternal deprivation occurs when an individual feels that his group is disadvantaged relative to another group. The working-class man who thinks that he is worse off than other working-class men, for example, suffers from egoistical deprivation; while the working-class man who looks at the gap between the working and middle classes is fraternally deprived. The individual who is both egoistically and fraternally deprived is said to be doubly deprived.

Ted Robert Gurr (1968a, 1968b, 1968c, 1969, 1970) turns Runciman on his head. If Runciman wonders why people do not rebel, Gurr asks why they do. In answer to his own question, he constructs an elaborate theory including sixty-eight hypotheses about the relationships among a dozen categories of variables. In Gurr's "process model" the magnitude of political violence varies according to the potential for political violence, the balance of the regime's institutional support and the dissidents' institutional support, and the balance of the regime's coercive control and the dissidents' coercive control. The potential for political violence, in turn, increases as the intensity and scope of relative deprivation increase. Relative deprivation is defined as "the discrepancy between 'ought' and 'is' " (1970, p. 23). Rendered algebraically, the proposition is

$$RD = \frac{Ve - Vc}{Ve}$$

where RD stands for relative deprivation; Ve stands for value expectations (the goods to which people feel entitled); and Vc stands for value capabilities (the goods which people feel they can attain).

Gurr identifies three patterns of deprivation. Decremental deprivation occurs when a group's value expectations are stable over time while the group's value capabilities decline. Aspirational deprivation occurs when a group's value capabilities are stable while the group's value expectations increase. Progressive deprivation involves the simultaneous increase of expectations and deterioration of capabilities. Gurr's model differs from the other four models of relative deprivation in that it is a dynamic model while the others are static.

A fourth model of relative deprivation has been proposed by Robin Williams (1975), a member of Stouffer's research team. Williams defines relative deprivation as the discrepancy between what one has and what one wants. He differentiates feelings of deprivation from feelings of disappointment, which involve expectations rather than desires, and from feelings of injustice, which involve the perception of deservingness. A better-off comparison other is a necessary, but not a sufficient, antecedent to felt deprivation. Williams is more interested in organized protest than in private discontent. Conditions that make a sustained protest most likely, as he lists them, include:

1. a collective relative deprivation, especially in
2. prestige . . . and political power, which
3. occurs suddenly . . . when
4. the deprived collectivity is large, commands substantial economic and political resources . . . [and]
5. the established regime . . . [is weak] (p. 373).

The final model is one I have developed (Crosby, 1976). Building upon the work of earlier scholars, especially Runciman, it equates felt deprivation with resentment or a sense of grievance and specifies that felt deprivation is one type of anger. Egoistical deprivation is experienced, according to my 1976 model, *when and only when* five preconditions are met. To feel deprived of some object or opportunity (X), people who lack X must want X; see that another has X; feel entitled to (deserving of) X; think it feasible to attain X; and not blame themselves (disclaim personal responsibility) for failing to have X now.

The five psychological preconditions of felt deprivation are viewed as the outgrowth of a variety of more objective determinants.

I group the determinants into those that have to do with (1) the individual's personality (e.g., need for achievement); (2) his personal past (e.g., recency of loss of X); (3) his immediate environment (e.g., number of others possessing X); (4) the wider society in which he lives (e.g., societal dictates about entitlements); and (5) biological needs (centrality of X to survival). Any one determinant affects one or more preconditions. The need for achievement, for example, affects the individual's expectations, while societal dictates about entitlements affect all five preconditions. The preconditions can also affect each other. People often convince themselves that they deserve what they want. The realization that some grapes are unattainable—to cite another example—has a well-known tendency to turn the grapes sour.

My model has undergone some revision. In the 1976 article, I note that Gurr and Runciman disagree about the role of expectations. For Runciman, deprivation happens when good things seem feasible; for Gurr, when they seem impossible. In 1976, I agree with Runciman. A year later, Cook, Crosby, and Hennigan (1977) attempt a reconciliation of Runciman and Gurr by distinguishing between past and future expectations. Using the distinction, Bernstein and Crosby (1978) suggest that deprivation varies as a positive function of past expectations and as a negative function of future expectations. Given the other preconditions, such as a sense of entitlement, the most aggrieved individual is one whose high hopes are irrevocably dashed. The housewife, for instance, who had expected a blissfully calm marriage but who now foresees decades of quarreling is likely to feel resentful.[1]

In sum, the five theorists agree that certain cognitions and emotions act as psychological preconditions of a sense of grievance. While they agree about the existence of preconditions, the theorists differ in the exact sets they propose. All state that individuals who are deprived of X must want X in order to experience deprivation. All but Gurr see the comparison to a better-off other as crucial, and all but Williams feature entitlement (deserving) as a precondition. The top portion of Table 2.1 illustrates the sets of preconditions specified by each model of relative deprivation.

Empirical research

The bulk of the empirical research falls into three types: survey studies of black unrest; survey studies of worker discontent;

Table 2.1 Hypothesized Preconditions of Resentment, Discontent, Dissatisfaction, or Anger

	Want	Comparison other	Deserving	Past expectations	Future expectations	Self-blame
Davis	present[a]	present	present			
Runciman	present	present	present		high[b]	
Gurr	present		present		low[c]	
Williams	present	present				
Crosby	present	present	present		high	absent[d]
Berkowitz	present			high		
Adams	present	present	present			
Patchen	present	present	present			absent

[a] According to the theorist, this element must be present if the objectively deprived person is to experience resentment or the other negative emotions.

[b] According to the theorist, expectations must be high if the objectively deprived person is to experience resentment or the other negative emotions.

[c] According to the theorist, expectations must be low if the objectively deprived person is to experience resentment or the other negative emotions.

[d] According to the theorist, self-blame (personal responsibility) must be absent if the objectively deprived person is to experience resentment or the other negative emotions.

and archival studies of violence. The first type of research flourished after the urban riots of the late 1960s. The researchers usually classified the respondents into groups, such as "riot participants" and "nonparticipants." The two groups were then compared in terms of their feelings of discontent, their reference groups, or various aspects of their backgrounds (e.g., Caplan & Paige, 1968). In surveys of workers, the researchers generally looked for associations among different attitudes. Runciman, for example, examined people's reactions to class differences as a function of their self-rated social class. Scase (1974) compared Swedish and English manual workers in their perceptions of and reactions to class differences. Gurr's (1968a) test of his model of civil strife typifies the archival research. He systematically searched a number of sources such as the *New York Times* and *Africa Digest* for "strife events" in 114 polities between 1961 and 1965. Over a thousand events were identified and for each polity pervasiveness, duration, and intensity scores

were calculated. Also calculated for each country were measures of short-term deprivation, long-term deprivation, and
several mediating variables (e.g., coercive force size). Gurr then
employed multiple regression techniques to determine which
variables statistically predict the magnitude of civil strife. Much
of the variance in strife, Gurr reports, is accounted for by the
deprivation measures.

The majority of the empirical studies can be said to corroborate the general theory of relative deprivation. Reviews of the
survey studies and of the few relevant experiments show that,
considered alone, each of the hypothesized preconditions of
deprivation is associated with dissatisfaction or discontent (Cook
et al., 1977; Crosby, 1976). The archival studies also tend to
show the expected associations between the presumed antecedents and the presumed consequences of felt deprivation.

Despite the general corroboration of relative deprivation
theory, the theory has generated controversy. Gurr claims a
victory for relative deprivation theory on the basis of his "ar-
mamentarium of techniques of causal inference" (Gurr, 1968a,
p. 1122), but others using similar techniques (e.g., Miller, Bolce,
& Halligan, 1977) reject relative deprivation. The lack of con-
sensus about the validity of the theory springs from several
problems. One concerns the proper level of analysis. Aggregate
level data are not always informative about events that occur in
the hearts and minds of individuals (Abeles, 1972), and references to emotional states may add nothing to accounts of political or social events (Spilerman, 1970, 1971). Even when the
information is about individuals, furthermore, information
about objective circumstances might prove inappropriate for a
theory about subjective experiences (Wallis, 1975).

Perhaps more problematic is the discrepancy between formal and operational definitions of some variables. In the studies of black unrest, the most popular way of assessing deprivation among blacks has been Cantril's Self-Anchoring Ladder
(e.g., Geschwender & Geschwender, 1973). It pictures a ladder
with eleven rungs. The respondent is asked to imagine that the
top rung represents the best possible life and that the bottom
rung represents the worst possible life. He then places himself
on the ladder. Yet no measure is made of the person's feelings

about his self-perceived position. Extrapolating from Crosby's (1976) model, it is conceivable that some people who place themselves toward the bottom of the ladder do not feel aggrieved about their lot because they hold themselves responsible for it. Nor are feelings of deprivation usually tapped in the studies of worker satisfaction. Even Runciman, in his survey of British workers, asked his respondents if they perceived that others were better off than themselves but did not ask the respondents how they felt about it. The slippage between operational and theoretical variables also appears in the archival studies (e.g., Butler, 1976; Feierabend & Feierabend, 1966; Feierabend, Feierabend, & Nesvold, 1969). Gurr's measure of persisting deprivation, for example, includes six items:

1. economic discrimination: exclusion of some groups from economic power positions
2. political discrimination: exclusion of some groups from political power positions
3. potential separatism: proportional size of geographic or ethnic separatist groups
4. dependence on private foreign capital
5. religious cleavages: number of organized religious groups
6. lack of educational opportunity

What, one wonders, have these to do with the discrepancy between 'ought' and 'is'? They seem more like measures of absolute well-being than like measures of relative well-being (cf. Parvin, 1973). Indeed, it seems intuitively probable that economic discrimination, political discrimination, and the lack of educational opportunity would all make the disadvantaged group believe it deserves its meager outcomes.

With so much imprecision, it is difficult to find direct evidence on the validity of any of the models of relative deprivation. To demonstrate the validity of a model, one must show that the preconditions listed in the model do, in fact, lead to deprivation. There have been at least three efforts to submit various models to validational testing. One effort involved a role-play experiment in which five of the hypothesized preconditions were manipulated independently (Bernstein & Crosby,

1978). In that study, the formulation put forward by Davis received firm support and Gurr's formulation received mixed support. No other model was confirmed. Another, more complicated laboratory study (Hennigan, 1979) produced inconsistent results, as did a small survey study of lawyers and legal secretaries (Crosby, 1978).

Connections

Relative deprivation connects in one way or another to many areas of research throughout the social sciences. It relates directly to four topics within social psychology: the frustration-aggression hypothesis, equity theory, justice theory, and hedonic relativism. The differences between relative deprivation research and the four other areas are generally a matter of emphasis. Issues of deserving or entitlement (the two are considered here to be synonymous) are focal to relative deprivation theory, but they remain in the periphery of the frustration-aggression hypothesis. Social comparisons are the *only* way in which we come to know what we deserve, according to the equity theorists. In relative deprivation theory, social comparisons can create discontent, but there are many ways in which we know if our outcomes are as good as they ought to be. While research on justice theory takes into account people's feelings about distributions in general, relative deprivation research concentrates on how they react to their own position in the larger matrix. The concern with reactions to one's own lot is shared by those working on hedonic relativism; but relative deprivation research is interested in determining people's reactions to the absence of a desired thing and hedonic relativism research in the consequences of the presence of a desired thing. We examine each of the four areas individually and in some depth. We dwell on equity theory because it has dominated social psychological approaches to justice since Thibaut and Kelley's (1959) provocative analysis of power and satisfaction.

In 1939, five psychologists at Yale University published *Frustration and Aggression* (Dollard, Doob, Miller, Mowrer, & Sears, 1939). It advances the frustration-aggression hypothesis, which states that aggression always follows frustration and that frustration is always followed by aggression. Frustration is defined as the interruption of an ongoing sequence of behavior directed toward obtaining a goal. Aggression means behavior performed with the intent of harming someone, including oneself. For two decades following World War II, the frustration-aggression hypothesis inspired hundreds of social psychological studies (Berkowitz, 1962). It soon became apparent that the purportedly causal relationship between frustration and aggression is not as invariant as Dollard and his colleagues would have it. Individuals perpetrate aggressive acts through obedience in the absence of frustration (Milgram, 1974). More importantly, a number of laboratory studies have demonstrated cases where neither direct nor displaced aggression follows from frustration (Berkowitz, 1968a).

Leonard Berkowitz, prominent in American aggression scholarship, has clarified and revised the frustration-aggression hypothesis. He defines frustration in terms of expectations as well as desires (Berkowitz, 1968b; 1972). The potential for aggression is greatest when one is denied something which one wants and had expected to have. (See Table 2.1) The hungry person who expected but is denied a meal is likely to become aggressive; the hungry person who had expected no meal is not. Whether the potential for aggression, which is loosely equated with discontent or hostility, eventuates in actual aggressive behavior depends on a variety of other factors, including one's habits, the norms of one's society, and the presence of aggressive stimuli.

Even more closely tied to relative deprivation theory is equity theory. Indeed, they are so intertwined that some scholars (e.g., Adams, 1965; Homans, 1974; Wheeler & Zuckerman, 1977) find them virtually indistinguishable. The basic proposition of what is sometimes called the exchange formulation of equity theory is that people evaluate their outcomes by comparing their own outcomes and inputs with those of a referent or comparison other (Adams, 1965; Berkowitz & Walster, 1976; Walster, Berscheid, & Walster, 1973; Walster, Walster, & Berscheid, 1978). A person will be satisfied with his outcomes when he perceives:

$$\frac{\text{own outcomes}}{\text{own inputs}} = \frac{\text{other's outcomes}}{\text{other's inputs}}$$

Guilt results when a person perceives:

$$\frac{\text{own outcomes}}{\text{own inputs}} > \frac{\text{other's outcomes}}{\text{other's inputs}}$$

Anger results, according to the equity theorists, when a person perceives

$$\frac{\text{own outcomes}}{\text{own inputs}} < \frac{\text{other's outcomes}}{\text{other's inputs}}$$

When the individual experiences guilt or anger, he acts to reduce or eliminate the feeling by changing one or more of the terms in the formula. The angry person, for example, might reassess the other's inputs and end his anger by deciding that the other's inputs are more valuable than he had thought, or he might lower the other's outcomes, perhaps raising his own outcomes in the process.

In an interview study of nearly 500 male workers of an oil refinery, Patchen (1961a, 1961b) discovered many workers who made discrepant comparisons that theoretically ought to have led to anger but that in fact did not. Anger failed to materialize when the men saw that the other's outcome-input ratio exceeded their own and blamed themselves for their own low outcomes. On the strength of these findings, Patchen concludes that the emotional consequence of perceived inequity depends on whether people accept personal responsibility for their predicaments. Like Crosby, Patchen considers the lack of self-blame as a precondition of deprivation.

Equity theory has elicited criticism. One problem is that it does not distinguish adequately between the perception of fairness and feelings of satisfaction (Jacobson & Koch, 1977). Certainly people do experience and seek to expiate guilt, but the distributions of rewards that people find most pleasing differ from those that they find most fair (Messick & Sentis, 1979). A related problem is that equity theory connot account for cases in which one individual reacts to another's outcomes without reference to his own situation. Yet we know that people sometimes perceive specific others (Crosby & Gonzalez-Intal, 1982) or generalized others (Kinder & Sears, 1981; Sears, Hensler & Speer, 1979; Sears & Kinder, 1971) to be overrewarded regardless of their own outcome-input ratio.

The problem of comparisons has prompted Berger and his associates to abandon the traditional approach to equity and to formulate, in its stead, the "status value" version of equity theory. According to Berger (Anderson, Berger, Zelditch, & Cohen, 1969; Berger, Zelditch, Anderson, & Cohen, 1972), a person's feelings of unfairness do not depend on comparisons with a particular other person. Rather, comparisons are with a generalized other thought to be typical of some class of people. To evaluate the fairness of his wages, for example, the mechanic contrasts his own pay with the pay that he thinks is typical for mechanics. He looks to the "average mechanic" in other words, and not to one individual or another in evaluating his own outcomes. Berger and his coworkers do not specify how the views of a generalized other develop. One suspects that the generalized other is a composite of many specific individuals.

In the traditional equity formulation, the divisions between comparison other, deserving, and distributive justice are fuzzy. Cohen (1979) distinguishes between individual deserving and distributive justice and notes that—equity theory notwithstanding—the two are sometimes opposed, especially in times of scarcity. Individual deserving "refers to the relationship between an individual's fulfilment of outcome preconditions and that individual's actual outcomes," while distributive justice concerns "a normative evaluation of a distribution of goods or conditions to distinct recipients" (p. 180). When resources are scarce, someone may feel entitled to a large amount of an outcome by the rules of individual deserving but to a small amount by virtue of distributive justice. Brickman, Folger, Goode, and Schul (1981) make a similar point in their treatment of micro amd macro justice.

The biggest problem with equity theory may be that it claims too much. The volume on equity edited by Berkowitz and Walster (1976), for example, contains the subtitle "Toward a general theory of social interaction." But equity may not be a general theory: we consider more than fairness in distributing outcomes (Leventhal, 1976; Morse, Gruzen, & Reis, 1976;

Schwinger, 1980) and, even more importantly, we consider more than inputs in determining which outcomes are fair. Morton Deutsch (1975; 1979) identifies three principles of distributive justice: equity, equality, and need. He proposes that equity is the dominant principle of distributive justice in relations centering around economic productivity but not in others. Equality is the dominant principle in relationships emphasizing socio-emotional well-being. Need is the dominant principle in relationships that center around growth and development. It is fair that the worker be paid in proportion to the hours worked. It is also fair that all members of a family receive equal helpings of dessert even though their contributions to the family's welfare differ widely. Similarly, it is fair that the child be given the attention and time he or she needs.

This brings us to the third area: justice theory. The scholar who has done most to promote an interest in justice among social scientists in recent years is Melvin Lerner. Lerner maintains that people have a need to believe in a just world (Lerner, 1975; Lerner & Miller, 1978) and that justice is an organizing theme for much human activity (Lerner, 1977). People differ in the strength of their need to see the world as just (Rubin & Peplau, 1975; Sampson, 1980) and in the techniques they employ to convince themselves that justice is done. Not only do people differ; situations differ. In some situations we convince ourselves that the world is a just place by denigrating the victim of misfortune (Ryan, 1971); in others, by compensating the victim.

Lerner and his associates take a much kinder view of human nature than do the equity theorists. The latter view power as "the more primitive phenomenon that lies behind distributive justice" (Homans, 1976, p. 243) and maintain that norms about deserving and about justice grow out of each greedy individual's desire to curb his neighbor's greed. Lerner believes that justice needs are as basic as power needs. Equity, he feels, may be "the consequence of trying to treat people who are in different circumstances (positions) on an equal basis" (Lerner, 1975, p. 17). The human commitment to personal deserving, furthermore, is linked to, but is not antecedent to, the human need for societal justice (Lerner, Miller, & Holmes, 1976).

Modern social science, in both its esoteric and its popularized forms, engages in a defensive denial of humankind's love of justice (Lerner, 1982). Experimenters contrive situations in which subjects may be seen as selfish and deceptive, but scientists ignore the wealth of data in and out of the laboratory that demonstrate the opposite.

The final area of research with which relative deprivation overlaps is the work by Philip Brickman and his associates on hedonic relativism. The pleasure that we take in a positive outcome, according to Brickman, depends on our past experiences and expectations and on the fate of our neighbors as well as on the outcome itself. Linsenmeier and Brickman (note 1) review a great number of studies that show that (a) the higher a person's expectations, the better the person's performance, but (b) at any given level, the lower the expectation, the greater is the satisfaction with one's performance. Dramatic support of the notion that happiness is relative is provided by a study of twenty-two major lottery winners, twenty-nine paralyzed accident victims, and twenty-two controls (Brickman, Coates, & Janoff-Bulman, 1978). The lottery winners take significantly less pleasure in mundane daily events than do the controls; the paraplegics do not significantly differ from the control group.

Brickman suggests that the phenomenon of adaptation carries some disturbing implications for the design of society. Assume, as a utilitarian does, that the best society is one with the greatest happiness for the greatest number. Given that the perception of a better-off other makes one less happy with one's own lot (Brickman, 1975), then "if the best can come only rarely, it is better not to include it in the range of experiences at all" (Parducci, 1968, p. 90). It is good, for example, to encourage the mass of people to develop their musical talents; but it is harmful to foster musical genius, which is inevitably rare. Another startling implication of Brickman's line of thinking is that a traditional society might promote happiness more than a modern society. In modern society, people are prone to experience improvements in their standard of living and then to expect continuous improvements. They may even feel dissatisfied unless the improvements occur at an accelerating pace; yet most who step on to the "hedonic treadmill" (Brickman &

Campbell, 1971) find in the end that it is like any other treadmill—exhausting and disappointing.

The theory of relative deprivation connects to many additional topics throughout the social sciences. It has direct ties to
social comparison theory (Latané, 1966; Suls & Miller, 1977)
and to reference group theory (Hyman & Singer, 1968) and
indirect ties to the concepts of status congruence (Benoit-
Smullyan, 1944; Geschwender, 1967; Lenski, 1954) and an-
omie (Seeman, 1975; 1977). The notion that satisfactions are
relative to a psychological standard informs much of the current theorizing about worker satisfaction (Dyer & Theriault,
1976; Lawler, 1968, 1971; Mizruchi, 1964; Porter & Steers,
1973; Smith, Kendall, & Hulin, 1969; Vroom, 1964, 1969;
Weitzel, Harpaz, & Weiner, 1977). Political scientists often consider Davies' famous J-curve theory of revolution to be a special
case of Gurr's progressive deprivation (Davies, 1962, 1969, 1974,
1978, 1979).[2] Given its conceptual proximity to the J-curve theory and to the theory of rising expectations (Geschwender, 1964,
1967), relative deprivation has become a staple of "the professional revolution scholars" (Kramnick, 1972, p. 62; see also Blasier, 1967; Stone, 1966).

Summary

Born of some paradoxical findings in World War II, the term
relative deprivation has enjoyed a long and controversial history. Five models of relative deprivation exist, and each one
proposes a unique set of preconditions. Most of the empirical
research has attempted to predict patterns of discontent. Archival studies of societal unrest, survey studies of black unrest,
and survey studies of worker dissatisfaction have provided evidence that the various preconditions are individually important
in determining feelings of resentment.

The research reported in this book contributes to the literature on relative deprivation. In Chapters 4, 5, and 6 we examine the extent of deprivation and of the hypothesized preconditions of deprivation among employed women, employed
men, and housewives. Of special interest are the contrasts that
can be made between three different types of deprivation that

we assess: grievance felt about one's own job situation; grievance felt about the job situation of women; and grievance felt about one's own home situation. Personal discontents (the rough equivalent of Runciman's egoistical deprivation) are, we shall see, minimal, whether they concern one's job or one's home life. Group discontent (roughly, fraternal deprivation) appears more pronounced. In Chapter 8 we employ the information we have about people's attitudes to submit the theory, in its many versions, to formal validational testing. At that time we see which of the hypothesized preconditions of deprivation actually do predict the extent of deprivation concerning one's own job, the job situation of women, and one's own home arrangements. How we have obtained the information about gratifications and deprivations and about the purported preconditions of deprivation is the subject of our next chapter.

Notes

1. Folger, Rosenfield and Rheaume (note 2) disagree with Cook et al. about the past-present distinction. Folger and his associates argue that grievances have less to do with the timing of expectations than with their reasonableness. They differentiate the likelihood of an outcome from the feasibility of an outcome. Likelihood refers to the probability that something will occur under present conditions. Resentments ought to be low when likelihood is high. Feasibility refers to the probability of an outcome under reasonable conditions which differ from the status quo. Resentments about missing things or opportunities ought to be high when feasibility is high. The woman who believes that her present marriage will not give her the peace she desires (likelihood low) but who can imagine another marriage which would (feasibility high) is prone to anger.

2. The name comes from the fact that the rise and fall pattern of prosperity (plotted along the y-axis) over time (x-axis) looks like a J lying on its side.

3

Methods

Whatever we conclude about the validity of relative deprivation theory and whatever we find about the deprivations and gratifications of working women, working men, and housewives, our ends are in some measure determined by our beginnings. What we conclude, in other words, depends in part on our methods, and our methods depend in part on our aims. In this chapter, we describe the sampling procedure of our survey, outline the contents of the interview schedule, and describe some of the characteristics of the sample.

Sampling procedure

The present study has, as we have noted, both a theoretical and a descriptive aim. To fulfill adequately the descriptive purpose of the study—that is, to document faithfully how paid employment influences women's attitudes—it seemed essential to sample women at both the upper and lower ends of the occupational spectrum. A diverse occupational sample would also serve the study's theoretical purpose. Because relative deprivation theory deals with the relationship between objective and subjective conditions, a test of the theory is likely to benefit from the representation of varied objective conditions.

Our desire to include women with both high- and low-prestige jobs in the study meant that a national probability sample was impossible. The percentage of working women throughout the country who hold high-prestige jobs is so small that we would probably have had to interview approximately two thousand people in order to include in the study ninety women with managerial and professional occupations. Even if we had possessed the resources for such a massive undertaking, there would be a danger in a national probability sample that the professional women might hold less prestigious jobs than the professional men (Etzioni, 1969).

Rather than interview women and men throughout the country, then, we decided to obtain our sample in a single town. Exactly which town was decided by several further factors. The first was our intention to examine the association between family status and feelings of gratification and deprivation. For men and perhaps especially for women, a worker's feelings about and commitment to the job may depend on domestic arrangements. The working parent certainly faces a different set of problems than does the single person. We decided, therefore, to partition the categories of high- and low-prestige working women and men into three groups each: single respondents, respondents who are married but childless (henceforth called "married") and married parents (henceforth "parents" or "parental group").

Because parents may be relatively rare in the cities and single women and men scarce in rural districts, a suburb seemed the most likely spot for obtaining all three types of employed men and women. Not any suburb would do. We specifically wanted an affluent suburb because an affluent suburb seemed the best place to look for the high-prestige working women required by our design.

Among the suburbs in the United States, those in Massachusetts held a special attraction for us. Every town in Massachusetts publishes annually a list of residents over the age of seventeen specifying, among other things, the person's age, address, occupation, and date of birth. Street Lists may be purchased by any member of the public; consultation of street lists involves no invasion of privacy. Using the Street List of a Massachusetts suburb allowed us to stratify the residents of the town on the basis of their sex and their job level and, by inference, into those who were married and those who were not.

Our search for a Massachusetts suburb with an accurate and up-to-date Street List soon led us to the Boston suburb of Newton. Preliminary inquiries indicated that Newton was uncommonly assiduous in its record-keeping. One resident told us of an incident in which the police paid a call on his neighbor because the neighbor had neglected to send in his data for the Street List. A small pilot study substantiated the impression of careful record-keeping. We attempted to contact women listed on several randomly selected pages of the 1976 Street List. We managed to reach more than 85 percent of the women with four or fewer phone calls and discovered virtually no mistakes in the information contained in the Street List.

The U.S. census of 1970 showed that Newton was also well suited to the aims of our research. In 1970 it had a population of 91,066 living in 26,958 separate households. The size of the town remained unchanged between 1960 and 1970. About 2 percent of the population was black. The median family income in 1970 was $15,381. About two-thirds of the men and half of the women aged twenty to forty-nine had attended college; more than 70 percent of Newtonites held white-collar jobs. The 1970 population included nearly 20,000 married couples. About half of the couples had children under eighteen.

Newton is representative of America in some ways. As Table 3.1 shows, Newton does not differ from most American towns in terms of household composition. Newtonites marry at the same rate as most Americans and have the same number of people in one dwelling. Newton is also close to the national average in its level of education. The town is, however, atypical in one critical respect, and all of the indicators of wealth in Table 3.1 point to Newton's distinctive affluence. The affluence of Newton should make us cautious about generalizing our findings to the entire United States. Living in a comfortable East Coast suburb, the 405 white and relatively young people whom we interviewed may sometimes react to their own jobs, the job situation of women, and their own home lives in ways that differ from most Americans. There is little reason to suspect, however, that the particular groups in our study—groups such as women with pretigious jobs—differ from similar groups throughout the country.

With the 1977 Newton Street List in hand, we set about to obtain samples of working women, working men, and house-

Table 3.1 Characteristics of Newton

	Newton	Mass.	U.S.A.
Average persons per household	3.2	—	3.1
Percentage of males (over 14) who are married	62.4	—	65.7
Percentage of females (over 14) who are married	53.2	—	61.2
Median years of schooling of males aged 25 plus	12.3	12.4	12.1
Median years of schooling of females aged 25 plus	12.3	12.4	12.1
Percentage unemployed	2.8	3.8	3.9
Percentage under poverty level	2.8	6.2	11.6
Percentage in white-collar occupations	72.1	52.7	—
Percentage earning over $15,000 per annum	51.1	25.2	19.2
Median family income	15,381	10,835	9,596

Source: 1970 United States Census

wives. First, we decided to limit the sample to people aged twenty-five to forty. This decision was dictated by our interest in family status. A sixty-year-old mother of a thirty-two-year-old offspring is a parent; but her situation differs in obvious ways from that of a thirty-year-old mother of an infant. Rather than attempt, with a small sample, to document the relationships among sex, job level, and family status throughout the cycle of one's life and of one's family life, we chose to restrict our attention to the early part of one's occupational and family careers. Our decision meant that we struck 48,729 names from the 63,551 in the Street List. We also eliminated students, retired people, foreign nationals, and individuals with androgynous names, leaving a total of 12,435 people.

The second step was to classify the remaining Newtonites on the basis of their job level. Of the numerous schemes for classifying occupations, social stratification researchers (Glenn, Alston, & Weiner, 1970; Treiman, 1977) recommend two: Duncan's Socioeconomic Index (Duncan, 1961) and the National Opinion Research Center (NORC) rating system (Hodge, Siegel, & Rossi, 1964). These are the only two schemes to include all occupations mentioned by the U.S. Bureau of Census

(1960). The two schemes are highly intercorrelated (Feather-man & Hauser, 1977; Treiman, 1977). To determine which scheme we wanted, we classified one hundred randomly selected individuals into those above the midpoint and below it, using first the Duncan SEI and then the NORC prestige rating scheme. Employed people were classified on the basis of their own occupations and housewives on the basis of their husbands' occupations. The results surprised us: only 40 percent of the individuals were classified the same way in both schemes. Most of the disagreements involved occupations such as teachers below the college level, which fell just above the midpoint on one scheme and just below on the other. We repeated the exercise with a tripartite division and found that ninty-eight of the one hundred names were classified into high, middle, or low by both schemes.

To avoid the instability of middling occupations and to help assure homogeneity within our groups of high- and low-prestige workers, therefore, we used the tripartite division in our sampling procedure and excluded from the study people with jobs of middle prestige. We selected the NORC rating scheme. Occupations such as sales clerk or laborer with a rating of forty or below were classified as low-prestige. Occupational ratings of sixty-one or above were classified as high-prestige. Physician, lawyer, college teacher, and dentist exemplify high-prestige occupations. Women who listed their occupation as "housewife" or "at home" were classified by their husbands' jobs. Of the 12,435 names in our Newton Street List aged twenty-five to forty (who were American and were neither students nor retired), the tripartite division yielded 3074 high-prestige individuals and 2259 low-prestige individuals. These people were distributed among the groups of employed females, employed males, and housewives in the way shown in Table 3.2.

Next we drew names randomly from each of the groups shown in Table 3.2 and obtained telephone numbers for them. Of the names drawn, 22 percent of the females and 18 percent of the males had no phone or had an unlisted number.[1] We sent a letter to each individual whose name was drawn and who had a listed phone number. The letter explained the nature of our study and said that the recipient would be telephoned in a

Table 3.2   Numbers of Names in Each Category (Size of Sample Pools)

| | Employed males | |
	High-prestige	Low-prestige
Apparently single	570	760
Apparently not single[a]	1454	576

| | Employed females | | Housewives | |
	High-prestige	Low-prestige	High-prestige	Low-prestige
Apparently single	177	358		
Apparently not single	277	195	596	370

[a]The nonsingle people were classified as married (but childless) or as parents during the telephone screening interview.

few days by a representative of Abt Associates, our interviewing firm. Within three weeks of mailing the letters, the firm telephoned the individuals, verified the information about their age, occupation and marital status, and in addition determined the number of children in the family. We invited individuals to join the study if they met our sampling criteria and if there were less than thirty in the pertinent cell of the design.[2] Fifteen and a half percent of the females and 15.8 percent of the males whom we invited to join the study declined. The numbers of respondents in each category of our sampling design are shown in Table 3.3.

The interview

Once an appointment had been made over the telephone, each of the 405 respondents was interviewed at home by a professional interviewer. All interviews took place between November 1978 and March 1979. The interview lasted about an hour. The interview schedule began with basic demographic information, such as the number of people living in the house or apartment. Working women and men were then asked about their jobs. All

Table 3.3   Design of the Study

| | Employed males | |
	High-prestige	Low-prestige
Single	n = 30	n = 30
Married	n = 31	n = 30
Parents	n = 31	n = 30

| | Employed females | | Housewives | |
	High-prestige	Low-prestige	High-prestige	Low-prestige
Single	n = 31	n = 30		
Married	n = 31	n = 22		
Parents	n = 28	n = 21	n = 30	n = 30

respondents were questioned about their views on the job situation of women. A section about domestic arrangements and especially about the division of labor at home followed. At the end of the interview came Radloff's (1975) CES-D depression scale, a question about salary and one about household income. Respondents were paid a ten-dollar honorarium.

Each of the three core segments of the interview contained questions about deprivation and about the hypothesized preconditions of deprivation. The selection of questions was dictated by the theory of relative deprivation. Concerning one's own job situation and one's home situation, we used open-ended questions to ask about the nature of gratifications and grievances. For a balanced picture, it was necessary to know what people like about their jobs and their home lives as well as what they dislike. Each segment included measures of the extent of discontent. Some questions measured the degree of deprivation and some the degree of dissatisfaction. The emotion of deprivation is conceived of as being akin to but distinct from dissatisfaction. By the feeling of deprivation, we mean a feeling of resentment or a sense of grievance. Deprivation is one type of anger. It is a sharper emotion than dissatisfaction. Unlike the person who is simply dissatisfied, the deprived person feels he has been the victim of an injustice. When considering how discontented someone is, the terms deprivation and gratification are used as antonyms: the greater the deprivation, the less the gratification. Because of our interest in contrasting various models of relative deprivation and equity, we also created scales for each of the six hypothesized preconditions of resentment. Table 3.4 contains examples of the questions. Answers to the close-ended questions like the ones displayed in Table 3.4 were combined according to a priori rules to yield quantitative scores for each variable. Answers to the open-ended questions were coded into classifications that suggested themselves after the data were inspected.

We have throughout attempted to use previously published items. Rather than create our own depression scale, for example, we used one with demonstrated psychometric virtues. In many instances, however, our questions were modeled after but did not reproduce existing items. Given the novelty of our specific study, it was often impossible to find ready-made measures for our variables. Job satisfaction scales are legion (e.g., Smith et al., 1969), but questions about what one deserves from or had expected from a job are rare. While there are many scales to measure attitudes toward women (e.g., Mason, Czajka, & Arber, 1976), very few published items tap the hypothesized preconditions of group deprivation. Rarest of all are suitable items for the section on domestic arrangements (Berk & Berheide, 1977). Studies of how people feel about their marriages are plentiful (Hicks & Platt, 1970) as are accounts of the division of labor at home (e.g., Blood & Wolfe, 1960; Scanzoni, 1978), but the current study is among the first to examine feelings about the division of labor (cf., Robinson, Yerby, Fieweger, & Somerick, 1977).

Confidence in our interview schedule rests on several types of evidence. The first is psychometric. Because our theoretical variables are assessed by scales composed of several questions, we can check the intercorrelations among questions. These are usually high, and they are higher than are correlations between items in different scales.[3] Thus, our measures appear to have both convergent and divergent validity (Campbell & Fiske, 1959). Intercoder agreement rates for the open-ended questions are also generally high. Furthermore, in the analyses of

Table 3.4 Examples of Questions Used to Assess the Factors

Factors	Job	Home	General for women
grievance	Within this last year, how often have you felt some sense of grievance concerning each of these aspects of your job: pay and fringe benefits number of hours chances for advancement challenge respect and prestige job security general working conditions	Within the last year, how often have you felt resentful about the amount of housework that you have had to do?	Would you say that you feel bitter or resentful about any of the following aspects of women's employment situations? In particular, are you bitter or resentful about: pay and fringe benefits number of hours chances for advancement challenge respect and prestige job security general working conditions
Preconditions 1. discrepancy between what one *has*, and what one *wants*	During the last month, how often have you felt that you wanted more from your job than you are getting from it now?	Here is a list of chores. Please tell me each chore that you do now but dislike doing.	In your opinion, does the "average" American working woman get what she wants in terms of . . . [pay and fringe benefits, etc.]?
2. perception that *others* are doing better.	[Concerning aspects of the job] would you say that you are better off, worse off, or about the same as [three people named by participant].	[Concerning work around the house] would you say that you are better off, worse off, or about the same as [three people named by participant].	Imagine a woman and a man with equal job training and experience. Which one would you expect to be better off in terms of . . . [pay and fringe benefits, etc.]?

42

3. discrepancy between what one has and what one *deserves*.	In view of your training and abilities, is your present job as good as it ought to be?	Taking all things into account, would you say that you do more or less work around the house than you deserve to do?	All in all, do you think that the employment situation of women in America is as good as it ought to be?
4. discrepancy between what one has and what one's *past expectations* were.	Could you think back now for a minute to the expectations you had when you first started working. How does your present job compare with those expectations?	When you finished your schooling, did you expect to spend x hours a week on housework? [x = the number of hours the participant now spends]	Now, think back to 1970 or 1971. At that time, did you think that women would make as many gains as they have made, or did you think more gains or fewer gains would be made?
5. pessimism about the *future*.	How do you feel about the kind of salary you'll be earning in the next five or so years?	What do you expect for the next 5 or so years?	What do you feel about the kinds of salaries that women will be earning in the next five or so years?
6. *no feelings of self-blame* for undesirable outcomes.	If your present job is not ideal, why is this?	If housework takes more time than it ought, why is this?	Which of the following statements do you agree with more? (a) If a woman can't get a good job, it's almost always her own fault. (b) Many women can't get good jobs through no fault of their own.

variance used to determine the relationships between attitudes and social characteristics in Chapters 4, 5, and 6, the results are the same whether we use raw scores or standardized scores. Finally, in testing the various models of relative deprivation (Chapter 8), the results of the regression analyses remain stable when we employ structural equation models that are designed to correct for measurement error. Taken together, the psychometric evidence shows that our information does not result from technical idiosyncracies in the interview schedule.

Our confidence is bolstered by the fact that the sex of the interviewer did not influence answers people gave to our questions. The large number of questions about women might have given a feminist slant to the interview schedule. To check for interviewer effects, therefore, approximately half of the single males and females with high-prestige jobs were interviewed by a male interviewer.[4] We then examined the answers which the two groups of single respondents gave to the male and to the female interviewers on the questions about women. Statistical tests showed some differences between the ways that males answer the questions and the way that females answer the questions. The tests also showed no differences in the answers given by either group to the male and female interviewers. In seven separate analyses of variance (ANOVAs), there were no main effects for the sex of the interviewer and no interaction effects between the sex of the interviewer and the sex of the respondent.[5] Nor did the sex of the interviewer affect how much interest people professed in women's affairs. Especially comforting is the knowledge that single men presented their views in exactly the same way to a male interviewer as to a female interviewer. The evidence allows us to infer that response bias does not account for the differences in attitudes that we shall be examining in the following chapters.

What of social desirability effects in general? Even though differences among the groups shown in Table 3.3 are real and are not an artifact of response bias, it is possible that all groups are more honest about some aspects of their lives than about other aspects. As we shall see in Chapters 4 and 6, people in our sample are more than moderately enthusiastic about their jobs, their home lives in general and, especially, about their marriages. Even if we do not confuse marital stability with marital satisfaction, things sometimes seem almost too good to be true. We are left to ponder the accuracy of our descriptions of people's attitudes.

There is no simple answer to this dilemma. Any self-reported measure is subject to distortion. It seems unlikely, however, that the respondents have reported to us attitudes that differ greatly from the attitudes they would report to a friend or to themselves. The respondents appeared to enjoy the interview and to feel involved in the study. We received several unsolicited cards, letters, and phone calls from the participants in the study offering positive comments about the interview. Virtually all respondents wanted to have reports of the study sent to them. Most answers to the open-ended questions, furthermore, appeared candid. When asked about the most gratifying aspect of home life, for example, one male respondent answered unabashedly "my boyfriend."

Even with no intentional dissimulation, the possibility of unintentional distortion remains. Perhaps our respondents are unwilling or unable to acknowledge their own discontents, especially when the discontents concern their families. We have no way of directly gauging defensiveness or self-deception among the residents of Newton, but—as we shall see in the next few chapters—some patterns in the results suggest a certain amount of denial among some groups in the study. Whether or not the consciously held attitudes of our respondents always match their unconscious feelings, we are primarily interested in explicating people's conscious reactions to some aspects of their worlds.

The sample

Assuming, then, the basic truthfulness of the information gathered, what are the characteristics of the people whom we include in the study using the sampling procedures described above? On the whole, the sample is relatively young. The average age of the respondents is thirty-four. The parents tend to be older than the married or single people, and the high-prestige workers tend to be older than the low-prestige workers. The sample is well-educated. Many respondents have attended college. The majority of the high-prestige workers have some graduate education as well. Employed females are slightly better educated than are employed males. High-prestige people are much better educated than low-prestige people.

Our attempt to equate women and men in terms of job level was by and large successful. Indeed, the average NORC prestige rating of the employed females is slightly but reliably higher than that of the males. As expected, the large contrast in NORC ratings concerns the high-prestige and low-prestige workers.

With prestige level so well controlled, it comes as a shock to discover that employed males in our sample earn significantly more than employed females. In a three-way ANOVA, three main effects emerge for salary: the expected one for job level, one for family status, and one for sex. This sex difference cannot be explained away by the argument that, for example, the female professionals are in less prestigious occupations than are the males (cf. Etzioni, 1969). Nor can age or education account for the differences. The women are as old and as well educated as the men. The contrast in earnings between women and men with equally prestigious jobs is illustrated in Figure 3.1.

If employed women face pay discrimination at work, it is the housewives who bear the largest burden of work at home both for housework and for child care. Housewives spend more hours per week on housework, exclusive of child care, than do employed women or employed men. Housewives work in the home an average of twenty-seven hours per week; employed women an average of ten hours; and employed men, six hours. The differences between the employed men, the employed women, and the housewives are especially marked, as Table 3.5 shows, among the low-prestige groups. Not only do housewives spend more time on housework in absolute terms; they also do so in relative terms. Employed men spend much less time in domestic labor than do others in their households. Among employed women, the picture changes according to family status and job level. Both high- and low-prestige housewives spend a great deal more time than others in their households in domestic labor.

In addition to long hours of housework, housewives spend

Figure 3.1 Salary and NORC Scores Among Employed Respondents

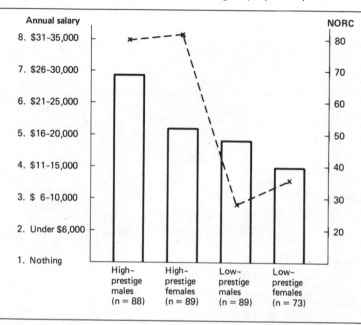

The bars show the mean annual salary for each group. The *X*s, connected by a line, show mean NORC ratings.

many hours on child care. As is obvious from Table 3.6, employed mothers devote about twice as many hours per week, on average, to child care as do employed fathers. Housewives double that number again, in part, no doubt, because of the greater number of children in their homes. The difference between the amount of work done by men and the amount of work done by women is great in both low-prestige high-prestige groups.

How closely do our data match other reports of household work? In one study, with a national probability sample, employed women and men report spending more hours per week on household labor than do our respondents (Pleck, 1979). In

Table 3.5 Hours Spent Each Week on Housework (Exclusive of Child Care)

| | Employed males | |
	High-prestige	Low-prestige
Single	7.23	4.80
	−32.83	−16.03
Married	7.16	4.63
	−5.03	−10.57
Parents	7.03	5.10
	−13.13	−36.03

| | Employed females | | Housewives | |
	High-prestige	Low-prestige	High-prestige	Low-prestige
Single	7.77	5.37		
	−21.39	−17.20		
Married	7.81	10.91		
	1.35	6.32		
Parents	13.71	17.48	23.77	29.90
	1.21	9.43	15.87	24.43

Note: The upper number is the average hours per week that the respondent spends on housework. The bottom number is average result of subtracting from respondent's hours per week the hours per week of 'others in your household.'

another study of over one thousand families in the state of New York, employed men, employed women, and housewives all report fewer hours than our sample (Walker & Woods, 1976). But while the exact number of hours may be different in our study than in some others, the patterns evident in Tables 3.5 and 3.6 are not unusual. Several researchers have found that employed women spend less time in housework and child care than do housewives and that the sex differential decreases when the wife works outside the home (Ericksen, Yancey, & Ericksen, 1979; Pleck, 1977; Robinson et al., 1977; Scanzoni, 1978; Vanek, 1974; Walker & Woods, 1976). Even when a woman is employed, furthermore, domestic labor is still primarily the female's responsibility. Whether the couples are white-collar (Epstein, 1971a, 1971b; Herman & Gyllstrom, 1977; Poloma & Garland, 1971; Thrall, 1978; Weingarten, 1978) or blue-collar

Table 3.6 Hours Spent Each Week on Child Care

	Employed fathers	Employed mothers	Housewives
High-prestige	14.16 −25.90 1.78	29.70 11.76 1.62	63.70 37.50 2.50
Low-prestige	13.13 −35.46 2.17	26.90 13.95 1.95	52.86 50.13 2.37

Note: The top number is the average hours per week that the respondent spends on child care. The middle number is the average for the group of the respondent's hours minus spouse's hours per week. The bottom number is the average number of children in the home.

(Araji, 1977; Clark, Nye & Gecas, 1978; Lein, 1979) is immaterial: women do most of the work at home.

The data on domestic labor in Newton contain one important departure from previous findings. In their classic study of marriage in America, Blood and Wolfe (1960) report that the division of labor is sharpest in high-status families. The information they obtained in 1955 shows that upper-class husbands contributed fewer hours at home, relative to the hours spent by their wives, than lower-class husbands. Twenty-two years later, we find the situation is reversed: the sex differential is smaller among the high-prestige groups than among the low-prestige groups. The change may reflect a genuine shift in middle-class practices.

Some may argue that a sex difference in home labor is only natural because men spend more hours than women in paid labor outside the home. To pursue this line of reasoning, we have counted the total hours worked per week by women and men in our sample. Total hours include time spent in paid employment, work around the house, and child care, as reported by the respondent. There is a relationship between family status and total hours. Single people work an average of 47 hours per week; married people, an average of 53, and parents an average of 81. Women work an average of 69 hours per week, significantly more than the 56 hours per week that men work. Somewhat surprisingly, people in the high-prestige groups work more hours each week ($\bar{x}=68$) than do people in the low-prestige groups ($\bar{x} = 58$). The groups that report the longest hours are high-prestige housewives, high-prestige working mothers, low-prestige working mothers, and low-prestige housewives. Their total working hours per week are 96, 90, 84, and 81, respectively. Among the residents of Newton, it is certainly not the case that women's hours within the home are balanced by men's hours outside the home.

Summary

Groups of employed women, employed men, and housewives have been interviewed about their attitudes. The groups were obtained in one suburban town in Massachusetts using a sampling technique that blended random stratified sampling and quota sampling. The sampling procedures and the survey instrument were developed with an eye to describing how employment affects women and, simultaneously, to contributing to the literature on relative deprivation theory. We have good reason to believe that the hour-long interviews yielded accurate information.

The sample resulting from our procedures is generally well educated and affluent. The high-prestige individuals earn more, are more educated, and are slightly older than the low-prestige individuals. Employed women equal employed men in terms of education and are very slightly superior to men in terms of occupational prestige ratings. When it comes to salary, however, there is a large and statistically significant difference between the sexes: men earn more than women. Housewives spend more time on housework and child care than do working women who, in turn, spend more time than working men. These are the facts about our Newtonites; in the next four chapters we shall examine their feelings.

Notes

1. In our small pilot testing, many individuals who were listed in the Street List but not in the phone book were traced and had moved

to nearby towns. It seems probable that the same was true for many individuals in the actual sample.

2. The criteria were that the person be between twenty-five and forty, white, and have an occupational prestige score of sixty-one or over or an occupational prestige score of forty or under. All employed respondents worked at least thirty hours per week. All housewives worked less than ten hours per week for pay and had an intact family including children. Single parents were excluded from the study. Due to the logistics of scheduling the interviews, we ended with thirty-one people in four of the fourteen cells. In three other cells, we fell short of thirty respondents. Among low-prestige employed married women and mothers, we exhausted the population of individuals who met our criteria and who were willing to participate in the study before filling the cells.

3. The average alpha coefficient was .59.

4. Ideally half of each group of respondents would have been interviewed by a male and half by a female. Male interviewers are rare, however.

5. Readers who are unfamiliar with analysis of variance are urged to consult Appendix I.

4

Gratifications and
Deprivations at Work

How do working women and men react to their jobs? What do
they like and dislike? How contented are they? Do they think
that they are receiving what they deserve from their jobs?

The answers to these and related questions derive from our
interviews with 163 employed women and 182 employed men.
Originally we viewed the information with an eye to sex differences. We wondered whether any differences in attitudes would
emerge for our samples, matched as they were in terms of job
level and family status. We were especially curious about how
employed women would appear in terms of the hypothesized
preconditions of deprivation. We wondered, for example, if
women would show more of a tendency to blame themselves
than men do or would be more reluctant to make comparisons
to better-off others.

We did not look only for simple sex differences. On the
contrary, previous studies of women and work alerted us to
potential complexities. We thought, for instance, that family
status might prove an important predictor of job attitudes
among females and not among males. We thought too that job
level would influence some attitudes among males and others
among females. We speculated about whether deprivation and
its preconditions would be greater among high-prestige women
or low-prestige women. About comparison others we were especially uncertain. With all the publicity about women's new-
found occupational mobility, it seemed possible that the low-
prestige women would see others as doing better than themselves. On the other hand, it also seemed possible that the high-

prestige women—working in the midst of men—might be especially prone to notice that others are doing better than they themselves.

Although we expected to see sex differences, we did not find them. The female workers and male workers in our sample are remarkably similar in their attitudes. And instead of the complex effects of sex, job level, and family status that we anticipated, we found a simple association between attitudes and family status. The strength of that association will become clear as we examine in turn the nature of worker gratifications and grievances, the extent of deprivation and dissatisfaction, and the level of the six hypothesized preconditions of deprivation. After looking at some additional factors that may help explicate our findings, we close the chapter with a summary.

Nature of gratifications and grievances

Employed women and men were asked: "What are the things about your work that you find especially gratifying or rewarding?" The answers were coded verbatim. They covered a wide range from succinct and concrete statements like "I love the bookkeeping end of it"; "travel—I like the travel idea"; or "being clever, working with students" to elaborate answers like these:

> There's a sense of accomplishment. I have respect from other people, and self-respect. I have to think a lot, which I enjoy. There is attraction to people—being appreciated.

and

> I like working with the people I work with. They are intelligent, easy to get along with. I have a lot of responsibility given to me, which I enjoy, and the place I work at encourages it. It gives me a sense of freedom to work under responsible individualistic conditions.

Scrutiny of the answers suggests seven categories of job gratification. The first is pay and fringe benefits. Answers such as "salary," "the money," "overtime, vacations," and "security" convey the sense of the first category. The second category covers feelings of accomplishment, fulfillment, or success expressed in answers like: "I enjoy my work"; "I feel I'm doing a good job"; "It's rewarding to obtain good results" as well as the straightforward "a sense of accomplishment." Similar to the second category is the third: learning, challenge, and intellectual stimulation. Here are statements such as "I can use my talents" and "intellectual stimulation." The fourth category, advancement and prestige, is typified by answers such as "moving up the corporate ladder"; "being a recognized authority in my field"; and "having students look up to me." A sense of independence or control was scored for answers that had to do with power and autonomy (e.g., "I feel I'm my own boss"; "no one to tell me what to do"; "directing and organizing other people"). The final two categories involve social interactions. Category six we call interpersonal relations. It includes references to colleagues (e.g., "everyone works together like a team"), employers (e.g., "my boss is great"), and others with whom one comes into contact on the job (e.g., "I get to meet a lot of sexy people"). The seventh and last category is reserved for specific references to helping other people or improving their condition in some way. Included here are answers like "making them better"; "showing people new things"; and the more general "making a social contribution."

Two coders scored the answers according to the seven categories.[1] Many respondents cite more than one gratifying aspect of their jobs. Indeed, two of the 345 employed respondents find as many as five different aspects of their jobs to be especially gratifying. Overall, there are 2.2 aspects cited per respondent.

What do people like most about their jobs? The simple answer is "a sense of accomplishment." Over 45 percent of the respondents generate answers that we classify as accomplishment. Nearly as important are interpersonal relations, cited by 43 percent of the workers. The remaining sources of gratification, in order of importance, include: learning and challenge—31 percent; helping other people—28 percent; advancement and

Figure 4.1 Work Gratifications as a Function of Sex and Job Level

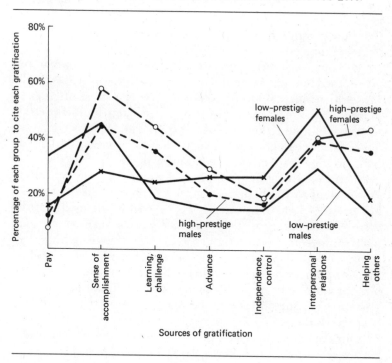

prestige—23 percent; independence and control—20 percent; and pay and fringe benefits—17 percent.

The small percentage of workers to cite pay as a source of job gratification probably testifies to the affluence of our sample. Most of our respondents are in the privileged position of working for rewards beyond the monetary. In support of this suggestion are the data depicted in Figure 4.1. As the figure shows, pay gratifies low-prestige men more often than it gratifies high-prestige men. One-third of the men with low-prestige jobs cite pay, compared with 13 percent of the high-prestige men, 14 percent of the low-prestige women, and 7 percent of the high-prestige women. Of course, it is not simply the absence of money that makes it salient. Sex-role socialization also seems to play a part. Even though low-prestige women have roughly the same household income and less personal income than low-prestige men, they are only half as likely as the men to refer to pay.

If women's indifference to pay accords with popular images, other findings evident from Figure 4.1 do not. Specifically we see that: (a) a sense of accomplishment is most often cited by high-prestige women and least often cited by low-prestige women; (b) among low-prestige respondents, interpersonal relations are less important for men than for women; but among high-prestige respondents, men and women are virtually identical; and (c) giving help to others is a much greater source of gratification to the high-prestige men and women than to the low-prestige men and women. It is sometimes claimed that the wish to help others motivates female professionals more than male professionals (Cartwright, 1972). Among our high-prestige groups, about 8 percent more women than men are gratified by the opportunity to help others. This difference—noticeable but not large to begin with—seems further diminished in comparison with the difference between high-prestige and low-prestige workers.

Our data also throw new light on the view that female workers are socially oriented (Lewis, 1976; Maccoby & Jacklin, 1974). Although half of the women with low-prestige jobs spontaneously cite interpersonal relations as a source of pleasure at work, this finding must be seen in context. Not only are women socially oriented; so are high-prestige men. Nor are women concerned with social relations to the exclusion of other motives. Indeed, among high-prestige women, a sense of accomplishment at work is more important than interpersonal relations. All in all, sex makes a difference in what people like about their jobs when it is considered in conjunction with job level; but in and of itself, sex does not predict the nature of job gratifications.

The nature of gratifications also depends on family status, especially as it interacts with gender. In Table 4.1 the sources of gratification are tabulated as a function of sex and family

Table 4.1   Work Gratifications as a Function of Sex and Family Status

	Pay		Sense of accomplishment		Learning, challenge	
	Male	Female	Male	Female	Male	Female
Single	20.0[a]	8.2	38.3	34.4	28.3	27.9
Married	16.4	5.8	52.4	48.1	19.7	38.5
Parents	32.8	17.0	44.3	55.3	32.8	40.4

	Advance		Independence, control		Interpersonal relations		Helping others	
	Male	Female	Male	Female	Male	Female	Male	Female
Single	20.0	34.4	18.3	19.7	41.7	59.0	23.3	27.9
Married	18.0	19.2	18.0	28.8	31.1	53.8	24.6	25.0
Parents	16.4	31.9	11.5	23.4	32.8	40.0	26.2	46.8

[a] Percentage of respondents in the cell to cite the code.

status. Each of the six groups, formed by considering these two factors in conjunction, contains roughly equal numbers of high- and low-prestige workers. In the table we see that pay pleases more parents than single or married people. Parents may be especially concerned with the economic rewards of their jobs because of their desire to provide financial security for their dependents. As before, there are hints of sex-role socialization with respect to pay. Fathers are approximately twice as likely as mothers to be pleased with pay. The breadwinner role must be more salient to the fathers in our sample of working people than it is to the mothers. All of the working mothers in our study have an employed spouse, but only 38 percent of the fathers do. We also see in the table that single people are much less likely than others to gain a sense of accomplishment from their jobs. Single people tend to be gratified by interpersonal relations, although the group differences are not large.

Unless we take job level and family status into account, the working women and men in our study generally like the same things about their jobs. But what a person likes about his or her job tells us very little about what the person dislikes. Perhaps certain aspects of work would prove especially nettlesome to women. To investigate the nature of work grievances, we asked "What are the things about your work that you find especially bothersome or distressing?" The first thing we looked for was an awareness of sex discrimination or sexual harassment. We did not find it. None of the men mentioned sex discrimination, and only a very few of the women did. One single woman in a low-prestige job said: "A lot of the men's personalities are hard to get along with. They say sexist and threatening things about women and will go to extraordinary lengths to say sexist comments." A female lawyer characterized the judges, unused to seeing women in courtrooms, as "outrageous." A woman banker alluded to "the discrimination against women in banking" and a sociologist noted the same for sociology. Statements such as these were the exception, not the rule.

If discrimination does not bother women or men, what does? A sense of the variation in answers may be gained from this smattering of responses:

There's poor administration in the department. It's also incompetent, unfair, biting, and malicious. Unethical too.

The money. Lack of recognition.

Job has little challenge. It's very easy.

Jealousy and hatred of my peers.

Constant interruptions. Unpleasant people. You've got to put up with customers who aren't always pleasant.

The pay. Unprofessionalism of the organization.

The woman I work for drives me crazy. She's unorganized in business and unpleasant to know. She's unpredictable. I wish she'd plan her store goods.

The inability of subordinates to accomplish tasks the way I would have them do it. I don't like the concern of my superiors over politics. They are afraid to make decisions.

Lousy customers. People don't appreciate what you're doing, thinking you're giving them the shaft. I'm bothered if a customer gives me a hard time. I'm waiting for parts and they don't show up and they get on me.

I don't like to file.

Table 4.2   Work Grievances as a Function of Sex and Job Level

	Pay		Insufficient resources		Lack of challenge	
	Male	Female	Male	Female	Male	Female
High-prestige	9.8[a]	13.3•	18.5	22.2	23.9	16.7
Low-prestige	4.5	8.6	21.3	10.0	10.1	17.1

	Lack of advance		Pressures, hours		Interpersonal relations		Frustrations	
	Male	Female	Male	Female	Male	Female	Male	Female
High-prestige	8.7	11.1	21.7	31.1	59.8	64.4	30.4	13.3
Low-prestige	10.1	15.7	19.1	20.0	52.8	62.8	31.5	17.1

[a] Percentage of respondents in the cell to cite the code.

After examining the verbatim answers, we developed seven categories of work grievances. They are: (1) pay and fringe benefits; (2) insufficient resources to complete a task; (3) lack of challenge; (4) lack of advancement; (5) pressure, long hours; (6) interpersonal relations (including bureaucratic and administrative problems); and (7) frustrations. Two coders scored the responses given by our Newtonites.[2]

An average of 1.7 sources of distress are cited by the workers in Newton. The majority of respondents cite only one aspect of their work as bothersome. Several respondents cite as many as four items. While interpersonal relations constitute a major source of gratification to workers, they also constitute the major source of distress. Sixty percent of all workers admit that they are bothered by interpersonal relations, including bureaucratic problems. The percentages of respondents citing other problems are quite small in comparison. Twenty-three percent mention pressure; 18 percent, insufficient resources; 17 percent lack of challenge; 11 percent, lack of advancement; 10 percent, pay and fringe benefits; and 10 percent, frustrations.

The nature of people's work grievances do not, on the whole, depend on sex, job level, or family status. Tables 4.2 and 4.3 reveal hardly any systematic variation among the groups of re-

Table 4.3   Work Grievances as a Function of Sex and Family Status

	Pay		Insufficient resources		Lack of challenge	
	Male	Female	Male	Female	Male	Female
Single	8.3 [a]	10.0	30.0	11.7	18.3	26.7
Married	10.0	20.8	13.3	26.4	18.3	13.2
Parents	6.6	4.2	16.4	12.8	14.8	8.5

	Lack of advance		Pressures hours		Interpersonal relations		Frustrations	
	Male	Female	Male	Female	Male	Female	Male	Female
Single	10.0	18.3	10.0	18.3	63.3	71.7	6.7	15.0
Married	6.7	15.1	25.0	24.5	51.7	52.8	8.3	9.4
Parents	11.5	14.9	26.2	38.3	57.3	66.0	3.3	8.5

[a] Percentage of respondents in the cell to cite the code.

spondents. The one exception concerns interpersonal relations. Single women are most bothered by interpersonal relations— including dealings with bureaucracies. The difference in percentage points between single women at one extreme and married men, at the other, is 20 on this one item. It ought to be remembered that single women also derive as much gratification from interpersonal relations as any other group. Clearly, social interactions loom large in the office life of single women.

Nor do group differences emerge if we approach the issue of job grievances from another angle. Believing that people might be more willing to find fault with their specific jobs than with their work in general, we asked: "Are there things you really want from your present job that you feel you will never get?" Fifty-seven percent of the respondents said yes. Of the people answering yes, 42 percent mentioned advancement and 30 percent mentioned pay. In all instances, the female workers and male workers tended to respond in similar ways.[3]

In sum, a sense of accomplishment pleases many workers. Interpersonal relations at work are both gratifying and distressing. The nature of gratifications depends on the respondents' sex and job level, but only when the two factors are considered simultaneously. Women and high-prestige men are relatively unconcerned with money. Family status also makes a difference in the nature of gratifications experienced. Single workers obtain less sense of accomplishment from their work than do others. Parents, and especially fathers, are pleased with pay. The nature of job grievances is more uniform across groups, but single women are most bothered by interpersonal relations.

Extent of discontent and of the preconditions

Although generally similar in *what* pleases and displeases them about their work, women and men may differ in *how* pleased they feel. In contrast to the open-ended questions used to discover the nature of people's gratifications and grievances were a series of close-ended questions to measure the extent of felt deprivation, of dissatisfaction, and of the six hypothesized preconditions of deprivation. For each variable, a score was obtained by summing the respondent's answers to the pertinent questions. Each respondent's Deprivation Score, for example, was derived by adding together his or her answers to four questions such as: "Within this last year, how often have you felt some sense of grievance concerning each of these aspects of your job: number of hours; chances for advancement; challenge; respect and prestige; job security; and general working conditions?"

The same procedure was used to create scales for work dissatisfaction and for each of the six hypothesized preconditions of felt deprivation.[4] The hypothesized preconditions include:

1. Wanting: the discrepancy between what one actually obtains from the job and what one would like to obtain;

2. Comparison Other: the extent to which others are seen as obtaining more from their jobs than does the respondent himself or herself;

3. Deserving: the discrepancy between what one actually obtains from the job and what one feels entitled to obtain;

4. Past Expectations: the discrepancy between what one actually obtains from the job and what one had expected to obtain;

Table 4.4   Frequency of Response to the Deprivation Question

The percentages of respondents to select each option in response to the question:

"Within this last year, how often have you felt some sense of grievance concerning each of these aspects of your job:"

	Always	Frequently	Occasionally	Seldom	Never	Total
Pay and fringe benefits	4.9	16.1	42.0	26.9	10.2	100%
Number of hours	4.4	13.7	24.2	30.3	27.4	100%
Chances for advancement	3.8	16.4	29.5	26.9	23.4	100%
Challenge	3.8	16.5	17.1	29.8	32.8	100%
Respect and prestige	2.0	10.7	22.9	33.9	30.4	100%
Job security	2.6	9.1	20.5	31.4	36.4	100%
General working conditions	3.8	12.5	31.1	28.2	24.4	100%

5. Future Expectations: the extent to which one is pessimistic about one's future job rewards; and

6. (No) Self-blame: the extent to which one refuses personal responsibility for current deprivations at work.

The quantitative approach substantiates the impression created by the qualitative data: as a group, our Newtonites tend to be positive about their jobs. They express little resentment and moderate satisfaction. The sample averages a score of 9.2 on the Deprivation Scale, where 1 means no grievance and 30 means much grievance. A general sense of contentment is visible in Table 4.4, which shows the distribution of answers to one of the items on the Deprivation Scale. For every aspect listed in Table 4.4, the distribution of responses is markedly, skewed toward the right side of the table. The percentages of workers who 'never' or 'seldom' feel aggrieved, in other words, far exceed the percentages who always or frequently feel aggrieved. Pay arouses more resentment than any other aspect of the job, but less than a quarter of the workers feel aggrieved about pay more than occasionally.

The positive tone persists if we look at the specific preconditions. For each and every scale shown in Table 4.5, the re-

Table 4.5 Work Attitudes Among Employed Respondents

Variables	Potential range	Scoring: a high score indicates	Overall mean	Sex		Job level		Family status		
				Male	Female	High	Low	Single	Married	Parents
Deprivation	1–30	strong feelings of deprivation	9.21	9.43	8.94	9.14	9.26	9.95	8.78	8.79
Dissatisfaction	2–10	great dissatisfaction	4.18	4.10	4.25	3.99	4.38	4.49	5.04	3.84
Wanting	3–21	a large discrepancy between what one has and what one wants	9.40	9.22	9.62	8.64	10.27	10.26	9.44	8.39
Comparison other	4–18	view that other(s) are better off than self	9.78	9.57	10.02	9.62	9.96	10.25	9.64	9.38
Deserving	3–14	a large discrepancy between what one has and what one deserves	7.40	7.28	7.55	7.42	7.39	7.85	7.42	6.88
Past expectations	2–10	disappointed prior expectations	5.54	5.40	5.69	5.58	5.49	5.64	5.62	5.34
Future expectations	3–12	pessimism	5.80	5.64	5.97	5.64	5.97	5.92	6.17	5.26
Self-blame	2–6	lack of self blame	3.17	3.21	3.12	3.20	3.13	3.10	3.06	3.36

For an exact account of each variable, see Appendix.

spondents average a score that is well below the midpoint. Workers feel that they are fairly close to obtaining what they want from their jobs. They feel that they are doing well as or slightly better than others are doing. They feel that they are receiving approximately what they deserve and what they had expected to receive. They are optimistic about their job situation. The workers tend to feel only partly responsible for present predicaments at work.

Given the contentment of our workers overall, do systematic variations occur? Does the degree of felt deprivation, of dissatisfaction, or of any of the preconditions vary as a function of sex, job level, or family status? To answer this critical question we performed a series of analyses of covariance (ANCOVAs).[5] In each analysis, we treated the respondents' sex, job level, and family status as independent variables. Age and salary were covariates because, as we saw in Chapter 3, single respondents in our sample are slightly but reliably younger and poorer than married people or parents. The quantitative measures of deprivation, of dissatisfaction, and of the various preconditions of deprivation were treated as dependent variables.

Table 4.6 shows the results of our analyses.[6] It is immediately apparent from the table that men and women react in the same ways to their jobs. Women are not more aggrieved than men. Women and men are equally satisfied. Nor does sex affect any of the preconditions, with the exception of Comparison Other. Among women, Comparison Other Scores vary according to family status, being highest for single women $\bar{x} = 10.73$) and lowest for mothers ($\bar{x} = 9.31$). In other words, single women perceive that others enjoy a slight advantage, but mothers do not. Among men, family status is unimportant. The mean Comparison Other Scores for the single, married, and parental males are 9.77, 9.48, and 9.44, respectively.

Perhaps we fail to find sex differences because we measure job attitudes with scales that cover many aspects of one's job situation. We know that, as a group, the women in our sample earn less than comparable men in our sample, but we cannot be certain that sex discrimination also exists in terms of, say, job security or opportunities for advancement. One may suppose that women feel positive about many aspects of their work

Table 4.6 Significant Effects Obtained in the Analyses of Covariance: F-values

Dependent variables	Sex (S)	Job level (JL)	Family status (FS)	S x JL	S x FS	JL x FS
			Independent variables			
		Main Effects			Interaction Effects	
Deprivation			3.645*			
Dissatisfaction			8.673*			
Wanting		5.241*				
Comparison other		4.095*			4.834**	
Deserving			3.850*			
Past expectations						
Future expectations			11.994***			
Self-blame						

Note: Age and salary were the covariates.
*p<.05
**p<.01
***p<.001

and that, on each scale, these positive feelings outweigh their negative reactions to pay in particular. Such a hypothesis is suggested by the gratification that high-prestige women derive from a sense of accomplishment and by the gratification that all women derive from interpersonal relations.

This hypothesis is not, however, supported by the facts. When we restrict our attention to questions that deal specifically with pay, the women's reactions remain by and large indistinguishable from the men's. In response to the question, "Would you say that your pay and fringe benefits are better than you deserve, what you deserve, slightly less than you deserve, or much less that you deserve?" for example, the average response of the women falls between "what you deserve" and. "slightly less." So does the average response of the men. For only one item does a sex difference emerge. When asked how their own pay compares with that of "the average lawyer's job," women say "slightly worse" while men say "the same." When the reference is to "the average factory worker's job," on the other hand, both women and men perceive their own pay as "much better." All in all, women feel as positive about their level of pay as do men. There seems to be a lack of correspondence between objective and subjective reality that is consistent with the theory of relative deprivation.

Also consistent with relative deprivation is the finding, evident in Tables 4.5 and 4.6, that job level is of limited importance for predicting how positive a person feels about his or her job. People with low-prestige jobs are no more dissatisfied than are people with high-prestige jobs. Nor do they report more deprivation. Low-prestige workers do experience a moderate gap between what they have and what they want, but they also claim the gap between what they have and what they deserve is small. The mean Want Score for low-prestige workers is 10.27, while for high-prestige workers, it is 8.64. The mean Deserving Scores are 7.39 and 7.42, respectively. When we control for age and salary, low-prestige workers are also significantly more aware of better-off others than are high-prestige workers. For none of the other hypothesized preconditions of deprivation do the high- and low-prestige groups differ from each other.

The limited importance of job level for predicting deprivation and its preconditions among our sample is not inconsistent with the literature on worker satisfaction. Examination of many studies with different sampling procedures and different interview schedules shows a lack of a strong relationship between one's job level and the positiveness of one's feelings about the job (Blauner, 1970; Ebeling et al., 1977; Gruneberg, 1979; Haavio-Mannila, 1971; Herzberg, Mausner, Peterson, & Capwell, 1957; Herzberg, Mausner, & Snyderman, 1967; Hunt, 1968; Lawler, 1971; Orden & Bradburn, 1969; Rice, Near, & Hunt, 1979; Schwab & Wallace, 1974; Vroom, 1969).

More predictive of job attitudes than either sex or job level is family status. Both the degree of dissatisfaction and the degree of felt deprivation vary as a function of family status, even when age and salary are controlled. Parents in our sample express the most satisfaction with their jobs and married respondents express the least. Single people whom we interviewed are much more resentful of their job situation than are married or parental groups. Parents, more than married or single respondents, also tend to feel that they receive what they deserve and to feel optimistic about the future. Finally, as we saw earlier, single women are more likely than mothers to think that other workers are better off than themselves.

In sum, when rendered in quantitative form, job attitudes do not seem to be linked in a simple or direct way to objective conditions on the job. The women in our study earn less than men with comparable jobs. Yet, subjectively, the employed women and employed men are virtually indistinguishable. Low-prestige workers also earn considerably less than high-prestige workers. Again, the attitudinal differences are not as great as the actual ones. While we did not find the expected sex differences, we did find some unanticipated differences relating to family status. Job attitudes are least positive among single people and most positive among parents. This finding may seem unexceptional in hindsight; but it would surprise many researchers to see the close association between job attitudes and home life among male and female workers.

Other factors

The lack of sex differences in the quantitative measures of discontent and in the possible preconditions of deprivation raise new questions. We could explain the female workers' contentment in spite of sex discrimination by observing that for them the hypothesized preconditions of deprivation are generally absent. According to this line of reasoning, explicated in Chapter 1, we might conclude that resentment about pay is low among women because, for instance, they do not feel entitled to greater pay, do not want greater pay, think others are not better paid, had not expected better pay, or think better pay will come in the future. The only potential explanation that we have eliminated concerns self-blame. We now know that women do not blame themselves for their predicament. With so many possible explanations remaining, we wonder why women do not feel entitled to greater pay, do not think others are better paid, and so on.

One possible reason that women and men workers react in apparently identical ways to their different job situations is that women feel less committed to working than do men. There is some evidence that work is more central to the lives of men than to women (Hulin, 1969; cf. Kavanagh & Halpern, 1977). Perhaps women remain pleased with their work despite unpleasantness and even discrimination because they do not have a strong emotional investment in their jobs. To explore this possibility, we asked two questions about job commitment.[7] When the answers were combined and treated as the dependent variable in a 2 (sex) by 2 (job level) by 3 (family status) analysis of variance, only one effect emerges. Like others (e.g., Lawler, 1971; Orden & Bradburn, 1969), we find an association between job level and job commitment. Low-prestige workers are less committed to their jobs than are high-prestige workers. Sex and family status are not important, either alone or in conjunction with job level. Indeed, the women in our sample are slightly (nonsignificantly) more committed to working than are men.

A second factor that may help explicate our findings is control. In some earlier work (Bernstein & Crosby, 1980), we reasoned that feelings of resentment or grievance might occur in response to an undeserved outcome that is thought to be under human control. Negative events—like flood and famine—that lie outside the realm of human agency may elicit depression or disappointment rather than a sense of grievance or deprivation. In our society males tend to overestimate their ability to effect positive outcomes; females tend to underestimate their efficacy (Deaux, 1976; Deaux & Farris, 1977). It seemed reasonable that the Newton women express contentment by every quantitative measure because they feel powerless to control their lives generally or their career life specifically.

Two questions tapped a sense of control on the job; another measured a sense of control over financial advancement; and a fourth measured a general sense of control.[8] On one of the job questions, high-prestige workers emerged with a stronger sense of control than did low-prestige workers. Concerning a general sense of control, no differences were found. Only for financial advancement did the analyses reveal any effects related to sex. On a 0 to 10 scale, men experience greater control ($\bar{x} = 7.47$) than do women ($\bar{x} = 6.60$). In sum, perceived control does not explain the pattern of our deprivation findings any better than job commitment.

A third possible explanation for the lack of sex differences concerns the target of one's anger. Freud (1933) characterized women as particularistic and as unable to make dispassionate assessments of justice. If Freud's ideas are correct, then women workers may fail to notice sex discrimination by attributing the inequities of the system to personal quirks of their bosses or their coworkers. If so, more women than men would select individual people as the target of any anger they feel about their job situations. Alternately, women may convince themselves that they are obtaining what they deserve because they feel unable or afraid to express anger at other individuals. If so, women would be less likely than men to select individuals as the targets of their anger. Following this line of inquiry, we asked the employed respondents:

> When you think of things that are wrong with your job, do you get angry, resentful, or bitter toward anyone in particular or do you get mad at things in general?
>
> It's always just things in general
> Usually things in general
> Half and half
> Usually some person or people
> Always some person or people.

Statistical analyses reveal no effects due to sex or family status. Women and men, in other words, react to frustrations in the same way. Job level, in contrast, is significant. People with high-prestige jobs are more willing than those with low-prestige jobs to direct their anger at people. Venting anger at others may be a luxury that most low-prestige workers can ill afford. Whatever the findings say about job level, they do not help much in explaining the contentment of female workers.

It is conceivable that women are unaware of males' advantages at work because they restrict their reference group to women. If women and men workers remain occupationally and socially segregated, the female worker may have little occasion to compare her situation with that of men. To pursue this idea, we asked the employed respondents to name three people whom they could or do use as points of comparison in evaluating their own jobs. We noted the sex of the comparison other. As Figure

Figure 4.2 Sex of Comparison Other

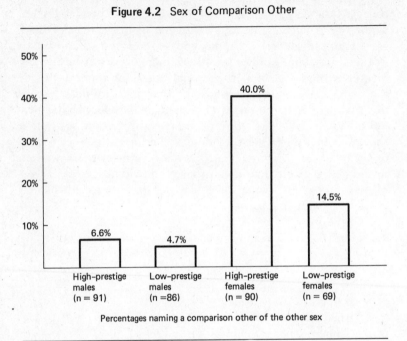

Percentages naming a comparison other of the other sex

4.2 shows, most people named first someone of their own sex. (The figures for the second and third names are very similar to the figures for the first name.) High-prestige women are more likely than men or low-prestige women to cross the sex barrier. That high-prestige women workers choose male referents fairly often makes sense. People tend to make comparisons with others in their immediate environment (Patchen, 1961b), and high-prestige women circulate in what is still a predominantly male world.

Although more likely to select a male as a referent than are low-prestige women, the professional women are no more likely to perceive others as better off than themselves. They do not score higher on the Comparison Other Scale than do low-prestige women. This pattern suggests that comparison other is not a critical precondition of felt deprivation. It also hints at

Table 4.7 Reactions to Deprivation

1. As a function of sex and job level

	% citing anger		% citing depressed emotions		% citing action		% citing resignation	
	Male	Female	Male	Female	Male	Female	Male	Female
High-prestige	21.1	48.0	25.0	28.0	21.1	14.0	25.0	18.0
Low-prestige	15.1	40.5	30.2	42.9	5.7	16.7	32.1	19.0

2. As a function of sex and family status

	% citing anger		% citing depressed emotions		% citing action		% citing resignation	
	Male	Female	Male	Female	Male	Female	Male	Female
Single	23.1	50.0	12.8	31.6	10.2	26.3	35.9	18.4
Married	9.3	44.4	39.5	38.9	20.9	5.6	23.2	13.9
Parent	26.1	33.3	39.1	33.3	4.3	11.1	26.1	27.8

[a] Percentage of respondents in the cell to cite the code.

a form of selective perception or perhaps selective processing among female workers in our sample. It is as if the high-prestige woman worker looks at but does not see her situation.

· Women's and men's reactions to deprivation are also informative. We asked people if there were some things they wanted but thought they would never attain from their jobs. Nearly 200 workers said yes, and we continued the question by asking them: "How does this make you feel?" The answers were coded into four categories.[9] The first includes angry emotions (e.g., anger, frustration, resentment). The second includes depressed emotions. It was scored if people said they felt sad, bad, disillusioned, disappointed, or depressed. Third is the category of action. It covers answers like "quitting," changing jobs, or changing something about the job. Finally, there is resignation, which includes avoidance (e.g., "I get things outside the job") and acceptance (e.g., "I don't mind it" or "I just remain optimistic").

Table 4.7 shows people's reactions to deprivation as a function of sex and job level. Women workers are much more likely than men to cite anger as a reaction, and anger is the reaction most often listed by women. Depression and resignation are the most common reactions among men. Low-prestige men are noticeably reluctant to cite the third category although popular images would feature this group as the most likely to leap into action. Single men are much less prone than any other group to become depressed.

The prevalence of anger among women on this one item seems at variance with the generally low level of resentment and of dissatisfaction. Perhaps working women do not wish to acknowledge the full extent of their resentments at work. They may repress their own emotional reactions until a pointed question leads them to voice their anger. Alternately, one can interpret the women's responses to this question as an indication that they are not afraid of expressing anger or dissatisfaction. If so, we would conclude that women have the ability to differentiate between their job on the whole and some particular aspects of the job. Perhaps they genuinely want some things and feel upset that those things are not attainable and, simultaneously, feel that those things constitute only a fraction of life at work.

Summary and speculations

The 345 employed respondents in our study tend to experience positive feelings about their jobs. Many derive a sense of accomplishment from them. Work is a place of both gratifying and bothersome interpersonal contacts. On the whole, bitterness about one's job or about various aspects of it is rare. Women react subjectively to their jobs in much the same way as men do. Similarly, people with low-prestige jobs are generally as satisfied with their work situations as are people with high-prestige jobs. Resentment and the hypothesized preconditions of resentment tend to be most marked among the single groups.

The present findings echo some earlier surveys of workers. Using a variety of instruments with assorted samples, industrial and social psychologists generally have found that American workers feel positively toward their jobs (e.g., Near, Rice, & Hunt, 1978). Another standard research finding to appear in the present study concerns the prestige of one's job; while job level relates to worker commitment, it is not consistently associated with worker satisfaction. Finally, despite a complex set of methodological precautions against sampling bias (described in the last chapter), our study hums with the sad and familiar refrain: employed women, as a group, face discrimination, but women are as content with their jobs as are men.

If our findings about the extent of discontent contain few departures from previous research findings, our discoveries about the nature of gratification and of grievance differ rather noticeably from earlier work in two ways. First, our sample seems generally unconcerned with money. Less than one-fifth of the respondents spontaneously mention money as a source of job gratification, and only one-tenth spontaneously mention it as a source of discomfort. Approximately 17 percent of the sample say that they would like to receive more pay than they think their present jobs will yield. When asked point-blank about pay and fringe benefits, as little as 21 percent of the working women and men admit that they have "always" or "frequently" felt "some sense of grievance." Figures such as these contrast starkly with the percentages that appear in some earlier studies. Herzberg et al. (1967) found, for example, that nearly 40 percent of their 200 male respondents thought that pay was a positive aspect of their jobs and that an equal percentage felt the opposite. Our sample's relative lack of concern with money and their relative concern with a sense of accomplishment and with interpersonal relations at work suggest a certain affluence. For a very large proportion of our respondents, employment seems to be less a matter of paying bills than of self-fullfillment.

The second departure from previous research findings is probably less important than the first, but it may also relate to the affluence of the sample. Unlike Herzberg and his associates (1967), we have found little evidence for the proposition that people like one set of factors about their jobs and dislike another set. True, nearly half of our respondents are gratified by a sense of accomplishment, and no one is bothered by a sense of accomplishment; but semantics probably play a large role in this difference. Certainly, interpersonal relations prove gratifying on the job as frequently as they prove distressing.

A final novel finding of the present study deserves attention: it is the contrast between single people, married people, and parents. As far as we know, no one before has documented a strong relationship between family status and worker attitudes among men and women. Psychologists and sociologists have speculated about how difficult it is for women to combine the role of mother with the role of worker, but they have not compared the degree of worker satisfaction among mothers and fathers with the degree among, say, single women and men. Had they made the comparison, they might have found—as we did—that single people are less positive about their jobs than are married people who are less positive, in turn, than parents. This pattern, although not reported before, makes sense intuitively. Perhaps single people have more time than married people or parents to dwell on problems and mishaps at work. For married workers and especially for parents the joys of home may wash away the concerns and smooth away the disgruntlements of the office, the factory, or the shop. Perhaps too, some of the woes of parenthood, woes as diverse as having a young one in the hospital, needing to plan for college tuition, or finding ways to restore a child's self-esteem, may put difficulties at work in a new, rather soft light. There may be nothing like the vicarious reacquaintance with the multiplication tables at home to diminish the impact of traumas at work.

What we have uncovered about people's attitudes toward their jobs, whether or not our knowledge differs from that of previous researchers, moves us a little closer to resolving the paradox of the contented female worker. We now know that self-blame is not a critical factor in women's contentment with their jobs. The women in our study are not more prone than the men to blame themselves when things go wrong at work. Nor does it seem that the women's positive outlook results primarily from a restricted choice of comparisons. High-prestige women tend to compare themselves with men more than low-prestige women do; but the two groups are equally convinced that they are doing well relative to others. By the process of elimination, then, it seems that the extent of job grievance or deprivation among the employed females in Newton is associated with one or more of the following four hypothesized preconditions of deprivation: wanting, deserving, past expectations, and future expectations. The women generally express optimism about their job prospects; their hopes seem to have been slightly exceeded rather than disappointed; they believe that they receive from their jobs what they ought to; and they claim to gain from working what they want to gain.

The importance of a sense of accomplishment and of good interpersonal relations at work for the employed women of Newton and the lack of attention accorded to money all make credible the women's claim that they derive from their jobs what they want. We are left to wonder, however, about the source of their optimism, about their view that their own expectations have been slightly surpassed, and especially about their opinion that they receive what they deserve to receive. We have tried without success to explain women's perceptions by looking at some additional factors. We see that women feel committed to their jobs; that they neither gravitate toward nor avoid specific individuals as the target of their angers at work; and that they are able to express anger about some aspects of their jobs while feeling contented about the job generally. When it comes to factors such as job commitment, sex differences are noticeably absent. The lack of sex differences undermines our ability to explain the working women's feelings of deserving, their past and future expectations in terms of these factors.

Two further answers to the question of deserving present themselves at this juncture. The answers are quite different from each other. First, it may be that despite sex differences in the objective conditions of employment (e.g., pay), there are virtually no sex differences in subjective reactions to employment because women (and maybe men too) are unaware of sex discrimination. They may, for example, mistakenly believe that women have now gained a position of equality with men. Alternately, the women may be cognizant of sex discrimination in general but unable to see it in their own personal cases.

We suspect that the second answer comes closer to the truth than does the first. It may be much easier psychologically to recognize cases of collective disadvantage than cases of individual disadvantage. Cases in which an individual is unfairly deprived of some desired outcome seem to require psychologically, albeit not logically, the existence of an individual harmdoer

(Crosby & Gonzalez-Intal, 1982). That is, it could be difficult for an individual to think that she or he is being personally disadvantaged unless the individual can also believe that some person or persons are responsible for the ill-treatment. Since it is emotionally noxious to view one's coworkers or one's bosses as villains, furthermore, people may avoid the conclusion of malice by denying the premise that they are personally ill-treated. When it comes to group or collective disadvantage, no such selective processing is required, because group harm does not seem to call psychologically for an individual harmdoer.

The denial of personal discrimination in the face of recognized discrimination against the group can be traced to cognitive as well as emotional reasons. H. L. A. Hart, the renowned legal philosopher, writing on the connections between justice, morality, and the law, equates the words "just" and "unjust" with the words "fair" and "unfair." He continues:

> references to fairness . . . are mainly relevant in two situations. . . . One is when we are concerned not with the single individual's conduct but with the way in which *classes* of individuals are treated. . . . The second situation is when some injury has been done and compensation . . . is claimed. (Hart, 1961, p. 154).

Only when an individual case represents a valid instance of general class or category can the claim of personal unfairness be pressed. Applying Hart's observation to equity theory, discussed in the second chapter, we see that it is easier to complete the equity formula for classes of people than for specific individuals. When dealing with categories of people, the "relevant" inputs and outcomes are rather easy to determine and the irrelevant idiosyncracies of individuals are averaged away. When one deals with individuals, in contrast, idiosyncracies tend to swamp the cognitive field. Applying Hart's observation to relative deprivation theory, we see that it is easier to know what a group of people deserve to obtain than it is to know what any individual person deserves. The contrast between the individual and the group should be equally dramatic whether the individual is oneself or another and whether the group is one's own group or another group.

Theoretical arguments like these incline us to think that an important element in working women's job contentment is the uncertainty that surrounds any decision about individual fairness or personal deserving. The story calls for empirical confirmation. The case would be much stronger, in other words, if we can show that the working women of Newton, contented about their own situations, express grievance about the situation of working women generally. It is to the question of group deprivation that we now turn.

Notes

1. While coding, the coders were blind to the characteristics of the respondents, as far as was possible. One hundred protocols were scored independently by two coders. Inter-rater agreement was 95 percent.

2. Coders were blind during the coding processes. One hundred protocols were scored independently by two coders. Inter-rater agreement was 92 percent.

3. Originally seven categories were scored. They were: (1) salary and pay ("money," "more money"); (2) better material ("good tools and on the job training"); (3) challenge ("I'd like to be using my degree and growing in my field"); (4) advancement ("to be in charge, have more control"); (5) personal satisfaction ("to be good at what I do and like to do it"); (6) interpersonal relations ("I don't get any kind of support or encouragement"); (7) ideal work conditions "a nicer office, with air conditioning"). Coders were blind during coding. For the seventy protocols coded by two independent raters, inter-rater agreement was 93 percent.

4. A complete and exact account of how each variable is operationalized may be found in Appendix II.

5. Readers who are unfamilirar with inferential statistics may consult Appendix I, where ANOVAS and ANCOVAS are briefly explained.

6. The eight dependent variables were also submitted to analyses of variance (ANOVAs). The ANOVAs revealed basically the same patterns as the ANCOVAs.

As an additional check on the scales, we performed analyses on measures created from standardized scores. The standardized Deprivation Scale, for example, was created by averaging the z-scores of the four questions that made up the raw Deprivation Scale. In virtually all instances, analyses with standardized scores yielded the same results as analyses with raw scores.

7. See questions 12 and 13 in Appendix III-B.

8. See question 120 in Appendix III-B.

9. For the seventy protocols scored independently and blindly by two raters, inter-rater agreement was 98 percent.

5

Views of the Job
Situation of Women

In his classic work on relative deprivation Runciman (1966) distinguishes between "egoistical" and "fraternal" deprivation. The former, as we have seen in Chapter 2, refers to grievances felt about one's own situation while the latter refers to grievances felt on behalf of one's group. Some scholars (e.g. Pettigrew, 1978, Rhodebeck, 1981) propose that collective deprivations have more political implications than do personal deprivations. Sucn propositions accord with Williams' (1975) model of relative deprivation. Aside from a few tantalizing studies that suggest that group and personal deprivations are empirically distinct (Abeles 1972; Hennigan & Cook, note 3; Martin, 1979; Vanneman & Pettigrew, 1972), however, very little is known about grievances felt on behalf of a group, whether or not it be one's own membership group.

To investigate group deprivation, we asked people in our study about their reactions to the employment situation of women in America. We wondered if the absence of personal deprivation among our working women, documented in Chapter 4, would also mean a lack of group deprivation. It seemed possible, if unlikely, that the employed females would deny the importance of sex discrimination in their own working lives because of a need to see the world as a just place (Lerner, 1975). The selfsame need for justice could make them underestimate the pervasiveness of sex discrimination in general. Consistent with this view is the observation that minority groups often engage in self-denigration (Allport, 1954). Perhaps the working woman believes that she is obtaining from her job what she deserves to obtain because of an internalized conviction that women are inferior to men.

What the data actually show is that employed women are the most upset about sex discrimination. Employed women are more resentful and dissatisfied about the fate of working women than are employed men or housewives. They are the most keenly aware of the discrepancy between what working women want and what they have, between what they deserve and what they have, and between what women obtain from their jobs and what men obtain from theirs. Coupled with the findings of the last chapter, the results strongly suggest that group deprivation may be a more acceptable emotion than personal deprivation. The data also show that deprivation and the hypothesized preconditions of deprivation are more intense among high-prestige groups than among low-prestige groups. These results echo the conclusions of Abeles (1972) and others (Caplan, 1970; Sears & McConahay, 1973) that ethnic consciousness and fraternal deprivation are most prevalent among well-educated blacks.

Deprivation and dissatisfaction

To measure deprivation, we asked the respondents if they felt "bitter or resentful" about seven aspects of "women's employment situation." The aspects are: pay and fringe benefits; number of hours; chances for advancement; challenge; respect and prestige; job security; and general working conditions. For each aspect, the options ranged from "very" (scored 6) to "not at all" (scored 1). Table 5.1 shows the frequency with which each option is selected for the different aspects of work life. Pay, advancement, and respect provoke resentment quite frequently.

When the responses to the different aspects are averaged, we obtain a summary Deprivation Score, with a potential range of 1 to 6 points. The actual overall mean Deprivation Score among the people in our study is 3.20. The distribution of Deprivation Scores among the fourteen groups in the study is shown in Table 5.2. From the table, we see that high-prestige working mothers are quite aggrieved. Low-prestige single men, at the other extreme, are fairly complacent.

Table 5.1   Frequency of Responses to the Deprivation Question

The percentages of respondents to select each option in response to the question:

"Would you say that you feel bitter or resentful about any of the following aspects of women's employment situation? In particular, are you bitter or resentful about:"

	Very	Somewhat	A little	Not certain	Not really	Not at all	Total
Pay and fringe benefits	12.1	24.7	20.7	5.2	18.0	19.3	100%
Number of hours	4.5	9.2	· 7.9	13.9	35.1	29.4	100%
Chances for advancement	17.0	23.4	23.0	6.2	12.6	17.8	100%
Challenge	10.9	19.8	17.3	9.1	22.2	20.7	100%
Respect and prestige	16.3	22.0	18.0	7.7	15.6	20.5	100%
Job security	8.9	18.3	15.3	9.6	24.4	23.5	100%
General working conditions	5.7	17.8	14.6	7.9	27.9	26.2	100%

It appears from Table 5.2 that employed women feel more resentful than either employed men or housewives. It also seems that high-prestige individuals feel more resentful than low-prestige individuals. To determine whether the apparent patterns are reliable, we can perform three separate analyses of variance.[1] In the first, we divide the sample into six groups by considering their employment group and job level. As in the last chapter, job level refers to high-prestige and low-prestige individuals, and the employed respondents are classified on the basis of their own occupations. Housewives, whom we did not consider in Chapter 4, are classified on the basis of their husbands' occupations. The three "employment groups" are: employed women, employed men, and housewives. Our first analysis is, thus, a 3 by 2 factorial.

One should remember that, by design, all the housewives in our sample are parents, while only one-third of the employed women and men are. It is possible, therefore, that what passes for an effect of employment group in the first analysis could

Table 5.2 Distribution of Deprivation Scores

	Employed males	
	High-prestige	Low-prestige
Single	x̄ = 2.88 (n = 30)	x̄ = 2.03 (n = 30)
Married	x̄ = 2.76 (n = 31)	x̄ = 2.39 (n = 30)
Parents	x̄ = 2.75 (n = 31)	x̄ = 2.29 (n = 30)

	Employed females		Housewives	
	High-prestige	Low-prestige	High-prestige	Low-prestige
Single	x̄ = 3.70 (n = 31)	x̄ = 3.70 (n = 30)		
Married	x̄ = 3.91 (n = 31)	x̄ = 4.17 (n = 22)		
Parents	x̄ = 4.30 (n = 28)	x̄ = 3.28 (n = 21)	x̄ = 3.75 (n = 30)	x̄ = 3.23 (n = 30)

The higher the score, the greater the deprivation. Potential range is 1 to 6.

actually be an effect of family status. To check this possibility, we perform a second analysis. We repeat the 3 by 2 ANOVA, but restrict the sample to parents.

In the third analysis, we exclude housewives and treat sex (male, female), job level (high prestige, low prestige), and family status (single, married, parent) as our independent variables. Age and salary are covariates in the 2 by 2 by 3 ANCOVA. This analysis is the one we used in Chapter 4. It is needed to determine whether deprivation or any of the other factors varies as a function of one's family status.

The analyses of variance confirm that the apparent results are reliable. The first analysis shows main effects for employment group and job level and no interactions. Employed females are the most resentful, and high-prestige individuals are more resentful than low-prestige individuals. The findings when one limits the sample to parents (in the second analysis) are virtually identical to the findings obtained from the entire sam-

Table 5.3 Distribution of Dissatisfaction Scores

| | Employed males | |
	High-prestige	Low-prestige
Single	$\bar{x} = 2.93$ (n = 30)	$\bar{x} = 2.53$ (n = 30)
Married	$\bar{x} = 2.90$ (n = 31)	$\bar{x} = 2.47$ (n = 30)
Parents	$\bar{x} = 2.83$ (n = 31)	$\bar{x} = 2.24$ (n = 30)

| | Employed females | | Housewives | |
	High-prestige	Low-prestige	High-prestige	Low-prestige
Single	$\bar{x} = 3.00$ (n = 31)	$\bar{x} = 2.70$ (n = 30)		
Married	$\bar{x} = 3.09$ (n = 31)	$\bar{x} = 2.91$ (n = 22)		
Parents	$\bar{x} = 3.18$ (n = 28)	$\bar{x} = 2.43$ (n = 21)	$\bar{x} = 2.70$ (n = 30)	$\bar{x} = 2.40$ (n = 30)

The higher the score, the greater the dissatisfaction. Potential range is 1 to 4.

ple. The results also remain stable if we exclude housewives from the analyses and treat gender, job level, and family status as three independent variables in an analysis of covariance, with age and salary as covariates. In such an analysis, sex and job level emerge as significant predictors of group deprivation. Employed women are more deprived than employed men, with the mean scores being 3.85 and 2.52, respectively. High-prestige respondents express more grievance ($\bar{x} = 3.37$) than do low-prestige employed respondents ($\bar{x} = 2.90$).

We also measured dissatisfaction. The respondents were asked, "All in all, how satisfied do you feel about the work situation for women in America today?" The options ranged from "very satisfied" (scored as 1) to "very dissatisfied" (scored as 4). The average score, overall, was 2.74. Table 5.3 depicts the distribution of mean scores among the groups in our study. Considerable variation is apparent, with high-prestige mothers scoring 3.18 and low-prestige fathers scoring 2.24.

Statistical tests reveal the same pattern of results for dissat-isfaction as for deprivation. In the first analysis, data from all respondents are used and we consider job level (high prestige, low prestige) and employment group (employed males, em-ployed females, housewives) to be our independent variables. The resulting 2 by 3 analysis of variance reveals main effects for job level and for employment group. High-prestige people are more dissatisfied than are low-prestige ($\bar{x} = 2.95$ for high and $\bar{x} = 2.52$ for low). Employed women are more dissatisfied than either of the other two groups. The mean scores are 2.91, 2.66, and 2.55 for employed women, employed men, and housewives, respectively.

In the second and third analyses, the results remain stable. Among parents only, job level and employment group are again important. High-prestige individuals are more dissatisfied than are low-prestige individuals. Group effects are also significant: working mothers are more dissatisfied than working fathers or housewives.

In the three-way ANCOVA, we obtain a main effect for sex. The average dissatisfaction score for females is 2.91, and for males it is 2.66. As in the other analyses, job level is important: high-prestige people feel more dissatisfaction ($\bar{x} = 2.99$) about the situation of working women than do low-prestige people ($\bar{x} = 2.54$). Family status does not affect satisfaction.

In sum, the extent of both dissatisfaction and deprivation vary as a function of employment group and job level. Em-ployed women, complacent about their individual situations, are more ready than either employed men or housewives to ex-press discontent about the situation of women in general. Among each of the three groups, furthermore, high-prestige individuals are more discontented about the situation of work-ing women than are low-prestige individuals. Family status, which proves an important determinant of people's feelings about their own jobs, plays no role in people's feelings about women's jobs.

Preconditions of felt deprivation

When we turn to the hypothesized preconditions of felt depri-vation, job level and employment group again appear as the

heroes of the piece. For each of the six hypothesized preconditions of group deprivation, we created a scale, analogous to
the scales created for the hypothesized preconditions of personal deprivation. Table 5.4 summarizes the significant effects
that obtain in the various analyses done for each scale. In the
table, we see that job level functions as a predictor in four of
the six cases. Employment group (and, similarly, sex in the
ANCOVAs) is equally important. The table also displays a re-
assuring consistency. In general, an effect that obtains in one
analysis also obtains in the other two.

Let us look at the variables one at a time. Our Want Scale
is derived by summing the respondent's answers to three questions such as this one:

Taking everything into account, what proportion of American
women get what they want from a job?

almost all
most
some
a few
none

The potential range of scores on the Want Scale was 3 to 12,
with higher numbers indicating a greater perceived discrepancy between what women have and what they want.[2] The
overall mean score of our Newtonites is 8.60. The perceived
discrepancy between real and ideal is greatest among employed
women ($\bar{x} = 8.78$) and least among housewives ($\bar{x} = 7.98$). High-
prestige individuals see the gap as larger than do low-prestige
individuals. Among high-prestige individuals, the average score
is 8.90; among low-prestige individuals, it is 8.26.

Do employed women differ from employed men and
housewives in their opinion of what women and men desire
from their work? A substantial literature has documented the
existence of negative stereotypes about working women. Like
many underprivileged groups, furthermore, women have traditionally shared the wider culture's negative view of themselves (Walster & Paté, 1974). Our findings and those of others
(Mason et al., 1976) suggest that times may be changing.
To gauge the extent of stereotyping, we asked: "Would you

Table 5.4 Summary of Significant Results for Preconditions

	Analyses and Independent Variables		
	2 × 3 ANOVA among entire sample Job level, employment group	**2 × 3 ANOVA among parents only** Job level, employment group	**2 × 2 × 3 ANCOVA among employed people only** Job level, sex, family status
Discrepancy between what women have and what they want	Level ($F = 26.464$; df = 1,396; $p < .0001$) Group ($F = 9.068$; df = 2,396; $p < .0001$)	Level ($F = 11.793$; df = 1,163; $p < .0001$) Group ($F = 8.496$; df = 2,163; $p < .0001$)	Level ($F = 13.622$; df = 1,320; $p < .0001$)
Discrepancy between what women have and what men have	Level ($F = 6.179$; df = 1,392; $p < .05$) Group ($F = 10.653$; df = 2,392; $p < .0001$)	Group ($F = 9.547$; df = 2,161; $p < .0001$)	Sex ($F = 14.495$; df = 1,318; $p < .0001$)
What women deserve to obtain	Level ($F = 46.057$; df = 1,397; $p < .0001$) Group ($F = 14.525$; df = 2,397; $p < .0001$)	Level ($F = 27.794$; df = 1,162; $p < .0001$) Group ($F = 4.097$; df = 2,162; $p < .02$)	Level ($F = 32.997$; df = 1,321; $p < .0001$) Sex ($F = 15.985$; df = 1,321; $p < .0001$)
Discrepancy between past expectations and present reality	—	—	—
Expectations for women's situation in the future	Level ($F = 8.277$; df = 1,397; $p < .004$) Group ($F = 8.360$; df = 2,397; $p < .0001$)	Level ($F = 7.042$; df = 1,163; $p < .009$) Group ($F = 3.819$; df = 2,163; $p < .05$) Level × Group ($F = 4.347$; df = 2,163; $p < .02$)	Level ($F = 13.500$; df = 1,321; $p < .0001$) Sex ($F = 6.365$; df = 1,321; $p < .02$)
Avoidance of blame of women for their own situation	—	—	Level ($F = 5.170$; df = 1,310; $p < .05$)

Dependent variables

say that men and women want the same or different things from a job?" Most of the respondents see no difference between men and women workers: 72.5 percent of the employed men, 72.2 percent of the employed women, and 58.0 percent of the housewives say that men and women want the same things. Clearly, stereotyping is not strong. Two hundred and eighty-five of the 405 respondents see no difference between men and women. Of the remaining 120 respondents, we asked: "What's the difference?" and coded the answers into five categories.[3] The categories are,

1. career and income are important for men
2. satisfaction and security are important for women
3. women need recognition from a job
4. women have other interests (e.g. children)
5. men have to work, while women work only if they want.

The most popular belief is that men work for a career and for money more than women do. About two-thirds of the employed men, employed women, and housewives mention this difference. Of the five categories, only one varies as a function of the respondents' characteristics. Nearly half of the housewives think that women especially need recognition or praise for their work; only a quarter of the employed men share this belief; and less than 10 percent of the employed women do.

Three questions composed the Comparison Other Scale. In one of the questions, for example, respondents were requested to "imagine a woman and a man with equal training and experience." They were then asked which one they would expect to be better off in terms of: (a) pay; (b) number of hours; (c) chances for advancement; (d) challenge; (e) respect and prestige; (f) job security; and (g) general working conditions. The options ranged from "woman much better off" (scored as 1) to "man much better off" (scored as 5). The potential range of scores on the Comparison Other Scale is 3 to 13. A score of 8 means that the respondent perceives men and women to be treated equally.

Looking at the sum scores, we see that virtually no group in the study thinks women are better off than men. Only 3 per-

cent of the sample scores 8 or less on the Comparison Other
Scale. For the sample as a whole, the mean score is 10.98. Although no group perceives men to be at a disadvantage, the
employed males in the study tend to minimize the extent of
male advantage. As Figure 5.1 shows, employed females and
the housewives both score higher on the Comparison Other
Scale than do employed males. The sex difference appears
equally strong if we look at the entire sample or at parents only.

What happens if we single out for attention the question
that concerns money specifically? Again, males in Newton minimize the male advantage. Table 5.5 summarizes the views of
employed men and women: 12.2 percent of the men and 2.5
percent of the women endorse the view that women are given
economic advantages over men. Low-prestige males are the least
aware of male advantage. Yet even among them, 62 percent
admit in effect that women are underpaid.

In addition to the Comparison Other Scale, we measured
the Newtonites' perceptions of sex differences in job rewards
by asking them to estimate the average yearly salary of women
and men with white-collar or blue-collar jobs. The average yearly
salaries estimated were:

$19,120 for white-collar men
$13,776 for white-collar women
$13,761 for blue-collar men
$ 9,507 for blue-collar women.

The estimates do not vary among the different groups of respondents. That our respondents guessed similar figures for
white-collar women and blue-collar men indicates a certain so-
phistication about economic realities among our sample. It also
suggests that our sample is considerably more aware of sex discrimination than samples in some previous studies. In 1973,
only 5 percent of workers interviewed in one investigation
thought that sex discrimination was a "problem area" (Quinn,
1973, in Hall, 1975). Highly educated groups have been more
realistic; but even among them awareness of sex discrimination
has not been widespread. McCune (1970), for example, polled
more than 6000 academics; only about a quarter of them knew
that women are subjected to discrimination.

Figure 5.1   Mean Scores on Comparison Other Scale as a Function of Job Level and Employment Group

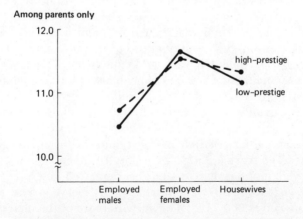

The higher the score, the greater the perceived advantage of men, relative to women. The potential range is 3 to 13. The overall mean is 11.0.

Table 5.5 Perceptions of Economic Advantage Among the Employed
Respondents

Q.70 Which of the following statements do you agree with more?	High-prestige males (n =91)	Low-prestige males (n =89)	High-prestige females (n =90)	Low-prestige females (n =73)
a. Women today are given economic advantages over men.	9.9	14.8	1.1	4.1
b. Men today are given economic advantages over women.	73.6	61.8	80.0	78.1
c. Neither men nor women are given economic advantage.	16.5	23.6	18.9	17.8
Total	100%	100%	100%	100%

Two questions were combined to form a Deserving Scale.
The first asked whether "working women in general get what
they deserve in terms of pay and fringe benefits, number of
hours, chances for advancement, challenge, respect and prestige, job security, and general working conditions." Options
ranged from women receiving "much more" than they deserve
to "much less" than they deserve. The second question read:
"All in all, do you think that the employment situation of women
in America is as good as it ought to be?" with potential answers
ranging from "definitely yes" to "definitely not." The sum scores
ranged, potentially, from 2 to 10 with a score of 5 meaning that
women are receiving what they deserve generally.

Once again working women average the highest score. This
time the gap is clearly between the working women, whether
they be single, married, or mothers, and the other two groups.
The average score among all employed women is 8.45. Among
employed mothers it is 8.40. The perceived discrepancy between what women have and what they deserve is least among
the housewives ($\bar{x} = 7.60$). The average score of the men is 7.82.
If the difference between the working women and the other
two groups is substantial, the difference between the high-
($\bar{x} = 8.45$) and low- ($\bar{x} = 7.60$) prestige individuals is even greater.
The Past Expectations Scale was created by summing the

scores on two questions that asked respondents to compare how well women are doing today with what they (the respondents) had expected a decade ago. Scores could range from 2 to 8. A score of 5 indicates that expectations have been met; a higher score that they have not. The overall average for our sample was 4.86. This indicates that, for the residents of Newton, expectations about the economic situation of women have, on average, been surpassed slightly. Scores on this variable, as Table 5.4 shows, do not depend on sex, employment group, or job level.

While past expectations are not sensitive to the respondents' characteristics, future expectations are. On a scale derived from the sum of three questions, the overall mean Future Expectation Score is 6.79. The scale ranges from 3 to 13, with scores of 8 or less indicating slight optimism. It is obvious from Table 5.6 that low-prestige people are more optimistic about the future situation of women than are high-prestige people. Employed women are slightly optimistic overall, but they are noticeably less buoyant than employed men or housewives.

The final hypothesized precondition of resentment is self-blame. Three forced-choice items assessed the extent to which one blames women for the situation they are in. One item, for instance, read,

> Which of the following statements do you agree with more?
> a. If a woman can't get a good job, it's almost always her own fault.
> b. Many women can't get good jobs through no fault of their own.

More than 80 percent of the respondents selected the system-blame rather than the victim-blame option in each instance, and the overall mean for our sample on the Blame Scale was 5.58 in a range from 3 (blame the woman) to 6 (blame the system). Perhaps because of a ceiling effect, no reliable systematic variations in scores appeared.

In sum, the residents of Newton tend to feel that working women do not receive as much from their jobs as they want or as they deserve. They perceive men to be better off than women.

Table 5.6 Mean Scores on Future Expectations Scale as a Function of Job Level and Employment Group

Among all respondents

Job level	Employed males	Employment group Employed females	Housewives	
High-prestige	6.62 (n = 91)	7.70 (n = 90)	6.48 (n = 30)	7.06
Low-prestige	6.35 (n = 90)	6.71 (n = 72)	6.42 (n = 30)	6.50
	6.48	7.26	6.45	

Among parents only

Job level	Employed fathers	Employment group Employed mothers	Housewives	
High-prestige	6.29 (n = 30)	7.97 (n = 28)	6.48 (n = 30)	6.88
Low-prestige	5.86 (n = 30)	5.91 (n = 20)	6.43 (n = 30)	6.08
	6.08	7.11	6.45	

The higher the score, the greater the pessimism.
The values can range from 3 to 13.
The overall mean is 6.79.

They also find the situation of working women to be better than they had thought it would be and seem optimistic that it will improve even more. They do not blame women for their current disadvantages. Employed women generally score higher on the hypothesized preconditions of felt deprivation than do either of the other groups. Perceived discrepancies between what working women have and (a) what they want; (b) what they deserve; and (c) what men have are largest among the employed women in our sample. Employed women are the least optimistic group. As with feelings of dissatisfaction and deprivation, the perceived discrepancy between what working women have and what they want is greater among the high-prestige samples than among the low-prestige samples. Newtonites with high-prestige jobs also see the gap between what working women have and what they deserve to be greater than low-prestige individuals see it.

Summary

The respondents in our study express considerable discontent about the position of working women in America today. Several scholars have traced the protean countours of sex-role stereotyping in different populations over time (Bass, Krusell & Alexander, 1971; Iglehart, 1979; Mason & Bumpass, 1975; Mason et al., 1976; Molm, 1978; Parelius, 1975; Scanzoni, 1978; Thorton & Freedman, 1979; Walster & Paté, 1974). Extrapolating from their findings, we had expected our sample to be more cognizant of and less accepting of sex discrimination than were people in previous studies. We were nonetheless surprised by the intensity of awareness and discontent that we actually found. We also found that people in high-prestige categories are more dissatisfied and aggrieved than are people in the low-prestige categories. The effect of job level on group deprivation repeats a pattern found among black Americans interviewed in the late 1960s. The third major finding in this chapter is that employed women are more distressed about sex discrimination than are employed men or housewives. Employed women differ from the other two groups in terms of deprivation, dissatisfaction, and four of the six hypothesized preconditions of deprivation.

The intensity of group deprivation among employed women contrasts sharply with the absence of personal deprivation. Similar contrasts have appeared in other studies. Taylor and Dubé-Simard (1981), for example, examined group and personal deprivation among a small sample of French-speaking Canadians. Approximately 60 percent of their respondents were dissatisfied with the treatment of Francophones as compared with Anglophones. Concerning their own individual situations, only 16 percent of the sample were dissatisfied when the comparison was to other Francophones and 36 percent were dissatisfied when the comparison was to Anglophones.

What prevents women from applying what they know about sex discrimination in general to their own personal cases? Why is it, in other words, that a working woman resents the job situation of women in general but feels complacent about her own job situation?

One mundane reason why women may find it easier to express group deprivation than personal deprivation concerns politeness. Females have traditionally been schooled in politeness and deference (Lakoff, 1975). While it seems loyal to stand up for one's group, to complain about one's own situation may appear to be simply discourteous. Declaring either to an interviewer or to herself that she is underpaid may thrust the woman worker dangerously close to the forbidden territory of impolite assertiveness. Given the willingness of the employed women in our survey to admit anger in response to some questions, we do not believe that politeness is a very important factor; but it could induce reticence in a few of the employed women.

More plausible but more complicated is an explanation that takes into account the preconditions of deprivation. According to this explanation, group deprivation leads to personal deprivation only when group deprivation creates the preconditions of personal deprivation. Sometimes awareness of the group's plight will influence a woman's perceptions about whether her own actual outcomes are as good as she wants, deserves, and so on. But perceptions of the group's predicament do not always influence a woman's assessment of her own situation in a simple or straightforward way.

The nature of comparison processes may help account for the dual findings of strong group deprivation and weak personal deprivation among working women. As we saw in Chapter 4, most people compare themselves with someone of the same sex in determining how good their own job is. Even high-prestige women, the group most ready to make cross-sex comparisons, compare themselves to men less than half the time. What do the working women see when they compare themselves with other women? When asked to compare themselves with "women who have jobs outside the home," 70 percent of the employed women in our sample think that they personally are better off than most working women. A slightly higher percentage think that they are also better off than women who do not have jobs outside the home. These percentages suggest that the working women in Newton may be so pleased with their own situation relative to other women in America that they willingly overlook differences between their own personal situations and the job situations of males with whom they work. Consistent with this line of reasoning is the slight (and nonsignificant) negative correlation among employed women between Comparison Other Scores concerning one's personal job situation and Comparison Other Scores concerning women's job situation relative to men's. Awareness of the discrepancy between the rewards of women and men, in other words, may make a woman slightly insensitive to discrepant comparisons in her own life.

Probably most important of all in accounting for the differential frequencies of group and personal deprivation among working women is the element of deserving. For reasons that are partly clear already and that will be obvious later, we believe that comparisons to better-off others do not affect feelings of deprivation directly but, rather, that they influence the extent of grievance by affecting feelings of deserving. As we noted in the last chapter, it is generally easier to see that a group lacks what it deserves than it is to see that an individual lacks what she or he deserves, even when the individual is oneself. One may feel certain, for example, that a group of women deserves to earn the same amount, on average, as a group of men if the two groups are, on average, comparable. In the individual case, averages are irrelevant and, as a result, comparability is hard to achieve.

From the differential frequencies of personal and group deprivation, the question arises as to whether women are especially prone to group deprivation or are perhaps especially immune to personal deprivation. Women are thought by many psychologists to be more socially oriented than men (e.g. Lewis, 1976; Maccoby & Jacklin, 1974). It is possible that females are especially sensitive to the plight of their group. The awareness of sex discrimination among men, and especially among high-prestige men, in our sample argues strongly against such a view. Nor does it seem likely that women are peculiarly immune to personal discontent. In the next chapter we shall see that women, particularly housewives, are no more unwilling than men to express resentment concerning their personal domestic arrangements.

Notes

1. In fact, all analyses were performed once using raw scores and once using standardized scores. The results were generally identical, indicating that our findings are reliable. The raw score analyses are reported in this chapter, as in Chapter 4, for expository ease.

2. See Appendix II for a complete account of the operational measure of each theoretical variable.

3. The categories were suggested by the data. One hundred and thirty-four protocols were scored by two independent raters, and the agreement rate was 99 percent.

6

Home Life

"My dog. My husband. My plants." These were the items listed by one high-prestige woman in response to our question: "What are the aspects of your home life that you find especially gratifying or rewarding?" "Nothing" was the answer of a single man with a low-prestige job. "When my middle child eats" said a housewife. Such answers were unusual.

More frequent were answers like these:

My children. I enjoy them. They give me love. My husband. He loves and respects me and likes me. We enjoy each other.

The ability, after all these years of working, to do exactly what I want and never had a chance to do, like taking courses or raising my son.

It's peaceful when I go home. I can do as I wish; don't have to answer to anyone.

Just the companionship of living with someone—just the sharing and good times together.

I've got a very good relationship with my husband. We have a very comfortable home. And the small luxuries.

Peace and tranquility—comfortable place to be with friends, solitude.

I'm happily married and love my wife. I'm happy with where I live and with my friends and with the way my life goes from day to day.

Having and watching the kids grow up. Doing things around
the house to make the house better. Having my wife at home.

Having somebody that cares for me.

People's feelings about their domestic arrangements and
particularly about the division of labor in the home are the subject of this chapter. As in the last chapter, we compare the reactions of working women, working men, and housewives.
Knowing that hostility is commonly displaced, we are watchful
for signs that working women, expressing no bitterness at work,
channel their frustrations into domestic complaints. Working
mothers—likely to be under the most stress (Coser & Rokoff,
1971; Holahan & Gilbert, 1979a; 1979b)—could be especially
negative about the division of labor at home (Haavio-Mannila,
1967) if not about the marital relationship (Axelson, 1963;
Burke & Weir, 1976; Epstein, 1971a; Poloma & Garland, 1971;
Rapoport & Rapoport, 1971a, 1976).

When we look at the nature of gratifications and grievances,
at the extent of deprivation and dissatisfaction, at the hypothesized preconditions of deprivation, and finally at marital satisfaction, the anticipated negative effects of employment on
women fail to materialize. Concerning feelings about one's home
life, and in particular about the division of labor, it is generally
the parents who differ from the single and married respondents. Our sample of housewives, all of whom are parents, ex-
hibit the least positive attitude about their home situation.

The nature of gratifications and grievances

Answers to the question about the gratifying aspects of home
life were sorted into six categories.[1] The first is children. This
was scored for any response that mentioned children directly
(e.g. "My children. I enjoy them") or indirectly (e.g. "It's great
being a parent"). More than three-quarters of the parents mention children as a pleasing aspect of home life. The second category is for mates, regardless of the degree of enthusiasm. Both
of the following, for example, fell under the heading:

"An intimate relationship with the man of my dreams"

and

"My husband and I get along reasonably well."

More than 60 percent of the married people and parents mention their spouses. Third comes any mention of people in one's environment, excluding specific references to one's children or one's mate. Responses such as "I like living with my parents," "my roommates," "the family unit is important to me" and "everyone loves me at home " give a flavor of the range of answers in the third category. The third category was coded for 31 percent of the respondents. So was the fourth, which reflects satisfaction with one's living space, home, or neighborhood. Examples of the fourth category include responses like "the neighborhood is nice" or "living in a big, warm house." Fifth, there are references to free time for personal interests (e.g. "having time to devote to volunteer activities"). Nineteen percent of the sample gave such answers. Distinct from the freedom to do things is the freedom from things. Freedom, independence, or privacy constitute the final type of gratification. Included in this code were responses such as "peace and tranquility," "no one bothers me"; and "I am a free spirit." This category was coded only 13 percent of the time. Of the 709 distinct answers given by our 405 respondents, 19 defied classification.

Only one individual in the study asserted that nothing at home was gratifying to him. Several individuals list as many as four aspects of their home lives which are particularly gratifying. Overall, the respondents cite an average of 1.75 gratifications. When it comes to the various sources of gratification at home, the data give overwhelming support to the common-sense notion that what people like at home is other people. All told, only one-fifth of the individuals whom we interviewed in Newton do not cite people—including children, mates, roommates, parents, and friends—as a source of gratification at home.

When we look beyond the nearly universal tendency to mention people as a source of gratification, some interesting patterns emerge. First, single respondents, and especially those with high-prestige jobs, like their independence, freedom and privacy. Among the single groups, 43 percent of high-prestige males; 42 percent of high-prestige females; 27 percent of low-prestige males; and 23 percent of low-prestige females cite independence. In contrast, about 5 percent of the married people and parents do. The direction of the difference between single people and others is hardly surprising; but the size of the difference is quite large.

A second important finding concerns children. It is clear from Table 6.1 that high-prestige housewives are most likely to cite children as a source of gratification. Among the high-prestige samples, the group differences reach statistical significance. Among low-prestige individuals, group differences are not significant. Almost exactly the same proportion of low-prestige and high-prestige fathers mention their children, stereotypes about class differences notwithstanding.

The effect of children on conjugal joy is a matter of some controversy. Several researchers find a decrease in marital happiness with the arrival of children (Hicks & Platt, 1970; Lemasters, 1957; Rollins & Feldman, 1970). Others disagree (Hurley & Palonin, 1967; Miller, 1976; Spanier, Lewis, & Cole, 1975). Conclusions vary, depending on methodology. Our own data also show the importance of methodology. Limiting our view to actual references to one's spouse, we see in the top figures of Table 6.2 that parents are less likely than married people to mention their spouse as a source of gratification. Among high-prestige individuals, the decline is a precipitous 35 percent. It is possible, of course, that many respondents who cite the family unit as a source of gratification mean to include their mate within the unit. The bottom figures in Table 6.2 give the percentages that result when we count as a reference to one's spouse either a specific mention (code 2) or a general mention (code 3). Children no longer appear detrimental to the marital relationship, but the percentages among housewives may give pause to the traditionalist. Housewives appear much less likely to take pleasure in their spouses than do employed women and men. Just as one of the implications of Chapter 5 was that marriage and parenthood enhances one's appreciation of the job,

Table 6.1 Percentage of Respondents Citing Children as a Home Gratification

Job level	Employed fathers	Employment group Employed mothers	Housewives
High-prestige	67.7 [a] (n = 31)	78.6 (n = 28)	93.3 (n = 30)
Low-prestige	66.7 (n = 30)	76.2 (n = 21)	80.0 (n = 30)

[a] Percentage of respondents in the cell to cite children as a gratification.

so one of the implications here may be that a job enhances one's appreciation of one's spouse.

Employed women are hardly more distinctive in their grievances at home than in their gratifications. Immediately after asking our Newtonites about the nature of gratifications at home, we asked them about the nature of their resentments. The answers were coded into seven categories.[2] The first, household chores, was coded for any mention of work that is

Table 6.2 Percentage of Respondents Citing Spouse as a Home Gratification

	Employed males High-prestige	Low-prestige		
Married	83.9 [a] (93.5)	66.7 (86.7)		
Parents	48.4 (87.1)	46.7 (76.7)		

	Employed females High-prestige	Low-prestige	Housewives High-prestige	Low-prestige
Married	80.6 (93.5)	68.2 (77.3)		
Parents	46.4 (85.7)	61.9 (85.7)	56.7 (66.7)	30.0 (53.3)

[a] The percentages in parentheses are calculated by counting as a reference to the spouse any general mention of people at home that might include the spouse as well as specific mentions of the spouse.

The other percentages include only specific mentions.

part of household maintenance, from "sorting socks" to "yard work." More general expressions of the same theme include responses such as: "coping with the clutter"; "I'm everybody's slave; picking up after everyone"; and "the chores never stop." The second category concerns problems with other people. Prominent here are references to children (e.g. "children when they misbehave") and to spouses (e.g. "I care about things she has no interest in"). Loneliness, isolation, or boredom are the third aspect, expressed by such responses as "I miss my family and friends on the West Coast"; "I never get out of the house"; or, more loquaciously: "lack of communication with other people. At the moment, it is difficult to get out. I feel the loss of friends. It's hard to wake up." Fourth comes problems with the building, which are cited directly (e.g. "water in the basement") or which can be inferred easily from references to one's "senile landlord" or the plumber who hasn't come in weeks. The fifth category is lack of time. It was scored for complaints such as "the lack of time to spend with the wife" or "the hecticness. That everybody's got such a busy schedule that the days go by before anybody looks up." Next is a lack of privacy, independence, or freedom to do what one wants. Answers like "there's no respect for my personal space" were coded in this category. Finally there are financial problems (e.g. "taxes"; "financial problems"; "I don't have enough money"; "It's a bit on the expensive side"). Of 438 separate items mentioned, twenty-eight did not fall within one of our codes. Fifty-seven respondents claim that there are no bothersome aspects to their lives at home. Overall, there are 1.08 items per respondent.

The bothersome items range from mundane to profound. One architect catalogued his woes:

> The storm windows don't fit right; the tenant hasn't paid his rent on time; and there are ants in the woodpile.

More disturbing are answers like these:

> Lack of accomplishment. Lack of self-discipline.

> The tentative nature of our living situation. Both of our futures individually as professionals. I've applied to school in

Washington, D.C., next year. So, do you buy a house or not?
Have kids or not? It's that kind of flux.

The fact that my father is in the hospital dying of cancer.

or

Feeling trapped.

If we tabulate the sources of distress, the percentages of all
respondents to mention each category are:

1. household chores   25 percent
2. interpersonal relations   29 percent
3. loneliness, isolation   10 percent
4. problems with building   5 percent
5. lack of time   15 percent
6. lack of independence   5 percent
7. financial problems   12 percent

The small percentage of respondents to mention financial
problems is consistent with the impression of affluence seen in
Chapters 3 and 4. Also apparent from the percentages is the
fact that although people are only about one-third as likely to
be irritated by others as to be pleased by others, interpersonal
relations constitute the most frequently cited source of grievance at home. As one father put it: "My kids: they provide the
joys and the agonies."

Partitioning the data according to respondents' job level
(high prestige, low prestige) and employment group (employed
men, employed women, housewives) reveals several variations.
Five findings are evident in Table 6.3. First, household chores
are a source of grievance for women but not for men. High-
prestige women are more likely to mention household chores
than are low-prestige women. Housework is most burdensome
for the high-prestige housewives. (This is so even though, as
we saw in Chapter 3, the average number of hours spent each
week on housework is greater among the low-prestige women
than among the high-prestige women.) Second, low-prestige
men are less bothered by interpersonal relations at home than
any other group. Third, only high-prestige housewives are prey
to feelings of loneliness and isolation. Low-prestige housewives

Table 6.3   Home Grievances as a Function of Job Level and
Employment Group

	Household chores			Interpersonal relations		
	Employed males	Employed females	House-wives	Employed males	Employed females	House-wives
High-prestige	8.7 [a]	47.8	66.7	37.0	34.4	26.7
Low-prestige	11.1	28.8	30.0	17.8	27.4	30.0

	Loneliness			Problems with building		
	Employed males	Employed females	House-wives	Employed males	Employed females	House-wives
High-prestige	8.7	7.8	33.3	6.5	4.4	3.3
Low-prestige	7.8	6.8	6.7	5.6	6.8	0.0

	Lack of free time			Lack of independence		
	Employed males	Employed females	House-wives	Employed males	Employed females	House-wives
High-prestige	17.4	26.7	10.0	4.3	5.6	0.0
Low-prestige	6.7	12.3	6.7	6.7	6.8	0.0

	Financial			Nothing is wrong		
	Employed males	Employed females	House-wives	Employed males	Employed females	House-wives
High-prestige	10.9	11.1	0.0	13.0	12.2	0.0
Low-prestige	16.7	11.0	20.0	25.6	12.3	10.0

[a] Percentage of respondents in the cell to cite the code.

are no more likely to cite loneliness than are any of the employed groups. Lack of free time is an issue for high-prestige employed women but not for most other groups. Low-prestige men are most likely to say that there is nothing wrong with their home life. At the other extreme are the high-prestige housewives. All of them find at least one aspect of their home life bothersome. Taken as a whole, these findings point to the

Table 6.4 Home Grievances as a Function of Family Status and Employment Group

	Household chores			Interpersonal relations		
	Employed males	Employed females	House-wives	Employed males	Employed females	House-wives
Single	6.7 [a]	16.4		21.7	26.2	
Married	14.8	39.6		21.3	30.2	
Parents	8.2	46.9	48.3	45.9	38.8	28.3

	Loneliness			Problems with building		
	Employed males	Employed females	House-wives	Employed males	Employed females	House-wives
Single	21.7	14.8		5.0	8.2	
Married	11.5	1.9		6.6	3.8	
Parents	1.6	4.1	20.0	6.6	4.1	1.7

	Lack of free time			Lack of independence		
	Employed males	Employed females	House-wives	Employed males	Employed females	House-wives
Single	8.3	3.3		11.7	13.1	
Married	11.5	22.6		4.9	1.9	
Parents	16.4	38.8	8.3	0.0	2.0	0.0

	Financial			Nothing is wrong		
	Employed males	Employed females	House-wives	Employed males	Employed females	House-wives
Single	6.7	14.8		23.3	14.8	
Married	13.1	11.3		18.0	15.2	
Parents	21.3	6.1	10.0	14.8	6.1	5.0

[a]Percentage of respondents in the cell to cite the code.

importance of social status in the nature of people's resentments at home. The things that employed women, employed men, and housewives dislike about their home life differ according to the individual's job level. The association between job level and distress, furthermore, is much stronger than the association between job level and the nature of gratifications at home. It is also stronger than the association between job level and grievances at work.

Further findings emerge when we divide the data about grievances at home along the lines of sex and family status. Table 6.4 shows the percentages of single, married, and parental women and men to mention each of the seven aspects we isolated in our coding. The figures reinforce the finding that more women than men experience chores as a grievance. Other results are:

1. Interpersonal problems depend on family status among the men but not among the women. Fathers are twice as likely as married and single men to cite other people as a source of distress at home. Although the figures are not shown here, further examination of the data reveals that of the fathers who complain about others in the home, about 40 percent single out their wives, about one-third cite their children, and the rest do not isolate individual irritants.
2. Loneliness is a special issue for single men. Disregarding job level, the percentage of single men who experience loneliness exceeds the percentage of housewives who experience loneliness.[3]
3. Concern over a crowded schedule varies according to the respondents' family status. The variation is much more noticeable among the employed women than among the employed men.

In sum, the different groups of people in our study tend to vary in what they like and dislike about their home lives. Some of the variations make sense simply in terms of the objective conditions of people's lives. Single men, for example, may be the group most bereft of companionship. Other variations suggest that people's gratifications and grievances occur relative to some psychological standard and not simply as a function of their objective status. The resentment of household chores among high-prestige women, compared with low-prestige women, illustrates the principle of relative deprivation.

Extent of deprivation and dissatisfaction

If the qualitative date are consistent with the concept of relative deprivation, so are the quantitative data. Parents in general, and housewives in particular, feel the most aggrieved about domestic matters. Employed women express no more deprivation

Table 6.5 Distribution of Deprivation Scores Among Married People
and Parents

	Employed males	
	High- prestige	Low- prestige
Married	x̄ = 7.63 (n = 31)	x̄ = 7.61 (n = 30)
Parents	x̄ = 10.42 (n = 31)	x̄ = 8.70 (n = 30)

	Employed females		Housewives	
	High- prestige	Low- prestige	High- prestige	Low- prestige
Married	x̄ = 8.37 (n = 31)	x̄ = 9.29 (n = 22)		
Parents	x̄ = 10.18 (n = 28)	x̄ = 9.12 (n = 21)	x̄ = 9.97 (n = 30)	x̄ = 11.62 (n = 30)

The higher the score, the greater the deprivation. Potential range is 2 to 34.

than do employed men, even though—as we saw in Chapter 3—the employed women in our samples do more housework than do the employed men. Nor does job level make a difference in the degree of deprivation.

Our measure of the extent of deprivation at home resembles closely our measure of deprivation at work.[4] To obtain the Deprivation Score, we summed the answers to five questions such as this one: "Within the last year, how often have you felt really good about the way things are going at home?" with options ranging from "almost never or never" (scored 6) to "almost all the time" (scored 1). The potential range of scores for the entire scale is 2 to 34. The actual range of scores is 2.1 to 31.6 with an overall mean of 9.3. Table 6.5 shows the distribution of Deprivation Scores among the married and parental samples in Newton. Single respondents are excluded from the table because some of the questions in the Deprivation Scale were not asked of single respondents. It appears from Table 6.5 that parents are more aggrieved about their home lives than are married people.

Three separate analyses confirm the impression given by Table 6.5. First, a 2 (job level) by 3 (employment group) ANOVA among all nonsingle respondents shows a main effect for employment group but no effect for job level and no interaction effect. Housewives express the most resentment ($\bar{x} = 10.80$), employed men the least ($\bar{x} = 8.59$), and employed women are in the middle ($\bar{x} = 9.18$). Because of the asymmetrical design of our sample, all of the housewives but only half of the employed women and men in the analysis are parents. To separate the effects due to employment status from effects due to family status, therefore, we must repeat the analysis but restrict the sample to parents. No significant effects emerge in the second analysis. The disappearance of a significant effect for employment group in the second analysis suggests that the apparent effect during the first, more comprehensive, analysis is an artifact of the design. In other words, housewives may appear most aggrieved because they are parents and not simply because they are nonemployed. Further support comes from the third analysis. Restricting our view to nonsingle employed respondents, a 2 (gender) by 2 (job level) by 2 (family status) analysis of covariance shows that the degree of deprivation varies as a function of family status but not as a function of gender or of job level. The average Deprivation Score among married respondents is 8.14; among parents, it is 9.64.

Slightly different findings occur for the Dissatisfaction Scale. With a potential range of 2 (very satisfied) to 10 (very dissatisfied), our sample averages a score of 3.47. Excluding again single people from the calculations, the mean Dissatisfaction Score for employed men is 3.31. For employed women, it is 3.37; and for housewives, 3.49. The group differences are not statistically significant.

In sum, quantitative measures of discontent show that people in Newton are generally pleased with their home lives. The level of resentment is low; the level of satisfaction high. Parents express the most resentment, but not the most dissatisfaction, with things at home.

Hypothesized preconditions

Concerning labor within the home, we assess the six factors that theorists have treated as preconditions of deprivation. Table 6.6 summarizes the significant effects obtained when each of the six scales is treated as a dependent variable. The table also shows the potential range and actual mean scores for each scale. Examination of the scores for the preconditions strengthens the impression of general contentment. Our Newtonites feel that they obtain at home what they want, what they deserve, and what they had expected to obtain. They do not, on the whole, see that others are better off than themselves, nor do they blame themselves for any present difficulties.

It is also clear from Table 6.6 that the domestic contentment of our sample overall is not a seamless robe. For each of the factors, in the two-way analysis of variance among the entire sample, there is either a significant main effect or a significant interaction in which employment group figures. In four instances the effects persist when the analyses are repeated with the more restricted sample of parents only. When we look at the actual average scores of each of the various groups, we see that parents in general and housewives in particular tend to obtain the highest scores. In other words, parents—and especially housewives—tend to feel the most negative about life at home.

Let us turn to the variables one by one. The Want Scale reflects the extent to which the person engages in tasks (e.g. shopping) which he or she wants to avoid. For this variable, the analysis among the entire sample reveals a main effect for employment group. The mean discrepancy between what one has and what one wants is greatest among housewives ($\bar{x} = 5.07$) and least among employed men ($\bar{x} = 3.26$). The employed women resemble the employed men, with an average score of 3.47. When we look only at the parents, the means for employed males and females rise to 4.11 and 3.81, respectively (and obliterate the main effect for employment group). Low-prestige housewives and high-prestige fathers report the largest gaps between what they have and what they want. In other words, there is no evidence that employment leads a woman to

Table 6.6 Summary of Significant Results for Preconditions

Dependent variables	No. of questions in scale	Potential range	Actual mean	Analyses and Independent Variables		
				2 × 3 ANOVA among entire sample Job level Employment group	2 × 3 ANOVA among parents only Job level Employment group	2 × 3 ANCOVA among employed people only Job level, Sex, Family status
Discrepancy between what one has and what one wants	2	0–22	3.64	Group (F = 9.665; df = 2,398; p <.0001)	Level × Group (F = 3.657; df = 2,163; p <.03)	Family (F = 5.07; df = 2,322; p <.007)
Discrepancy between what one has and what others have	2	2–5	3.28	Level × Group (F = 3.042; df = 2,386; p <.05)	Level × Group (F = 3.131; df = 2,159; p <.05)	Level × Sex (F = 4.777; df = 1,311; p <.03)
Discrepancy between what one deserves to obtain and what one has	3	2–25	5.62	Group (F = 14.101; df = 2,365; p <.0001)	Group (F = 6.870; df = 2,163; p <.001)	Sex (F = 12.247; df = 1,289; p <.001) Level × Family (F = 5.564; df = 2,289; p <.004)
Discrepancy between past expectations and present reality	1	0–1	0.15	Group (F = 13.595; df = 2,398; p <.001) Level × Group (F = 3.729; df = 2,398; p <.03)	Group (F = 8.518; df = 2,163; p <.0001)	—

Dependent variables	No. of questions in scale	Potential range	Actual mean	Analyses and Independent Variables		
				2 × 3 ANOVA among entire sample Job level Employment group	2 × 3 ANOVA among parents only Job level Employment group	2 × 3 ANCOVA among employed people only Job level, Sex, Family status
Expectations for the future	1	1–3	1.59	Group (F = 3.012; df = 2,398; p <.05)	—	Level × Family (F = 4.645; df = 2,322; p <.01)
Avoidance of self-blame	2	1–5	3.67	Group (F = 9.075; df = 2,398; p <.0001)	—	Sex (F = 5.734; df = 1,322; p <.02) Level × Family (F = 3.224; df = 2,322; p <.05)

feel that she is engaging in domestic tasks that she would like
to avoid. Our final analysis of the Want Scale is the three-way
analysis of covariance from which housewives are excluded. The
analysis shows a significant effect for family status: the reported discrepancy is greatest among parents ($\bar{x} = 4.08$), next
among married people ($\bar{x} = 3.41$) and least among single people
($\bar{x} = 2.75$).

The findings concerning Comparison Other are less clear-
cut. All three analyses show interaction effects, but the nature
of the interactions changes. When we consider all of the respondents, the high-prestige men and the high-prestige
housewives are more alert to better-off others than are the low-
prestige men and the low-prestige housewives, while among the
sample of working women, prestige operates in the opposite
way. Similarly, among the employed men and women (excluding housewives) the high-prestige men and the low-prestige
women are most aware of the advantage of others. In the two-
way analysis of variance among parents, however, the figures
are reversed. High-prestige employed mothers, like high-prestige housewives, are more aware of better-off others than are
their low-prestige counterparts. Among fathers, awareness increases as job prestige falls. In short, scores on the Comparison
Other Scale do not seem to be related in a stable way to the
respondents' social group. The lack of stability makes good
sense: as we shall see in Chapter 7, people are much less likely
to use comparison others in determining how happy their home
life is than in determining how happy their work life is.

For the factor of deserving, employment group is important
among the entire sample and among the parents only. Employed men generally perceive a smaller gap between what they
have and what they deserve than do employed women who, in
turn, perceive a smaller gap than do housewives. The scores on
the Deserving Scale are 4.85 for employed men; 5.89 for employed women; and 7.08 for housewives. Similarly, employed
fathers ($\bar{x} = 4.97$) obtain a lower average score than do employed mothers ($\bar{x} = 6.02$). In addition to the sex difference, an
interaction between family status and job level emerges in the
three-way ANCOVA of Deserving Scores among the employed
respondents. Examination of the means in the interaction shows

that high-prestige single respondents and low-prestige married respondents report the largest discrepancy between what they have and what they deserve. Neither of these groups scores as highly as do the housewives. In other words, housewives are especially prone to feeling that they do more than their fair share of housework.

Not only do housewives experience the largest discrepancy between current and deserved outcomes; they are also the ones to feel that their current situation is not as good as they had expected. About 10 percent of the employed men and 20 percent of the employed women feel disappointed. One-third of housewives do. Interestingly, housewives are also the most optimistic of all the respondents. Average scores for the various groups on the Future Expectations Scale are: 1.61 for employed men, 1.63 for employed women, and 1.40 for housewives, where a low score denotes optimism. Among the employed sample, parents are the most optimistic group; high-prestige single respondents and low-prestige married respondents are the least optimistic.

Finally, among our Newtonites, housewives accept significantly more personal responsibility for their domestic problems than do employed women. Employed women, in turn, accept more blame than do employed men. Using a scale where a high score means an avoidance of self-blame, housewives average a score of 3.37; employed women, 3.64; and employed men, 3.78. (It is worth recalling that employed men and women do not differ in their tendency toward self-blame for problems at work.) In addition to the main effect of sex among the employed sample, there is an interaction effect between family status and job level: high-prestige married respondents and low-prestige single respondents are the least prone to self-blame.

In sum, although our respondents express quite positive feelings about the division of labor in the home, housewives tend to differ from the employed men and women. There is no evidence that employment creates the hypothesized preconditions of deprivation about the division of labor at home among women. If anything, the opposite is true. The housewives perceive some discrepancy between their present situation and their desired, deserved, and expected one; the employed women, like

the employed men, perceive hardly any. Looking only at the
employed people, family status is an important variable, especially in conjunction with job level and gender.

Marital satisfaction

Although primarily interested in people's feelings about the division of labor in the home, we were curious about marital satisfaction. We asked respondents, "everything considered, how
happy has your marriage been for you?" and seven other questions relating to the hypothesized preconditions of deprivation.
To measure future expectations, for example, we asked: "What
does the next five or so years hold in store for your marriage?"
Virtually every study in the last two decades has found that
marital satisfaction is high among Americans (Bernard, 1973;
Blood & Wolfe, 1960; Clemente & Sauer, 1976; Iglehart, 1979;
Scanzoni, 1972; Weiss & Aved, 1978). Our study is no exception. Seventeen percent of the married people and parents see
their marriages as "nearly perfect"; 64 percent as "extremely
happy"; 17 percent as "fairly happy"; and less than 2 percent
as "average in happiness." Nobody admits to a marriage that is
"fairly unhappy" or "very unhappy." Less than 10 percent of
our 284 married people and parents think that their marriage
is not as good as that of their friends or not as good as it should
be. In response to the question, "If your marriage is not perfect
now, why is this?" approximately one-fifth of the respondents
select the option, "doesn't apply to me: my marriage is perfect."
Only 1.4 percent are even fairly (let alone very) pessimistic about
the future. Sixteen percent of the sample admit that their marriages are not up to their prior expectations; but more than
twice that figure find their marriages to have surpassed their
expectations.

Are some groups less panegyric in describing their marriages than are others? Most (e.g. Blood & Wolfe, 1960; Renne,
1970; Scanzoni, 1972) but not all (e.g. Jorgensen, 1979) researchers have found a positive relationship between marital
satisfaction and social status. Some scholars have also found
marital satisfaction to be affected by whether the wife works
outside the home (Staines, Pleck, Shepard, & O'Connor, 1978).
Among our sample, neither statistical analyses nor examination

of the mean scores reveals systematic variations. Although less likely than the employed parents to mention their spouse as a source of gratification at home, housewives are no more nor less positive than the employed women and men on the eight quantitative measures of marital satisfaction. Parents do not, on the whole, differ from the married but childless respondents. High-prestige groups resemble low-prestige groups.

The lack of group differences attests to the fact that the people in our study differentiate between their marriages and the way in which labor is divided in the home. It seems that the housewives, for example, may resent the laundry arrangements but be satisfied with, say, companionship. A woman may be aggrieved at the lack of egalitarianism in the division of labor but may feel that the division of labor constitutes only a small part of the marital relationship. She may also feel that her relationship with her husband constitutes only a fraction of her home life. In the housewife's differentiation between marriage and domestic labor we hear a faint echo of some findings in Chapter 4. More specifically, it recalls to mind the employed woman's ability to feel angry with one aspect of her job while remaining free from a general sense of resentment.

Summary

The people whom we interviewed tend to feel gratified about their home lives. Sources of gratification outnumber sources of grievance. Resentment and dissatisfaction, when approached quantitatively, are low. The same is true of the hypothesized preconditions. Although the groups do not differ in their enthusiastic endorsement of their marriages, some groups are less pleased than others with the division of labor in the home. Parents experience the most deprivation; housewives constitute the least positive group of all.

Notes

1. The categories were created after inspection of the data. One hundred and five protocols were scored independently by two coders.

They agreed 97 percent of the time. Coders were blind to the respondents' characteristics while coding.

2. Eighty-one protocols were scored independently by two coders. They agreed 96 percent of the time. Coders were blind to the respondents' characteristics while coding.

3. Loneliness bothered high-prestige and low-prestige single males equally.

4. For a precise account of how each variable is operationalized, see Appendix II.

7

Comparisons Across Domains

In this chapter we take a different approach to the issues surrounding women and work. First, we continue the search for evidence of a conflict between work and home by seeing how attitudes toward work correlate with attitudes toward home. We then examine the positiveness of people's feelings, their reactions to frustrations, and the nature of comparison processes at work and at home. Looking at the perceived characteristics of the work environment as contrasted with the home environment can help us to understand how both environments may affect women and men.

Correlations

One of the major themes in the literature on working women, as we have seen, is the conflict between work and home. In 1971 Coser and Rokoff published their seminal paper outlining how women are expected to place family demands ahead of career demands. Psychological as well as physical stress results from the cross-pressures. This stress, the authors argue, might be one reason that women are so underrepresented among the professions. In support of their analysis, Coser and Rokoff note that the percentages of Ph.D. holders who have achieved the rank of associate or full professor are 53.8 for men; 47.1 for unmarried women; 23.7 for married (but childless) women; and 22.6 for mothers. Other statistics provide further presumptive evidence for Coser and Rokoff's conflict hypothesis. Several studies have documented a direct link between marriage and

117

success among males and between bachelorhood and success among females (Feldman, 1973; Havens, 1973; Mueller & Campbell, 1977). An eight-year longitudinal study found that interstate migration increased as the husband's occupational prestige rose but was unaffected by the wife's occupational prestige (Duncan & Perrucci, 1976). Finally, with marriage, absences from work decrease for males but increase for females (Hedges, 1977).

Most studies of attitudes or feelings show that dual-worker couples do experience conflict, although less intensely than Coser and Rokoff would expect or than the statistics suggest. The strains of two careers under one roof, furthermore, are usually more than offset by enhanced life satisfaction for all members in the family unit (Fogarty, Rapoport, & Rapoport, 1971; Rapoport & Rapoport, 1971b). Traditionally, it is the wife who accommodates her career to the husband's career and to the demands of the family, and traditionally the accomodation is made with little intrapsychic or interpersonal conflict (Holahan & Gilbert, 1979a, 1979b; Young & Willmott, 1973). The most comprehensive recent study on the conflict between work and home suggests that the picture may be changing (Pleck, Staines, & Lang, 1980). According to the study, about 35 percent of workers interviewed in the 1977 Quality of Employment survey (Quinn & Staines, 1978) report that family life and work interfere with each other "somewhat" or "a lot." Most of these are parents. Husbands are as likely as wives to report interference, but the nature of the interference is different for men and women. Men are more likely than women to cite excessive work time; women are more likely than men to cite scheduling problems and negative spillover (e.g., exhaustion, preoccupation) from their jobs. About 23 percent of employed wives and single parents admit that child care arrangements cause them problems with their work, such as being late to work. Only 2.1 percent of the employed husbands experience similar problems.

If the employed people in Newton experience a great deal of conflict between work and home, then we would expect those who are the most satisfied with work to be the least satisfied with home and vice versa. If time is short, it might be allocated either to work or to home but not adequately to both. On the basis of Coser and Rokoff's paper, furthermore, the negative association between contentment at work and contentment at home ought to be stronger among the females than among the males.

The correlations that actually occur in our data give little support to the conflict hypothesis. The correlations are positive. They are of equal or greater magnitude for women than for men. The Pearson's *r*s between dissatisfaction at work and dissatisfaction at home are .13 for all nonsingle respondents and .22 for working women. For deprivation at work and at home, they are .27 for all nonsingle respondents and .28 for working women. The correlations are statistically significant; they might have appeared higher if there were more variability among our respondents.

If we examine other attitudes toward one's job and toward one's home life, we find very small and nonsignificant correlations. The Pearson's *r* between scores on the Wanting Scale at work and scores on the Wanting Scale at home, for example, is .06. Knowing that there is a large discrepancy between what someone has and what someone wants at work, in other words, tells us virtually nothing about the size of the discrepancy at home. The lack of a relationship between any hypothesized precondition of deprivation at work and its counterpart at home implies strongly that the significant association between contentment at work and contentment at home results neither from people's personality traits nor from a tendency toward naysaying. It is not the case that some people are consistently pessimistic and others consistently optimistic. It is not the case that some people are especially sensitive to the outcomes of others, no matter what the context. It seems unlikely, therefore, that some people simply complain more than others.

The reliable correlations between discontent at work and at home probably indicate that, to a certain degree, people's attitudes toward work both affect and reflect their attitudes toward home. Our data are consistent with Piotrkowski's (1979) account of how the joys and sorrows of work often spill over into a working man's home life and also with her speculations about how the events at home can color life at work.

The degree of spillover should not be overemphasized, however. The mutual influence of work and home attitudes is not great enough, among our sample, to undermine the protective value of multiple roles. The married people and parents in our study are probably cushioned against jolts at work by the fullness of their home lives because the two worlds are, by and large, separate. Similarly, the very separateness of work from home may afford the employed women and men a protective distance from domestic problems.

Positive and negative feelings at work and at home

The impressions given in Chapters 4 and 6 are that the people of Newton like their jobs, love their homes, and are euphoric about their marriages. The impressions are strengthened when we contrast people's feelings about their own lives with their generally gloomy view of the situation of working women depicted in Chapter 5. Let us now substantiate these impressions with an item-by-item comparison of people's positive and negative feelings at work and at home.

The first comparison concerns the extent of deprivation and dissatisfaction. Deprivation Scales for one's own job situation, the job situation of women, and one's own home situation had different potential ranges. So did the Dissatisfaction Scales. To allow at least a rough comparison across domains, we can standardize the mean scores by converting them to a percentage of the maximum possible scores. (High scores indicate discontent.) Table 7.1 presents the findings for the Deprivation Scales and Table 7.2 for the Dissatisfaction Scales. In both tables, mean scores of various subsamples are given to ensure that variations in the scores reflect true shifts rather than changes in the samples.

Looking down the columns of Table 7.1, we see that the Deprivation Scores remain stable across modifications in the samples. Looking along the rows, we see that the scores shift across domains. The average Deprivation Score occurs halfway along the scale for women and only one-third of the way along the scales for one's own work and one's own home life. Our respondents express much more resentment about the situa-

Table 7.1 Converted Deprivation Scores

Domain Sample	Personal job situation (range 1 to 30)	Personal home situation (range 2 to 34)	Situation of working women (range 1 to 6)
Among all respondents	—	—	53.33 (n = 405)
Among employed respondents	30.67 (n = 341)	—	52.50 (n = 345)
Among employed married and parental respondents	29.27 (n = 280)	32.11 (n = 224)	53.00 (n = 224)
Among all married and parental respondents	—	33.19 (n = 284)	—

The scores represent percentages of the maximum possible score. High scores indicate resentment.

tion of working women than about their own home or job situations. For dissatisfaction, the differences are even more dramatic. The respondents feel most satisfied with their home arrangements. They are also very satisfied with their jobs. Concerning the situation of working women, they are quite dissatisfied.

Comparisons based on converted percentages are admittedly rough. They may be misleading if the scores are distributed differently on the different scales. To achieve a more precise comparison, Figure 7.1 depicts the percentage of respondents selecting each of five options to indicate how satisfied they feel with their jobs and their family lives. The figure shows that three-quarters of the Newtonites are very or somewhat satisfied with their jobs and that 90 percent of them are very or somewhat satisfied with their family lives.

We can make another direct comparison between feelings at work and feelings at home by seeing which specific emotions, from a list of thirty-eight, people claim to have felt in the previous two days at work and at home. Table 7.3 presents the percentages of respondents to have experienced each emotion

Table 7.2 Converted Dissatisfaction Scores

Domain / Sample	Personal job situation (range 2 to 10)	Personal home situation (range 2 to 10)	Situation of working women (range 1 to 4)
Among all respondents	—	—	68.50 (n = 404)
Among employed respondents	35.33 (n = 344)	—	69.50 (n = 344)
Among employed married and parental respondents	33.44 (n = 223)	25.67 (n = 224)	69.25 (n = 223)
Among all married and parental respondents	—	26.11 (n = 284)	—

The scores represent percentages of the maximum possible score. High scores indicate dissatisfaction.

at work or at home. Although the Roseman Mood List (cf., Roseman, 1979) contains twenty-six negative moods and only twelve positive ones, the Newtonites are more likely to report positive than negative emotions both at work and at home. The percentages in Table 7.3 remind us of Parson's characterization of the socioemotional aspects of home life (Parsons & Bales, 1955). Looking only at cases where there is a difference of fifteen or more percentage points, we see that five emotions are felt more often at home than at work. These are grateful, happy, loving, relieved, and trusting. Three of the emotions require another person as their object; happiness does not require a human referent but often involves one. No emotion is experienced much more frequently at work than at home.

It is possible that not all Americans are as positive about their home and work lives as are our Newtonites. We suspect, however, that our sample is not atypical. In a culture in which mental health is a moral issue (Szasz, 1961), unhappiness may be the equivalent of damnation. We do well to remember the positiveness of people's feelings toward home and work when we think about the protective function of multiple roles. A bad

Figure 7.1 Satisfaction with Present Job and with Family Life

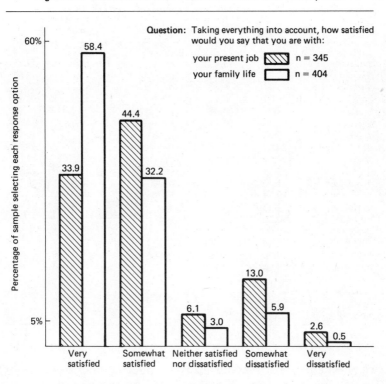

home life may not diminish the salience of negative events at work; and an unhappy job could amplify rather than reduce domestic tensions.

That our sample feels most richly rewarded by home life augurs well for them. One thoroughly substantiated finding is the importance of people's home lives for general life satisfaction. The research literature shows that for women in England (Bailyn, 1970) and Canada (Laurence, 1961) and for men and women in America (London, Crandall, & Seals, 1977; Spreitzer, Snyder, & Larson, 1979; Weaver, 1978a) family life is the single most important factor in life satisfaction. Although it is un-

Table 7.3   Roseman Mood List

| | Percentage of respondents who felt the mood | | | | |
	At work (n = 345)	At home (n = 405)		At work (n = 345)	At home (n = 405)
angry	25.51	27.41	elated	20.29	15.31
annoyed	50.43	45.43	excited	28.70	34.81
anxious	35.65	23.46	grateful	19.71	39.01
ashamed	3.77	4.20	happy	53.04	80.99
bitter	6.67	6.42	hopeful	33.91	38.27
bored	25.51	17.78	joyous	7.25	19.26
depressed	13.33	19.75	loving	9.57	64.20
deprived	3.77	3.71	proud	34.21	46.42
discouraged	24.93	18.76	relieved	2.67	19.01
disgusted	14.54	10.12	satisfied	48.70	49.63
dislike	5.51	3.70	self-confident	57.39	42.96
dissatisfied	21.16	16.30	trusting	17.97	36.54
distressed	10.44	8.62			
fearful	4.35	5.43			
frustrated	40.29	28.89			
guilty	6.09	12.34			
hating	3.19	2.47			
indignant	5.80	5.19			
infuriated	8.98	9.14			
lonely	9.23	18.52			
unhappy	12.17	14.57			
upset	22.90	21.98			
worried	23.48	31.36			

clear whether the relationship is stronger among husbands or wives, a number of studies also demonstrate a strong relationship between global happiness and marital happiness (Bernard, 1973; Bradburn, 1969; Bradburn & Caplovitz, 1965; Glenn, 1975; Gurin, Veroff, & Feld, 1960), and between family adjustment and global well-being (Andrews & Withey, 1976; Campbell, Converse, & Rodgers, 1976). Employed married American men and women both report more involvement with family than with work (Pleck & Lang, 1978).

Frustrations

Although negative or frustrating events are equally rare at home and at work, people may interpret and react to frustrations differently in the two environments. First, problems at work might seem less—or more—remediable than problems at home. People may feel that problems at work are beyond their grasp because of a diffusion of responsibility that can arise in group situations. Or they may feel better able to cope with problems at work than with problems at home because of the problem-solving mode that seems to operate at work. To measure efficacy, we asked: "When something does go wrong at work, no matter who is to blame, is it generally within your control to fix things?" The same question was repeated for home life.

People experience a sense of control about both work and home life but not about the situation of women. Although perceived control is slightly greater for matters in one's home life than for matters on the job, approximately 85 percent of the respondents believe that it is in their control to rectify matters at work and at home. The lack of perceived control concerning the job situation of women makes the feelings of efficacy about problems at work and at home seem even greater. When asked how much they—alone or with others—could do to improve the situation of working women, less that one-quarter of the sample think they can do more than "a bit." The exact percentages are displayed in Figure 7.2.

Concerning the target of their anger, people's reactions to frustrations at home and at work are again fairly similar to each other and distinct from their reactions to the situation of working women. We asked respondents whether they get angry at people or at things when they think about things that are wrong at work, at home, or for women. Table 7.4 shows the proportions of respondents to select each option for the three attitude domains. The bimodal distribution of answers to the question on women looks very different from the more bell-shaped curves for work and home. As the table illustrates, almost three-fourths of the respondents target their anger at "things in general" when they think about the predicament of women. With regard to work and home, fewer than one-third blame "things in general" when all does not go well.

Comparison others

According to traditional equity theorists (e.g., Adams, 1965; Homans, 1974; Walster et al., 1973), a person never feels unjustly treated unless a better-off other is present, if only in the

Figure 7.2 Feelings of Efficacy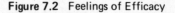

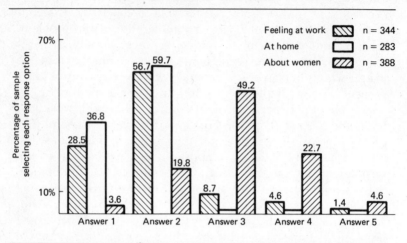

For work and home, we asked "When things go wrong . . . is it generally within your control to fix things?" Options were: (1) almost always within my control; (2) sometimes within my control; (3) rarely within my control; (4) usually beyond my control; and (5) almost always beyond my control.

For the situation of women, we asked "How much do you think you — alone or with others — can do to change things for the better?" Options were: (1) a very great deal; (2) a great deal; (3) a bit; (4) not too much; and (5) nothing.

person's imagination. One factor that may contribute to modern industrial unrest is the visibility of people for whom the outcome-input ratio far exceeds the outcome-input ratio of the average worker (Lawler, 1968). The lack of referents against whom to compare herself, furthermore, might have prevented inchoate anger in the pre-"liberation" housewife from developing into a coherent sense of grievance (Friedan, 1963; Greer, 1970).

How do comparison processes function at work and at home for the residents of Newton? Eighty percent of the employed people report that they compare themselves with others when

Table 7.4 Target of Anger

	Percentage of respondents who select each response when they think of things that are wrong		
	At work (n = 337)	At home (n = 280)	For women (n = 404)
It's always things in general	5.93	3.93	50.00
Usually things in general	26.71	25.71	22.52
Half and half	35.01	39.28	4.95
Usually someone or some people	28.78	29.29	1.48
Always someone or some people	3.56	1.79	21.04
Total	100%	100%	100%

trying to decide how good their job is; only 50 percent claim to use comparison others when deciding how good their home life is. Whether or not they spontaneously compare themselves with others, the respondents were asked to cite as many as three people with whom they might compare their lot at work and at home. In every instance, the respondent was asked if he or she were better off, worse off, or the same as the comparison other. An average score was derived ranging potentially between one (respondent better off) and three (respondent worse off). The frequencies of each response appear in Table 7.5. Fifty-eight

Table 7.5 Respondent's View of Own Position Relative to Three Comparison Others

		Percentage obtaining each score concerning:	
	Score	Job (n = 339)	Home (n = 395)
Respondent is better off	1.00	17.99	19.75
	1.33	10.03	15.44
	1.50	1.18	2.02
	1.67	14.45	20.51
	2.00	16.52	19.75
	2.33	15.93	11.90
Respondent is worse off	2.50	0.59	1.01
	2.67	8.55	4.05
	3.00	14.75	5.57
Total		100%	100%

percent of our respondents see their own home situation as better than that of their friends; 44 percent of the employed respondents see their own work situation as better.

Other data echo the tendency of our respondents to feel in a privileged position at work and even more so at home. To determine how people think of their comparative earnings, we asked the employed respondents: "For a person with your experience and your type of job, what would you say about your earnings?" The response options and the percentages of respondents selecting each are:

I am paid far above average	6.1 percent
I am paid somewhat above average	32.0 percent
My pay is average	36.9 percent
I am paid somewhat below average	19.2 percent
I am paid far below average	5.8 percent

We see that more people perceive themselves to be above average than to be below average in their compensation.

If a self-congratulatory strain is audible at work, it is deafening at home. We asked the nonsingle respondents in the study: "Taking everything into account, how does your own marriage compare with that of your friends?" The answers and percentages of respondents selecting each option are:

Mine is much better	38.5 percent
Mine is slightly better	30.0 percent
Equal	26.5 percent
Theirs are slightly better	3.5 percent
Theirs are much better	1.1 percent

It is hard to know whether one ought to congratulate our respondents or to send condolences to their friends. There are a few reasons why the percentages might be biased toward the positive side. Even more than the size of one's paycheck, the health of one's marriage may be interpreted as a sign of competence. Our respondents may want to see their own marriages as better than those of their friends because they would like to maintain an image of themselves as able and accomplished. Alternately, the residents of Newton may be under the impression that most marriages are in peril. The divorce rate increases yearly throughout the United States, and the increases are heavily publicized. Although specialists distinquish between marital stability and marital satisfaction, the average respondent may not. Perhaps when someone says his marriage is better than his friends' marriages, he means that his own minor misery looks better to him than does his media-fostered vision of their domestic inferno. Of course, we would expect people to rely on the media for information about their friends' marriages only to the extent that the information does not come directly from their friends.

Summary

There is no evidence of direct interference between work and home, and there is evidence of some spillover of feelings from one domain to the other. The correlations between dissatisfaction and resentment at work and at home are low but reliable. The general separateness of work and home is consistent with the idea that multiple roles offer psychological protection.

Feelings toward work and feelings toward home bear many similarities. In both, the tone is quite positive. The members of our sample certainly feel better about their own personal situations than about the situation of working women. They also experience a greater sense of control over their personal lives. The major difference between work and home feelings concerns the role of comparison others. Comparisons are avoided in the domestic sphere. When we force comparisons upon our respondents, it is the unusual person indeed who does not think that his or her own family and marriage is far above average. While the average employed respondent may also overestimate his or her outcomes at work, the extent of the overestimate is much less than at home.

8

Testing the Theory

Our survey—like many studies before it—bristles with findings that are consistent with the concept of relative deprivation. The employed women of Newton are satisfied with their jobs in general and with their salaries in pàrticular despite objective sex discrimination. Low-prestige workers, including low-prestige women workers, are less distressed about the situation of working women than are their high-prestige counterparts, even though the latter are better off than the former. Nor do subjective deprivations at home correspond isomorphically with objective conditions: low-prestige women, for example, are subject to an especially unequal division of labor in the home, but they are no more resentful than are high-prestige women.

While corroborating the theory of relative deprivation, our results leave undemonstrated the validity of any specific model. In this chapter, we perform a series of validational tests of the five models of relative deprivation (Crosby, 1976; Davis, 1959; Gurr, 1970; Runciman, 1966; Williams, 1975), the frustration-aggression hypothesis (Berkowitz, 1972), and the two equity models (Adams, 1965; Patchen, 1961a, 1961b) summarized in Chapter 2 and displayed in Table 2.1. The tests tend to confirm the proposition that deprivation depends on cognitions and emotions rather than on objective factors. The tests show, in other words, that the theory is generally correct. At the same time, they call into question the validity of any specific model. We emerge from the technical details of validation at the end of the chapter to propose a tentative new model.

Validating models

How does one test the validity of a model or theory? Theories and models specify how variables relate to one another (Bunge, 1959; Nagel, 1961, 1965). Each of the models outlined in Chapter 2 proposes how feelings of resentment, grievance, or deprivation relate to other cognitive and emotional factors and to objective reality. For each model we have derived a list of factors that are hypothesized to act as preconditions of felt deprivation. It follows that to test any model, we should see if the proposed factors do, in fact, act as preconditions of felt deprivation. *If feelings of deprivation or grievance vary as a function of the hypothesized preconditions, the model is valid.* If not, it is invalid.

The most straightforward method for validation is multiple regression analysis.[1] In a multiple regression analysis, the dependent or criterion variable would be the level of deprivation, resentment, or grievance as measured by the Deprivation Scale. The six hypothesized preconditions and the demographic variables such as sex would be treated as predictor variables. The multiple regression analysis could be performed once for the data about one's own job, once for the data about women's jobs, and once for the data about one's own home life.

Each regression analysis allows us to answer two basic questions: first, do the psychological factors, as a group, explain any of the variance in the level of deprivation over and above what is explained by the demographic factors? To answer this question, we can perform a two-step hierarchical multiple regression. In the first step are entered demographic characteristics. In the second are entered scores on the various scales (e.g., the Wanting Scale).

If Step 2 increases the amount of variance explained by the regression equation, then we know that psychological factors, as a group, help to predict the level of deprivation, and we can infer that the theory of relative deprivation is generally valid. We are then ready for the second question: which of the hypothesized preconditions do, in fact, predict the level of deprivation? The answer to this question constitutes a measure of the validity of any specific model of relative deprivation. We can use Davis's model to exemplify the approach. Imagine that the regression analysis shows that scores on the Wanting Scale, the Comparison Other Scale, and the Deserving Scale all predict scores on the Deprivation Scale, and that none of the other scores do. Imagine, in other words, that the hypothesized preconditions of wanting, comparison other, and deserving are significant and that no other factors in the equation are. This would demonstrate that the model proposed by Davis is valid. If wanting, comparison other, or deserving fails to explain a significant amount of the variance in deprivation, then the model is invalid. If some other factor, like future expectations, predicts the level of deprivation as well as wanting, comparison other, and deserving, then the model proposed by Davis is valid but incomplete.

While a multiple regression analysis provides the most straightforward procedure for validational testing, ambiguities in the models and limitations in our data make it an imperfect procedure. The relatively small size of the sample prohibits the creation of an interaction term in the regression equation. This means that a regression analysis is not strictly appropriate for models in which the preconditions combine in a multiplicative fashion. Crosby, for example, states explicitly that resentment is felt when all the preconditions are met. If even one precondition is lacking, according to Crosby's (1976) model, resentment is not felt. A regression analysis which assumes that the preconditions combine in an additive, linear fashion is not totally suitable for testing such a complex model. In fairness to the specific models, we have devised two additional procedures for testing their validity.

The second procedure circumvents the problems of the regression analyses. In it, we dichotomize scores on each of the hypothesized preconditions into two categories—present and absent in some cases, high and low in others. The division is performed according to a priori rules. Table 8.1 illustrates the sorting rules for the precondition, wanting X. As the table shows, wanting is scored "present" if the individual feels "not very close" or "not at all close" to obtaining things he desires from a job (Question 19); if he feels he wants more from his job at least "a couple of times a week" (Qestion 20); or if he ranks his job as low in fulfilling his wants (Question 21). In general, then, the variable is scored "present" if there is any

Table 8.1 Typical Dichotomizing Rules

Want is present for any respondent who provides *any one* of the answers by which there is an *X*. For all other respondents, want is scored absent.

Q.19

How close does your job come to actually giving you these things [which are desired things cited in Q.18]?

    very close
    somewhat close
X not very close
X not at all close

Q.20

During the last month, how often have you felt that you wanted more from your job than you are getting from it now?

X constantly
X at least once each day
X a couple of times a week
   once a week
   not very often
   never

Q.21

Thinking about your job right now, and taking everything into account, how much does your job fulfill your wants? Give the job a score between zero (if it fails totally) and 10 (if it succeeds absolutely).

X 0
X 1
X 2
   3
   4
   5
   6
   7
   8
   9
  10

indication of a large discrepancy between what the individual has and what he wants. Otherwise, wanting X is scored as "absent." Analogous rules exist for each of the six hypothesized preconditions as they relate to one's own job, the job situation of women, and one's own home life. (The rules are presented in Appendix II-B.)

After each respondent has received a dichotomized score

for each hypothesized precondition, we divide the sample into two categories: the constellation group and the remainder. The constellation group comprises the individuals who meet the particular set of preconditions specified by the model. Davis's constellation group, for example, includes all individuals for whom wanting is present, comparison other is present, *and* deserving is present. The remainder includes all respondents for whom wanting is absent, comparison other is absent, *or* deserving is absent. The test of any version of the theory is whether the mean Deprivation Score of the constellation group is significantly higher than the mean Deprivation Score of the remainder. If the model proposed by Davis is correct, for instance, people who want X, see another has X *and* feel entitled to X themselves (i.e., his constellation group) will have an average Deprivation Score that is significantly higher than that of the remainder.

The second procedure, like the first, has drawbacks. We lose information when we transform scores from a scale into nominal (on-off) data. Also, the "constellation group" for some of the more complex models can be quite small. The number of people whose scores conform to five criteria is likely to be minute, but Crosby's model specifies five preconditions of felt deprivation.

To avoid the problem of small numbers without assuming that the factors combine in a linear, additive fashion, there is a final validational procedure. In it, we do not start with the preconditions, but rather with the Deprivation Scores themselves. We select a group of the most deprived individuals (i.e., those with the highest scores) and the least deprived individuals (i.e., those with the lowest). We then compare the two groups in terms of their average scores for wanting X, comparison other, deserving, past expectations, future expectations, and self-blame. The critical test of any model is whether the most deprived group differs from the least deprived group on the preconditions hypothesized by the model. If Davis is correct, to continue the example, the most deprived people should have higher average scores than the least deprived people on the Wanting Scale, the Comparison Other Scale, and the Deserving Scale. The two groups should not differ in terms of past expectations, future expectations, or self-blame if Davis's model is complete as well as valid.

With three procedures for testing each model in the three separate attitude domains, each model is submitted to nine tests of validity. The large number of tests is justified by the nature of the theory and by the nature of the data. We employ three separate procedures in order to give the models a fair hearing. Regression analysis is the critical procedure, but both the constellation approach and the extreme scorers approach are needed to compensate for inadequacies of the multiple regression analysis. We repeat the three tests for attitudes toward work, toward the position of women, and toward home because the dynamics of deprivation may be different in the three domains. Like others, we have found personal deprivation and group deprivation to be empirically distinct. We have also found that comparison processes play a different role in how people feel about their homes than in how they feel about their jobs. Conceivably, one model is valid for one attitudinal domain but not for the others.

Resentments at work

Our first test of relative deprivation theory, using as data the employed respondents' feelings about their jobs, is straightforward. It is a multiple regression analysis to determine which background factors and which psychological factors statistically predict feelings of resentment about one's job. Because several researchers (e.g., Spilerman, 1970, 1971) have claimed that the level of discontent can be accounted for entirely by sociological variables and that psychological variables are superfluous, we perform a two-step hierarchical regression analysis. In the first step are entered six background factors; in the second, six psychological factors. If the amount of variance explained in the criterion variable, felt deprivation, is greater after the second step, then the psychological factors are statistical predictors of felt deprivation. Determining which among the six psychological variables predict felt deprivation tests the various versions of relative deprivation and cognate theories.

The six background characteristics to be entered as a block

Table 8.2 Attitudes Toward the Job: Summary of Regression Analysis

	Step 1	Step 2
Variables in the equation	Sex, family status, education, salary, household income, prestige rating of occupation	Sex, family status, education, salary, household income, prestige rating of occupation, wanting, deserving, comparison other, past expectations, future expectations, self-blame
Multiple R	0.186	0.564
R square	0.034	0.318
Adjusted R square	0.015	0.290
Standard error	3.506	2.976
degrees of freedom	6,295	12,289
F	1.765	11.261

n = 302
Criterion variable: extent of deprivation about one's job

into the regression equation are: (1) sex; (2) family status; (3) education; (4) salary; (5) household income; and (6) prestige of occupation. Sex is a dummy variable with female scored as one and male as two. Family status is coded on a three-point scale (1 = single; 2 = married, without children; 3 = parents). Education varies from 1 (some high school) to 5 (graduate study). Salary stretches from 1 (nothing) to 12 (over $50,000 per annum). So does yearly household income. Prestige of occupations is rated according to the National Opinion Research Center rules (Center for Political Studies, 1977). The actual range of occupations among our sample is 17.3 to 81.2.

In the second step of the regression are entered as a block the six hypothesized preconditions of felt deprivation. The measures of each psychological factor, and of the criterion variable, resentment, are the same as those described in Chapter 4. (For exact operationalizations, see Appendix II.)

When the demographic variables are entered but the psychological variables are not, the one variable to predict resentment reliably is family status. The negative beta weight confirms the descriptive findings reported in Chapter 4: single people experience the most grievance about their jobs. The to-

Table 8.3 Attitudes Toward the Job: Regression Coefficients

Variable	B	Beta	Std. error B	F
Sex	0.477	0.067	0.380	1.575
Family status	−0.257	−0.059	0.223	1.326
Education	0.224	0.078	0.236	0.899
Salary	0.190	0.115	0.117	2.625
Household income	−0.012	−0.009	0.087	0.019
Prestige rating	−0.043	−0.025	0.013	0.102
Wanting	0.366	0.418	0.057	39.992
Comparison other	0.075	0.044	0.117	0.417
Deserving	0.276	0.050	0.382	0.521
Past expectations	−0.105	−0.049	0.133	0.627
Future expectations	0.392	0.179	0.126	9.641
(No) self-blame	0.465	0.101	0.230	4.090

n = 302
Criterion variable: extent of deprivation about one's job

tal amount of variance explained by the demographic variables is, as Table 8.2 shows, insignificant. In other words, people's feelings of deprivation are not simply a function of their objective social characteristics.

Total variance explained jumps when the psychological variables are entered into the regression. The F-value for the entire equation after step two is 11.26. Entering the psychological variables into the equation also causes the demographic variable of family status to shrink into insignificance. Table 8.3 presents the regression results after step two. The regression analysis confirms the general validity of relative deprivation theory. Demographic variables cannot predict the level of resentment about one's job, but psychological variables can.

If the overall findings support the theory in general, the particular pattern of results proves less heartening for relative deprivation theorists. As Table 8.3 shows, two factors reliably predict the criterion variable: wanting and future expectations. The greater the discrepancy between what one has and what one wants, the more grievance one feels. The more pessimistic one is, the more grievance one feels. In addition, self-blame is marginally significant: the freer one is from self-blame, the more prone one is to a sense of grievance. No model of relative deprivation, equity, or frustration-aggression, explicated in Chapter 2, proposes that deprivation varies as a function of this particular constellation of preconditions. All models include wanting, and Gurr's model includes low future expectations as well. But Gurr also includes deserving in his model, and deserving does not predict the level of deprivation in the regression analysis. Davis's, Adams's and Patchen's models envision deserving as a precondition, and they are thus disconfirmed. So are Runciman and Crosby. Indeed, Runciman and Crosby are doubly damned, for they predict that deprivation is greatest when future expectations are high. Williams includes comparison other and Berkowitz includes past expectations.[2]

If the regression analysis invalidates all the models, the second procedure confirms them all. In the second procedure, we compare, model by model, the constellation group with the remainder of the respondents. Table 8.4 summarizes the outcomes of the comparisons. For each model, the constellation group experiences more deprivation than do others. Gurr's model, which comes closest to being confirmed by the first procedure, is the least strongly supported model in the second. As we can see in Table 8.4, there are twenty-two respondents for whom want is scored present, deserving is scored present and future expectations are scored low. These twenty-two respondents obtain an average score of 10.84 on the Deprivation Scale, which is reliably but not enormously different from the 9.09 obtained by the least deprived group.

The wreath of victory won by the models in the second validational test has a thorn. With all models being supported, it is impossible to choose among them. Contrast the equity models of Patchen and Adams. The only difference between the two is Patchen's inclusion of low self-blame. Both models are valid. Yet relative to Patchen, Adams lacks completeness. Relative to Adams, Patchen lacks parsimony.

What do we find with the third method, in which we contrast the most deprived group and the least deprived group? The potential range of scores on the Deprivation Scale is 1 to 30. The actual range is 1 to 24. We aimed to select the top 15 percent and the bottom 15 percent of the scorers. Examination of the frequency distribution revealed clusters, and we consequently selected the top-scoring twenty-three individuals (most

Table 8.4 Second Validational Test of Relative Deprivation Theory Using Attitudes Toward the Job as Data

Theorists	Characteristics of constellation group	Mean deprivation scores — Constellation group	Mean deprivation scores — Remainder	Test of significance — t	Test of significance — df	Test of significance — Two-tailed probability
Deprivation theorists						
Davis, Adams	want present C.O. present deserve present	$\bar{x} = 11.16$ (n = 109)	$\bar{x} = 8.29$ (n = 233)	−7.45	340	0.0001
Runciman	want present C.O. present deserve present future exp. high	$\bar{x} = 11.24$ (n = 87)	$\bar{x} = 8.51$ (n = 255)	−6.52	340	0.0001
Gurr	want present deserve present future exp. low	$\bar{x} = 10.84$ (n = 22)	$\bar{x} = 9.09$ (n = 320)	−2.24	340	0.03
Williams	want present C.O. present	$\bar{x} = 10.56$ (n = 153)	$\bar{x} = 8.11$ (n = 189)	−6.70	340	0.0001
Crosby	want present C.O. present deserve present future exp. high self-blame absent	$\bar{x} = 11.25$ (n = 59)	$\bar{x} = 8.78$ (n = 283)	−5.01	340	0.0001
Others						
Patchen	want present C.O. present deserve present self-blame absent	$\bar{x} = 11.32$ (n = 73)	$\bar{x} = 8.63$ (n = 269)	−5.98	340	0.0001
Berkowitz	want present past exp. high	$\bar{x} = 10.88$ (n = 94)	$\bar{x} = 8.57$ (n = 248)	−5.57	340	0.0001

deprived) and the bottom-scoring twenty-three individuals (least deprived) from our sample of 345 employed Newtonites.

Table 8.5 shows the contrast between the top group, the bottom group, and the total employed sample for each of the hypothesized preconditions of felt deprivation and for felt deprivation itself. The table also shows the results of a series of *t*-tests in which the top- and bottom-scoring group are contrasted. It is clear from the table that the two groups differ significantly on each and every precondition. The differences are always in the expected direction.[3] Crosby and Runciman are again refuted: they are wrong about future expectations. The other models are valid but incomplete.

In sum, concerning people's attitudes toward their jobs, the validational tests produce discrepant results. The regression analysis confirms the central proposition of relative deprivation theory but disconfirms every model. The relative deprivation models of Davis, Gurr and Williams, the equity models of Adams and Patchen, and the frustration-aggression hypothesis are all confirmed by both the second and third procedures. We see from the third test, however, that none of the models is complete.

Resentments about the position of women

We repeat in this section the three tests of validity. Instead of data about one's own job situation, this time we use data about one's view of the job situation of women. In all but one analysis, we use data from the entire Newton sample. Again, the results of our tests are inconsistent.

The hierarchical multiple regression again involves two steps. In the first, six demographic variables are entered as a block. The six variables in this analysis are: (1) sex; (2) family status; (3) education; (4) salary; (5) prestige rating of own (or, for the housewives, of husband's) occupation; and (6) employment status. Employment status is a dummy variable (1 = employed; 2 = not employed). The other variables are scored as in the multiple regression analysis for deprivation about one's own job. The six hypothesized preconditions of deprivation are entered as a block in step two. These variables are scored as before. (See Chapter 5 and Appendix II.)

Table 8.5 Third Validational Test of Relative Deprivation Theory Using Attitudes Toward the Job as Data

Hypothesized preconditions	Potential range	Mean scores for each group			Significance tests (contrasts extreme groups)		
		Most deprived (n = 23)	All employed respondents (n = 345)	Least deprived (n = 23)	t-value	df	Two-tailed probability
Deprivation	1–30	17.17	9.21	3.05	−5.57	44	0.0001
Wanting	3–21[a]	12.61	9.40	5.96			
Comparison other	4–18[b]	10.18	9.78	8.19	−3.55	42	0.001
Deserving	3–14[c]	8.63	7.40	5.90	−5.79	44	0.0001
Past expectations	2–10[d]	6.20	5.54	4.89	−2.77	43	0.008
Future expectations	3–12[e]	6.18	5.80	4.45	−4.06	44	0.0001
Self-blame	2–6[f]	3.39	3.17	2.87	−2.21	44	0.032

[a] The higher the score, the greater the discrepancy between what one has and what one wants.
[b] The higher the score, the greater the perception that other is well off relative to self.
[c] The higher the score, the greater the discrepancy between what one has and what one deserves.
[d] The higher the score, the greater the gap between past expectations and present realities.
[e] The higher the score, the greater the pessimism.
[f] The higher the score, the greater the freedom from self-blame.

Table 8.6   Attitudes Toward the Position of Women: Summary of
Regression Analysis

	Step 1	Step 2
Variables in the equation	Sex, family status, education, salary, prestige rating, employment status	Sex, family status, education, salary, prestige rating, employment status, wanting, deserving, comparison other, past expectations, future expectations, self-blame
Multiple R	0.478	0.628
R square	0.229	0.395
Adjusted R square	0.216	0.375
Standard error	1.280	1.143
degrees of freedom	6,365	12,359
F	18.092	19.570

n = 372
Criterion variable: extent of deprivation about the position of working women

The demographic variables explain nearly 50 percent of the
variance in felt deprivation. The F-values of sex, education, and
employment status after step one are 57.342, 7.732, and 4.637,
respectively. F-values for the other demographic variables are
quite small. When the psychological variables are entered in
step two, there is an increase in the overall variance explained
(as Table 8.6 shows), while education and employment status
drop into nonsignificance. But if psychological factors increase
our ability to predict the level of grievance about the situation
of women, one demographic characteristic remains important.
Table 8.7 shows that sex remains the single most important
predictor of felt deprivation and that comparison other and
deserving are also important.[4]

The regression analysis offers some support of the general
theory, although less strongly than in the case of one's own job.
Again, no model is confirmed by the regression analysis with
data concerning women's jobs. Every model includes 'wanting
X' as a precondition of deprivation, but this variable does not
emerge as a significant predictor of deprivation in the regression analysis.[5]

Table 8.7 Attitudes Toward the Position of Women: Regression Coefficients

Variable	B	Beta	Std. error B	F
Sex	−0.887	−0.304	0.141	39.260
Family status	0.051	0.030	0.081	0.410
Education	0.014	0.012	0.080	0.031
Salary	−0.022	−0.039	0.352	0.426
Prestige rating	0.036	0.053	0.004	0.671
Employment status	−0.179	−0.043	0.243	0.545
Wanting	0.091	0.079	0.064	2.032
Comparison other	0.237	0.209	0.054	19.221
Deserving	0.272	0.245	0.067	16.264
Past expectations	0.039	0.034	0.051	0.584
Future expectations	0.051	0.067	0.037	1.891
(No) self-blame	−0.060	−0.031	0.089	0.461

n = 372
Criterion variable: extent of deprivation about the position of working women

What happens when we perform the second validational test? Here we score the hypothesized preconditions of group deprivation in a dichotomous fashion following a priori rules. (See Appendix II.) A constellation and a remainder group are formed for each model: each constellation group contains individuals for whom the pattern of scores matches the constellation of factors thought to produce deprivation. Table 8.8 gives the mean scores and the results of *t*-tests in which the constellation and remainder groups are contrasted. Runciman and Crosby are again refuted. How to select among the other five valid models may be a matter of personal preference. Those who fancy parsimony might find the frustration-aggression hypothesis to be most useful, those who are attracted to completeness may prefer Patchen's model.

The third procedure, in which extremes are contrasted, confirms some models. The Deprivation Scale concerning women's situation has a potential range of 1 to 6. In the entire sample of Newtonites, eight women and 50 men have a score of 1 on the scale. These fifty-eight individuals constitute the least deprived group. For contrast, we selected forty-two individuals who score at the other end of the scale.[6] Table 8.9 shows the mean scores for the most and the least deprived groups

Table 8.8 Second Validational Test of Relative Deprivation Theory Using Attitudes Toward Women as Data

Theorists	Characteristics of constellation group	Mean deprivation scores Constellation group	Mean deprivation scores Remainder	Test of significance t	Test of significance df	Test of significance Two-tailed probability
Deprivation theorists						
Davis, Adams	want present C.O. present deserve present	$\bar{x}$ = 3.33 (n = 365)	$\bar{x}$ = 2.02 (n = 40)	−5.63	403	0.0001
Runciman	want present C.O. present deserve present future exp. high	$\bar{x}$ = 3.11 (n = 276)	$\bar{x}$ = 3.40 (n = 129)	1.92	403	p > .05
Gurr	want present deserve present future exp. low	$\bar{x}$ = 4.01 (n = 90)	$\bar{x}$ = 2.97 (n = 315)	−6.26	403	0.0001
Williams	want present C.O. present	$\bar{x}$ = 3.26 (n = 383)	$\bar{x}$ = 2.31 (n = 22)	−3.02	403	0.003
Crosby	want present C.O. present deserve present future exp. high self-blame absent	$\bar{x}$ = 3.13 (n = 271)	$\bar{x}$ = 3.35 (n = 134)	1.43	403	p > .10
Others						
Patchen	want present C.O. present deserve present self-blame absent	$\bar{x}$ = 3.35 (n = 360)	$\bar{x}$ = 2.01 (n = 45)	−6.09	403	0.0001
Berkowitz	want present past exp. high	$\bar{x}$ = 3.42 (n = 223)	$\bar{x}$ = 2.93 (n = 182)	−3.44	403	0.001

and for the entire sample. The significance tests are also shown. With the exception of blame, the most deprived and least deprived groups differ significantly from each other on every hypothesized precondition. The similarity between Table 8.9 and Table 8.5 is marked.

As before, the conclusions we draw from the data depend in part on our predilections. Both Runciman's and Crosby's models of relative deprivation are refuted by the data because the deprived group is significantly more pessimistic than the gratified group. Patchen's equity model is disconfirmed because the two groups do not differ in the degree to which they blame women for their current plight. The data provide support for the the models of relative deprivation proposed by Gurr, Williams, and Davis, as well as for the frustration-aggression hypothesis and Adams's equity model. None of the models is complete.

In sum, concerning attitudes toward the position of women, no model is unequivocally supported. The relative deprivation models of Davis, Gurr, and Williams are confirmed by the second and third procedures. So are the models of Adams and Berkowitz. Patchen's model is confirmed by the second test but disconfirmed by the third. Runciman's and Crosby's models are disconfirmed by all tests.

Resentments at home

When we use as our data base people's attitude toward domestic arrangements, and especially toward the division of labor in the home, both the first and third validational tests end in a rout for relative deprivation theory. In the second validational test, five of the seven models are confirmed.

The regression analysis of resentments at home uses information from the married people and parents. Many of the single respondents live alone and are, therefore, unable to answer most of the questions. In the first step of the two-step hierarchical multiple regression, the six demographic variables shown in Table 8.10 are entered as a block. In the second step, the six hypothesized preconditions are added in a block. The psychological variables increase the amount of explained variance quite

Table 8.9 Third Validational Test of Relative Deprivation Theory Using Attitudes Toward Women as Data

Hypothesized preconditions	Potential range	Mean scores for each group			Significance test (contrasts extreme groups)		
		Most deprived (n = 42)	All respondents (n = 405)	Least deprived (n = 58)	t-value	df	Two-tailed probability
Deprivation	1–6	5.53	3.20	1.00	−4.92	96	0.0001
Wanting	3–12[a]	9.65	8.60	8.39			
Comparison other	3–13[b]	11.95	10.98	10.31	−6.48	96	0.0001
Deserving	2–10[c]	9.25	8.05	7.38	−7.76	98	0.0001
Past expectations	2–8[d]	5.58	4.86	4.56	−4.24	98	0.0001
Future expectations	3–13[e]	7.96	6.79	5.86	−5.28	98	0.0001
Blame	3–6[f]	5.74	5.58	5.42	−1.84	92	0.069

[a]The higher the score, the greater the perceived discrepancy between what women have and what they want.
[b]The higher the score, the greater the perceived discrepancy between what women and men have.
[c]The higher the score, the greater the perceived discrepancy between what women have and what they deserve.
[d]The higher the score, the greater the discrepancy between past expectations and present realities.
[e]The higher the score, the greater the pessimism.
[f]The higher the score, the less women are blamed for problems.

Table 8.10 Attitudes Toward the Home: Summary of Regression Analysis

	Step 1	Step 2
Variables in the equation	Sex, family status, education, salary, prestige rating of occupation, employment status	Sex, family status, education, salary, prestige rating of occupation, employment status, wanting, deserving, comparison other, past expectations, future expectations, self-blame
Multiple R	0.280	0.529
R square	0.078	0.280
Adjusted R square	0.057	0.246
Standard error	3.777	3.377
degrees of freedom	6,258	12,252
F	3.679	8.188

a lot, as the table shows. From Table 8.11, we see that resentment at home varies as a function of deserving, wanting, and past expectations.[7] The results support Berkowitz's (1972) version of the frustration-aggression hypothesis. Berkowitz features discontent as a function of desires and past expectations. Berkowitz's formulation is, however, incomplete. None of the other models is confirmed, but the increase in explained variance when psychological variables are entered in the regression equation confirms the general theory.

The second procedure, using as data people's feelings about home, provides more support for the various models. With Crosby's model the constellation group fails to differ from the remainder in terms of average Deprivation Scores. With Patchen's model, as Table 8.12 shows, the two groups are marginally different from each other. The other five comparisons all yield highly significant differences. It might be worth noting that the constellation groups formed for both Crosby and Patchen are tiny. Perhaps the incomplete model proposed by Davis and Adams is more useful than the model proposed by Patchen, not only because the former is more parsimonious but also be-

Table 8.11   Attitudes Toward the Home: Regression Coefficients

Variable	B	Beta	Std. error B	F
Sex	−0.246	−0.031	0.509	0.234
Family status	0.976	0.129	0.461	4.482
Education	−0.095	−0.031	0.291	0.108
Salary	0.255	0.174	0.122	4.331
Prestige rating	0.075	0.040	0.016	0.199
Employment status	1.169	0.123	0.766	2.329
Wanting	0.290	0.213	0.081	12.748
Comparison other	−0.011	−0.002	0.273	0.002
Deserving	0.884	0.232	0.244	13.042
Past expectations	1.674	0.158	0.639	6.844
Future expectations	0.283	0.045	0.344	0.678
(No) self-blame	−0.323	−0.061	0.325	0.990

n = 265
Criterion variable: extent of deprivation about one's home life

cause the phenomena it describes occur more frequently in the realm of feelings about one's home life.

The third procedure provides no support for any model when we use data about life at home. Again excluding single respondents, we have selected the fifteen most deprived and the fifteen least deprived individuals. Table 8.13 shows that the two groups differ significantly from each other in terms of deserving and wanting. The most deprived group is not, however, more likely than the least deprived group to view others as better off than they themselves are. This invalidates Davis, Runciman, Williams, and Crosby, as well as Adams and Patchen. Nor do extreme scorers differ in their past or future expectations, thus refuting the frustration-aggression hypothesis and Gurr.

In sum, concerning people's attitudes toward their home, the results are motley. The regression analysis supports the theory generally and Berkowitz's frustration-aggression hypothesis, but it disconfirms other models. By the second procedure, the models of Davis, Runciman, and Gurr, as well as those of Adams and Berkowitz, are confirmed. None of the models is supported when we look at extreme scorers.

Table 8.12 Second Validational Test of Relative Deprivation Theory Using Attitudes Toward Home as Data

Theorists	Characteristics of constellation group	Mean deprivation scores Constellation group	Mean deprivation scores Remainder	Test of significance t	Test of significance df	Two-tailed probability
Deprivation theorists						
Davis, Adams	want present C.O. present deserve present	$\bar{x} = 12.66$ (n = 30)	$\bar{x} = 8.87$ (n = 254)	−5.30	282	0.0001
Runciman	want present C.O. present deserve present future exp. high	$\bar{x} = 12.48$ (n = 21)	$\bar{x} = 9.02$ (n = 263)	−4.05	282	0.0001
Gurr	want present deserve present future exp. low	$\bar{x} = 12.31$ (n = 19)	$\bar{x} = 9.06$ (n = 265)	−3.62	282	0.0001
Williams	want present C.O. present	$\bar{x} = 10.84$ (n = 69)	$\bar{x} = 8.77$ (n = 215)	−3.96	282	0.001
Crosby	want present C.O. present deserve present future exp. high self-blame absent	$\bar{x} = 12.03$ (n = 3)	$\bar{x} = 9.25$ (n = 281)	−1.24	282	p > .10
Others						
Patchen	want present C.O. present deserve present self-blame absent	$\bar{x} = 12.73$ (n = 5)	$\bar{x} = 9.21$ (n = 279)	−2.03	282	0.05
Berkowitz	want present past exp. high	$\bar{x} = 11.69$ (n = 48)	$\bar{x} = 8.78$ (n = 236)	−4.93	282	0.0001

Table 8.13 Third Validational Test of Relative Deprivation Theory Using Attitudes Toward Home as Data

	Potential range	Mean scores for each group			Significance tests (contrasts extreme groups)		
		Most deprived (n = 15)	All nonsingle respondents (n = 265)	Least deprived (n = 15)	t-value	df	Two-tailed probability
Deprivation	2–34	18.97	9.28	3.22	-3.04	28	0.005
Wanting	0–22 [a]	6.33	3.64	2.73			
Comparison other	2–5 [b]	3.33	3.28	3.05	-0.85	27	0.404
Deserving	2–25 [c]	8.33	5.62	4.13	-2.45	28	0.021
Past expectations	0–1 [d]	0.20	0.15	0.13	-0.48	28	0.638
Future expectations	1–3 [e]	1.67	1.59	1.60	-0.27	28	0.790
(No) self-blame	1–5 [f]	3.40	3.67	3.93	1.80	28	0.083

[a] The higher the score, the greater the discrepancy between what one has and what one wants.
[b] The higher the score, the greater the perception that other is well off relative to self.
[c] The higher the score, the greater the discrepancy between what one has and what one deserves.
[d] The higher the score, the greater the gap between past expectations and present realities.
[e] The higher the score, the greater the pessimism.
[f] The higher the score, the greater the freedom from self-blame.

Revising the models

Several conclusions follow from our analyses. First, it is unquestionably true that feelings of grievance depend on cognitive and emotional factors and not simply on objective factors. Psychological factors predict felt deprivation better than demographic factors do in the regression analyses. When we contrast people who experience a great deal of resentment about their own jobs or about the job situation of women with people who experience little resentment, the two groups vary in terms of the hypothesized preconditions of deprivation. In short, deprivations are relative and not absolute.

Second, we conclude that none of the models is unambiguously valid. Berkowitz's model is confirmed in six of the nine validational tests; some of the relative deprivation and equity models are confirmed nearly as often. But none of the models is always confirmed. Even when they are confirmed, the models appear incomplete.

The third conclusion relates closely to the second: some of the models seem better than others. Runciman's and Crosby's relative deprivation models and Patchen's equity model are clearly the weakest. Crosby's model is confirmed only once, Runciman's twice, and Patchen's three times. Crosby and Runciman are wrong about the role of future expectations; contrary to their models, resentments are greatest when the goal appears unattainable. Crosby and Patchen are wrong about self-blame. They claim that people feel aggrieved only when they reject personal responsibility for their own predicament; the facts seem otherwise.

These conclusions leave us in an uncomfortable position. Where the theory of relative deprivation departs most sharply from common sense is in specifying the particular set of factors that act as preconditions of resentment. To confirm the general theory without opting for a specific model is, therefore, unsatisfying. We could simply say that the models of Davis (and Adams), Gurr, Williams, and Berkowitz are all valid, but we must acknowledge that the models differ in their sets of preconditions. We could decide that resentment varies as a function of wanting, comparison other, deserving, past expectations, and future expectations, because these are the preconditions that figure in one or more of the valid models. Such a construction lacks elegance. It begs the question: are some factors more important than others?

Data from a laboratory test of relative deprivation can help answer the question. In the laboratory study (Bernstein & Crosby, 1980) more than 500 students read a story about a student who wanted a certain grade or about an engineer who wanted a promotion. Half the time, there was a better-off comparison other, half the time not. Half the time, the character felt entitled to the goal, half not. In this way each of the hypothesized preconditions of felt deprivation, except wanting, was independently varied. After reading the story, the student answered a series of questions about how he or she would feel in the circumstances. Two dependent measures were created. One was a simple measure of resentment. The other was a composite score, where feelings of resentment, anger, dissatisfaction, disappointment, and unhappiness were all combined. Analyses of variance revealed that both the simple resentment measure and the composite score varied as a function of deserving, of future expectations, and of self-blame. Scores were higher when deserving was high, future expectations were low, and self-blame was high. (The last finding, which was unexpected, probably resulted from a confound in the self-blame manipulation.[8])

Taken together, the findings of the present survey study and of the laboratory study suggest a revised model, in which wanting and deserving are the two essential preconditions of felt deprivation. To feel aggrieved about a situation, people must feel that there is a discrepancy between what they have and what they want and a discrepancy between what they have and what they deserve. Support for this revised model is contained in Table 8.14. The table illustrates which of the hypothesized preconditions actually do predict resentment in the various tests. Looking across the rows, we see that wanting and deserving each fail to predict deprivation in only one instance. Wanting does not emerge as a predictor in one of the multiple regression analyses, deserving in another. Perhaps the problem

Table 8.14   Predictors of Felt Deprivation

	Regression [a]			Extremes contrasted [b]			Lab study ANOVAS [c]	
	Job	Women	Home	Job	Women	Home	Resent-ment	Compo-site
Wanting	X		X	X	X	X	—[d]	—
Comparison other		X		X	X		X	
Deserving	X	X	X	X	X	X	X	X
Past expectations			X	X	X			X
Future expectations	X			X	X		X	X
No self-blame				X			X[e]	X

[a] The X indicates that the variable emerged as a significant predictor of the criterion variable in the regression analysis.

[b] The X indicates that the most deprived group differed from the least deprived group on this variable.

[c] The X indicates that there was a significant main effect for this variable in the Bernstein & Crosby (1980) analyses.

[d] Wanting was not manipulated in the experiment.

[e] The self-blame variable affected the variables in a way opposite to the expected way (i.e., the greater the self-blame, the greater the deprivation).

in both instances is one of multicollinearity. Scores on the Wanting and Deserving Scales are very highly correlated. Concerning attitudes toward one's own job, the Pearson's r is .57; concerning attitudes about women's jobs, it is .63. For no other psychological factors are the correlations nearly this high.

The revised model features wanting and deserving as the essential but not as the only preconditions of resentment. Comparison other and past and future expectations are also included. The perception that others are better off than oneself, the thought that one is less well off than expected, and the belief that conditions will not improve probably all amplify feelings of grievance. They also contribute, no doubt, to creating resentments by affecting what people want and what they feel they deserve. Sibling rivalry is not the only situation in which people want something simply because another person has it. It is also common to feel entitled to that which others have and which we had expected to have. Figure 8.1 illustrates the relationships among variables in the revised model.[9]

Figure 8.1 Mechanics of Grievance

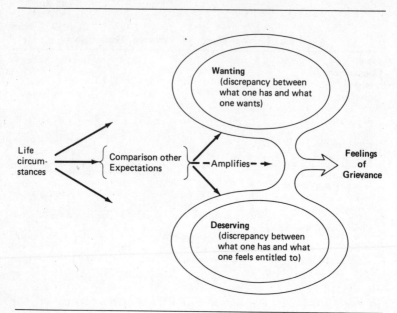

Summary

Using three separate procedures, we have tested the various models of relative deprivation, equity theory, and the frustration-aggression hypothesis. As a general statement, relative deprivation theory appears correct; but none of the specific models is confirmed. This is true even though the dynamics of grievance appear to be the same in the three attitudinal domains. The models proposed by Davis, Gurr, Williams, Adams, and Berkowitz all receive a fair amount of support. Although they are validated by several of the tests, these models are incomplete. Runciman's, Crosby's, and Patchen's models are all disconfirmed. The test results, combined with some previous findings, lead us to propose, tentatively, a revised model. It features wanting and deserving as the essential preconditions of felt deprivation and includes comparison other, past expectations, and future expectations as amplifiers.

Notes

1. For readers who are unfamiliar with multiple regression, an idea of what is involved can be grasped by thinking of the regression as a series of correlations. Where multiple regressions differ from simple correlations is in allowing us to examine simultaneously the relationships between a criterion variable (in this case, felt deprivation) and a number of other variables (e.g., wanting, deserving).

2. The possibility exists that the theory is valid and that the fault lies in our measurements. We therefore repeated the first test of the theory using the LISREL IV program of structural equation modeling (Goodman, 1972, 1973; Joreskog, 1974). Each of the demographic variables was assumed to be measured perfectly by a single item in the survey instrument. The six hypothesized preconditions and the criterion variable (deprivation) were each assessed by at least two measures. In the structural equation, we entered all twelve predictor variables simultaneously. The results of the structural equation model are remarkably close to the results of the standard regression analysis. Wanting emerges as the single most important predictor of felt deprivation (gamma equals 2.352). We also repeated the two-step hierarchical multiple regression analysis using standardized rather than raw scores. Each of the psychological factors was assessed by a scale composed of the standardized scores of each question that contributed to the scale. The results here were virtually identical to the results obtained when raw scores were used. Finally, we should note that the results of the regression analyses concerning one's own job situation, women's job situation, and one's own home situation remain the same among different subsamples.

3. Future expectations act in the way expected by Gurr (1970): the deprived group is more pessimistic than the gratified group.

4. If we repeat the analysis using standardized scores, the same results emerge. LISREL IV shows sex and comparison other are the most important predictors of resentment about the position of women.

5. Why doesn't wanting emerge as a significant predictor of deprivation? Perhaps the problem is one of group identification. Concerning group deprivation, we assess the discrepancy between what women are seen as wanting and what they are seen as having. Perhaps we

ought to have asked the respondents not about what women want for themselves but rather about what they, the individual respondents, want for women. We cannot directly test this possibility with the data at hand, but we can indirectly test it by repeating the multiple regression for the group deprivation data and restricting the sample to employed women only. Among employed women, the desires of the respondents and the desires of the group are, presumably, quite close. In the multiple regression with a restricted sample, comparison other and deserving emerge as predictors of felt deprivation, but wanting does not. Indeed, the regression analysis using only the employed women's data produces results very similar to the results produced using the entire Newton sample.

6. Forty-two respondents represents slightly over 10 percent of the sample. We were unable to take exactly 10 percent due to clustering.

7. If we repeat the regression analysis using standardized scores, we obtain essentially the same results. The LISREL IV program yields slightly different results than the regression, due primarily to a change in the measurement of self-blame. The factors of wanting and deserving are still important predictors of felt deprivation in the structural equation model.

8. The confound had to do with foreseeability. In the self-blame condition, the negative outcome could have been foreseen. In the no self-blame condition, it could not have been foreseen.

9. Secondary analysis indicates support for the revised model (Muehrer, note 4).

9
Conclusions

From a narrow concern with the discontents of working women our study has evolved into an investigation of the gratifications and the resentments of women and men about their jobs, their home lives, and the job situation of women. The theory of relative deprivation has shaped the contours of the investigation. This theory centers on the proposition that one's subjective status depends less on objective conditions than on certain psychological factors, such as feelings of entitlement.

Descriptive findings

Whether we use qualitative information on the nature of people's gratifications and grievances, quantitative measures of discontent, or quantitative measures of the hypothesized preconditions of deprivation, we see the people in our study as very positive about their jobs and their home lives. The level of satisfaction is high; the level of resentment is low. Most people report that they have what they want, what they deserve, and what they had expected to have. They are optimistic. When things do go wrong, they tend not to blame themselves. People typically rank their jobs as slightly above average in the rewards given, their home lives as moderately above average, and their marriages as well above average. They derive pleasure from a sense of accomplishment at work. Interpersonal relations are a source of gratification and of irritation both at work and at home.

The general contentment with one's personal life that we

find in Newton, Massachusetts, is consistent with the picture that emerges from surveys throughout the nation. Life satisfaction and happiness seem high among Americans (Wilson, 1967). Most Americans claim to feel satisfied with their jobs (Vroom, 1969), their home lives (Bernard, 1973), and especially with their marriages (Rollins & Feldman, 1970). Skeptics could wonder if Americans avowed happiness is sometimes at variance with their behavior. If people are so happily married, why do a high percentage of American marriages end in divorce? The answer is, of course, that marital stability and marital satisfaction bear no necessary connection. Indeed, in a culture that values action, the quest for happiness could lead to instability. The discontented person may move rapidly out of the unhappy situation, even if this means changing his job or leaving his marriage.

While the people of Newton display a typically American impatience with personal discontent, they are much more distressed about the situation of working women that we had expected. Resentment about the situation of employed women—that is, group deprivation—is strongest among employed women; but employed men and housewives also report high levels of group deprivation. From the fact that the sex of the interviewer had no measurable effect on the views people expressed about the plight of working women, we infer that the respondents' desire to please the interviewer has not contaminated the information they provide.

We do not, however, claim that the enlightened views expressed by the residents of Newton reflect the climate of opinion throughout the United States. The groups of people included in our study—groups such as women with high-prestige jobs—are probably representative of similar groups in the nation at large; but our sample overrepresents some groups, underrepresents others, and excludes still others altogether. It remains to be seen whether the attitudes expressed today by the relatively young, well-educated, white women and men of one affluent East Coast suburb will be expressed tomorrow in other parts of the United States by other types of people (ef. Bronfenbrenner, 1958).

The extent of group deprivation is not the only surprise. Another unanticipated finding is the association between job attitudes and family status. Researchers have traditionally conceived of work as a male domain and of family as a female domain. Many scholars have speculated about the conflicts between a woman's work and family, but few have actually *examined* the relationship between job attitudes and domestic arrangements of male and female workers. When we included family status as a variable in our design, we expected it to interact in complex ways with sex and job level. We had not foreseen the simple and direct relationship between family status and job attitudes.

With hindsight it seems reasonable that single people should feel the least positive about their jobs. A full and happy home life probably prevents a person from brooding about problems that arise at work.[1] Involvement with one's spouse and one's children may blunt one's awareness of intrigue or unfairness at the office, the shop, or the factory. Perhaps, too, domestic problems such as a spouse or a child in poor health cause the married people and parents to see problems at work in a different perspective than do single people. The mother of a sick child, for example, may be aware of office intrigue but may consider it unimportant in the context of other worries.

The protective value of multiple roles is also obvious when we examine attitudes toward the division of labor at home. Housewives, all of whom are parents in our study, express more dissatisfaction and resentment about life at home than do the employed women and men. Housewives feel that their expectations have been somewhat disappointed, and they perceive a gap between their actual and their ideal home situations. Housewives also tend to mention their spouses less often than do employed people as a source of gratification at home.

It would be simplistic to conclude from the housewives' relative discontent about the division of labor at home that paid employment causes women to feel even happier than they would otherwise be about their home lives. Similarly, it is not necessarily true that employment opens a woman's eyes to the predicament of working women. Our cross-sectional data make it difficult to partition reality into neat causes and effects. Perhaps a happy home life or a good marriage frees a woman to seek paid employment. Perhaps the kinds of women who desire employment differ in some fundamental ways from those who desire to remain at home. Personality traits that predispose some women to work are also likely to be reinforced by education and especially by professional training. Without making causal inferences, it is nevertheless interesting to note that the employed women in our study differ from housewives in their attitudes toward the division of domestic labor and in their views about the situation of working women. In the latter respect, employed women also differ from employed men.

Theoretical findings

While the theory of relative deprivation has provided the structure of our descriptions, the descriptive information has been used to test the theory. The validational tests support relative deprivation theory in its general form, call into question the specific models, and provide the groundwork for a revised model. The new, tentatively proposed, model states that deprivation, resentment, or grievance arise when people feel there is a discrepancy between what they have and (a) what they want and (b) what they deserve. Comparisons with others who are better off can influence people's desires and their perceptions of what they deserve. Comparisons can also amplify feelings of grievance, once these feelings are established. But comparisons with better-off others do not, in and of themselves, produce feelings of grievance. Expectations function in the same way as comparisons in the new model: they contribute to wanting and deserving and they augment feelings of grievance.

The contented female worker

Combining the descriptive and theoretical conclusions, we are ready to return to the paradox of the contented female worker that originally helped incite our interest. Why do the women in our study, like women in earlier studies, feel positively about all aspects of their jobs, including pay? The simple answer is that *for our women, as for our men, there is little discrepancy between what they obtain from their jobs and what they want to obtain and there is little discrepancy between what they obtain and what they feel entitled to obtain.* The simple answer immediately raises two further questions. First, why do the women feel that they obtain what they want from their jobs? Second, how can we account for the finding that the working women in our sample, who earn significantly less money than men with comparable jobs, feel that they receive from their jobs what they are entitled to receive?

The first question presents little difficulty. Quite simply, it seems that the employed women of Newton see little gap between their actual and their desired job rewards, even though they are underpaid relative to men, because pay does not constitute a critical desire for them. Money matters less to the women in our sample than does a sense of accomplishment or good interpersonal relations. Among the high-prestige women, 7 percent mention money as a gratifying aspect of their jobs; 50 percent cite a sense of accomplishment; and 42 percent cite interpersonal relations. Among the low-prestige women workers, 14 percent mention money; 28 percent a sense of accomplishment; and 51 percent interpersonal relations. When asked what they want from a job, about half the women and half the men cite a sense of accomplishment. Half the men and only one-third of the women also think money is important.

The females' relative disregard of money is no doubt determined in large measure by their life circumstances. The lack of concern with pay among the women, and to a certain degree among the men in our study, reflects the affluence of our sample and of Newton. We do not wish to rule out biology entirely in accounting for sex differences in the relative weights given to money, accomplishment, and interpersonal relations as sources of reward on the job, but the importance of job level as a determinant of people's job gratifications undermines a purely biological explanation. High-prestige and low-prestige working women are as dissimilar as are women and men. Women with high-prestige jobs, for example, are the most likely to be gratified by a sense of accomplishment, while women with low-prestige jobs are the least. Family status also counts. Money is a source of job gratification to more parents than to married or single people. This suggests that financial dependents make money important. As long as employment remains an option rather than a necessity, self-fulfillment is critical.

While the agreement between women's actual outcomes and their desired outcomes lends itself to an easy explanation, the women's belief that they are receiving what they deserve presents more of a puzzle initially. The working women in our study are aware of and upset about the extent of discrimination that faces most women on the job. Yet they appear quite naive about the discrimination that they themselves must overcome.

What prevents a woman from seeing that she herself receives less than she ought even though she perceives that women in general receive less than they ought? Three observations, all of which have been made earlier in the book, prove especially helpful in explaining the gap between a woman's perception of her own situation and her perception of the situation of women in general. Each of the three merits elaboration here.

First, we observe that the notion of deserving cannot be extricated from the concept of categories. The essence of justice, says the moral philosopher Perelman (1963), is that one must treat like alike. Since everyone is the same as others on some but not all dimensions, the trick is to decide which dimensions are pertinent to the issues at hand and which are irrelevant. The trick, in other words, is to create viable categories. As a result, "justice constitutes one segment of morality primarily concerned not with individual conduct but with the ways in which classes of individuals are treated" (Hart, 1961, p. 163).

It follows that one can sustain more easily the claim that a class of individuals have been denied their just deserts than the claim that a particular individual has not received her or his just deserts. When one asserts that a particular woman is the victim of sex discrimination, one treats the individual woman as a member of the larger class, women. To the extent that we relate to the particular woman as an individual human being, complete with a unique set of attributes and behaviors, we lose sight of the woman as the representation of an abstract or nominal group. In short, it is cognitively more difficult to process ideas about deserving when we deal with real individuals than when we deal with classes of individuals.

If it is difficult to perceive any individual whom one knows personally as simply the embodiment of an abstract category, how much more difficult is it to perceive oneself in such a way!

The first reason why the employed women of Newton are aware of a discrepancy between what women workers generally deserve and what they receive while being simultaneously unaware of such a discrepancy in their own lives is, no doubt, that the women conceive of themselves as individuals and not as representatives of a nominal group.

The second reason is that individual suffering, unlike group suffering, appears to call for individual villains. When one is dealing with general categories of people, the perception of suffering does not seem to entail the role of harmdoer. Indeed, the more numerous and depersonalized the victims, the more likely it seems that some impersonal force (e.g., the monsoon or the stock market) has occasioned their suffering. When one is dealing with a specific individual, on the other hand, it is difficult to focus on the effects of harm and, at the same time, resist the impulse to uncover some human agent of that harm. Logic permits us to recognize cases in which one individual suffers through the fault of no person or persons—not even himself; but psycho-logic yearns for primitive symmetry. As soon as one perceives that some individual is the victim of discrimination, in other words, one runs the risk—due to what we might term the fallacy of symmetry—of also perceiving some other person or people in the individual's environment as the perpetrator of discrimination.

When the individual in question is oneself, furthermore, the person tends to assume, again fallaciously, that any agent of harm intends to produce the harm (Jones & Davis, 1965). People can discriminate by accident and people can discriminate in spite of (and sometimes because of) the best intentions. We all know this in the abstract, but we rarely remember it when we consider our own case. The woman who perceives that she receives less than she deserves from her job is propelled into an examination of whether someone at work wishes her ill. Once articulated, the thought of a malefactor may be debated or dismissed, but the very process of articulation may itself be painful. Small wonder that some women avoid the risk of such pain by seeing themselves as exceptions to the sex discrimination that they acknowledge in the world around them.

The third reason that an employed woman may separate

her perceptions about the plight of women in general and her perceptions of her own case is that, in many situations, to define oneself as a victim is to invite denigration. As we saw in Chapter 2, Lerner (1981; Lerner & Lerner, 1981) and others Walster et al., 1978) have amassed empirical demonstrations of the theoretical argument that people need to believe in a just world. Sometimes the need to see justice impels people to compensate the victim of an injustice. More often, the need to see the world as a just place causes people to denigrate those who suffer. Rather than see injustice, for example, many affluent Americans convince themselves that welfare recipients cannot or will not hold a decent job and so deserve their fate (Ryan, 1971). It seems reasonable to suppose that many victims know intuitively our third observation. The typical working woman may, in short, see herself as the lucky exception to the discriminatory rule because at some level she knows that to do otherwise simply courts further problems.

Consideration of the three factors illuminates how cognitive and emotional processes can act in concert to produce faulty reasoning. One issue which cognitive social psychologists debate hotly is the role of motivation in misattributions. The dominant camp in the debate claims that attributional errors can generally be explained in terms of information-processing mistakes (Miller & Ross, 1975; Nisbett & Ross, 1980; Ross, 1977). Others maintain that emotions, and especially the desire to see oneself in a positive light, count a great deal in human inferential processes (Bradley, 1978; Miller, 1976; Orvis, Kelley & Butler, 1976; Riess, Rosenfield, Melburg, & Tedeschi, 1981; Stevens & Jones, 1976). However the employed women of Newton might make attributions about their own behaviors or their "selves", the way in which they make inferences about their *outcomes* certainly seems to contain a large portion of emotion. The emotional content, furthermore, can hardly be extricated from the cognitive content.

A brief foray into logic shows why. Two logical strategies allow a woman to deduce that she is the individual victim of sex discrimination. The first requires her to trade in counterfactuals. For each woman, her own case is a single datum. As such, it precludes a demonstration of covariation between sex and treatment on the job; but co-variation is essential if one is to argue that there is a causal link. In other words, the woman cannot logically conclude that she is mistreated because she is a female unless she argues that she would be treated differently if she were a male.

Logic permits a second argument. The woman can look for covariation between her treatment and the attitudes of her employers or co-workers. If the working woman holds several jobs over several years, she may see that she does well in jobs where her boss is non-sexist and that she does poorly in jobs where her boss is sexist. The more well-established the pattern, the more certain can the woman be that any current problems derive from the attitude and behavior of her employer. In such a way may she conclude that she is the individual victim of sex discrimination. Note how this cognitive strategy impells the woman to seek a malefactor or agent of discrimination. Trying to separate motivational factors from sheer information-processing factors would be a false effort in this instance (cf. Tetlock & Levi, 1982).

By no means do the three factors we have considered entirely explain the gap between group discontent and personal contentment. Politeness no doubt influences the women's perceptions as well as their statements. The lack of communication structure among women may also serve to keep each woman uninformed about her own position (Kidder, Fagan, & Cohn, 1981). It also seems that men and women use different norms about deserving, especially in the case of money (Major & Konar, note 5). While other factors may reinforce the separation between one's own fate and the fate of the group, the three factors we have observed suffice to illustrate how the step from knowledge of the group's situation to an understanding of one's own situation, which is quite a small step logically, can become a chasm psychologically. No longer do we marvel at the reluctance of women to apply what they know about sex discrimination in general to their own personal situations. The wonder now appears to be that anyone could make the application at all.

A few women in our study do bridge the chasm. What distinguishes these women from the working women who refuse to perceive that they obtain less than they ought to obtain, individually, from their jobs? Some answers emerge in a post-hoc analysis in which we compare two subgroups from our sample of employed women. The two subgroups have been selected by examining the distribution of Deserving Scores among the employed female respondents. For each woman, we look at (a) the extent to which she feels that she receives less from her job than she deserves; and (b) the extent to which she feels that women receive less from their jobs than they deserve. The former score, taken from the personal Deserving Scale described in Chapter 4, provides a summary measure of feelings of personal injustice. The latter score, taken from the group Deserving Scale described in Chapter 5, gives a summary measure of feelings of group injustice. When we plot the employed women's scores on both personal and group injustice, as we do in Figure 9.1, we can for the purposes of analysis isolate a small number of women who experience both personal and group injustice. The cluster that is circled in the upper-right-hand corner of Figure 9.1 perceives a large gap between what women ought to receive and what they do receive and a similar gap between what they themselves ought to receive and what they do receive. The cluster might be termed the congruent subgroup. In the upper-left-hand corner of Figure 9.1 is the incongruent subgroup for whom a sense of group injustice is great while a sense of personal injustice is low. The boundaries of the subgroup are obviously somewhat arbitrary, but the incongruent subgroup serves as a control for the congruent subgroup. The incongruent subgroup numbers thirty.

The congruent and incongruent subgroups differ from each other materially. The two groups are very similar in the average prestige ratings of their $\bar{x} = 60$ for the incongruent subgroup and jobs $\bar{x} = 64$ for the congruent subgroup); they contain about the same proportion of high-prestige and low-prestige women workers. But the two subgroups differ in terms of their average salaries and their average household incomes. The fifteen women represented in the upper-right-hand corner of Figure 9.1 earn, on average, about $15,000 a year. Those in the upper left earn slightly over $20,000 a year. The difference, which is nearly as great as the difference between men and women,

Figure 9.1 Group Deserving and Personal Deserving

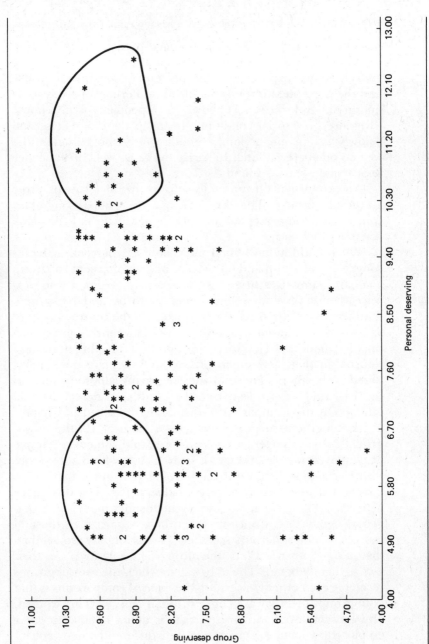

reaches statistical significance. It suggests that, at some point, economic difficulties can help a woman to jump the cognitive and emotional gap between the perception of group injustice and the perception of personal injustice. Perhaps there is some minimum level of comfort above which people typically choose to ignore how social conditions relate to their own lives and below which people no longer indulge in the morselization that we and others (e.g., Lane, 1962; Kinder & Kiewet, 1979; Kinder & Sears, 1981) have found.[2]

The congruent group is also distinctive in terms of three attitudinal factors. The three factors are comparison other, control, and the perception of a harmdoer at work. Let us look briefly at each factor.

When deciding how good their job is, 21 percent of the incongruent subgroup and 60 percent of the congruent subgroup compare themselves first of all with a man. Women who perceive themselves and women generally to be underrewarded, in other words, are three times as likely as the control group to select a male referent. Not only is the congruent subgroup distinct in whom they choose as a comparison other; they are also unusual in their assessment of how well they are doing compared with others. Those in the congruent subgroup tend to feel that they receive less from their jobs than do comparable others. On the Comparison Other Scale described in Chapter 4, the congruent subgroup averages a score of 12, the incongruent subgroup averages a score of 9, and the entire sample of employed people averages a score of 9.8, where a low score means that one feels relatively advantaged and a high score means that one feels relatively disadvantaged. The difference between the congruent and incongruent subgroups reaches statistical significance. Concerning earnings in particular, those in the congruent subgroup see their pay as slightly worse than that of most other workers; the incongruent subgroup sees their pay as slightly better. The only way in which the two subgroups resemble each other concerning the issue of comparisons is that both groups feel they are better off than most working women. How an employed woman feels she is doing relative to other employed women, to state the matter differently, does not influence the size of the perceived gap between actual and deserved outcomes. What does influence the perceived gap is the woman's assessment of how well her own rewards match those of a more abstract and sex-unspecified referent person. The association between feelings of deserving and the awareness of a better-off comparison other suggested by these data is consistent with the revised model of relative deprivation presented in the last chapter and pictured in Figure 8.1.

The second major attitudinal difference between the congruent and the incongruent subgroups concerns control. Forty-seven percent of the incongruent subgroup believe that there are things they want from work that they will never obtain in their present jobs. In this regard the incongruent subgroup resembles closely the majority of working women and men in the study. Quite different is the predominant view of the congruent subgroup: thirteen of the fifteen women in that subgroup believe they will never obtain some of the things they desire from their jobs. The congruent subgroup is also much less likely than the incongruent subgroup to believe that advancement on the job depends on how well a person works. They are much less sanguine about their ability to rectify matters when things go wrong at work.

While the band of women who perceive both personal and group injustice tend to feel little control about their own jobs, they are not unusually low in their feelings of control generally. They do not, for example, differ from the incongruent group in their willingness to view American society as a meritocracy. Whether the sense of low control at work has preceded or has followed from the women's sense of injustice is so complex a question that we cannot even speculate about it. Perhaps the perception that one cannot control aspects of one's job and the perception that one receives less from the job than one ought are both expressions of a general disenchantment with or alienation from one's job.

The final difference between the congruent and incongruent subgroups concerns agency. In response to the question, "Within the last month, how often has your boss let you down?" the incongruent subgroup averages an answer between "hardly ever" and "sometimes." The congruent subgroup answers halfway between "sometimes" and "fairly often." The difference between the two subgroups, when measured quantitatively, appears highly reliable. The pattern represents exactly what we would expect on the basis of our observation that personal harm requires, in a primitive and illogical way, a personal harmdoer. Our cross-sectional data render causal inferences hazardous, and it seems inappropriate to claim either that disenchantment with one's boss always causes women to feel their rights have been violated or that the reverse is always true. Probably some of the congruent women initially perceive a violation of their rights while others initially attend to some problems with their superiors. Whichever cognition happens to occur first for a woman, it seems likely that the two cognitions reinforce each other. The erosion of either one might lead to a decay in the other.

Before leaving the two extreme subgroups it should be noted that only a portion of the fifteen women represented in the upper-right-hand corner of Figure 9.1 express grievance about their personal job situations. Indeed, out of the 163 employed females in the study, only five score high on both the personal and the group Deprivation Scales. The great majority of working women express much resentment about the job situation of women but little resentment about their own job situation. What accounts for the drop from fifteen, when we look at feelings of deserving, to five, when we look at feelings of grievance? The basic explanation for the drop is that the emotion of grievance comes not only from a perceived discrepancy between ought and is; grievance also depends on desires. About two-thirds of the women in the congruent subgroup, in short, feel that they have what they want even though they have less than they deserve.

Epilogue

What do our final observations and findings bode for the future? Will the American woman worker become more aggrieved during the next decade or decades? Will her feelings of resentment about her own job situation change if she comes to want new rewards from her job or to feel that she deserves more from her job?

Most likely they will not. We do suspect that what American women want from their jobs will change as social realities change. Single-parent families are increasingly common (Grossman, 1977, 1978; Veroff et al., 1981). As white and middle-class women find themselves or define themselves more and more often as the head of household, they will probably become concerned with money, and the financial rewards of employment should assume new salience among the list of gratifications that women seek from employment. Sex-based inequities in pay, prestige, or chances for advancement, were they to continue, would with increasing regularity lead women to perceive a discrepancy between what they have and what they want.

But while the employed female's wants change, her feelings of entitlement are not likely to outstrip her actual outcomes. The participants in our study have a surprisingly great awareness about sex discrimination in general, and the employed women seem even more aware than the men or the housewives. Yet strong psychological barriers seem to prevent women from translating their general awareness into knowledge of their own personal situations. Nothing in the forseeable future will make women more agile at leaping the barrier. There will probably continue to be a small core of women who recognize personal injustices and a scattered few women who feel upset about the injustices they recognize. For the great majority, however, group discontent and personal contentment will probably continue their coexistence.

In closing we ought to consider a second, more optimistic reason for believing that widespread group deprivation will not lead to a proliferation of personal deprivation. Since World War II, sex discrimination in employment has become morally offensive to increasing numbers of people. It is now illegal as well. In our sample, people no longer deny the predicament of working women. Sex discrimination may not prove to be as transient as are some of the attitudes and feelings we have described in this book; yet it may not be too ingenuous to hope that from a recognition of the problem will come social change.

Notes

1. Remember that the sample, by design, excludes single parents. Virtually none of our respondents was divorced. The sample was also privileged in terms of their age, health, and geographic location.

2. If this view is correct, then minority groups ought to compartmentalize their lives less than do majority groups concerning minority issues. A recent study by Miller (1981) finds that symbolic racism operates among blacks much less than it does among whites. Racial attitudes among blacks, unlike racial attitudes among whites, tend to be closely tied to aspects of one's personal situation.

Reference Notes

1. Linsenmeier, J. A. W., and Brickman, P. Expectations, performance and satisfaction. Unpublished manuscript, University of Michigan, 1980. (Available from P. Brickman, Institute for Social Research, The University of Michigan, Ann Arbor, Michigan, 48106.)

2. Folger, R., Rosenfield, D., Rheaume, K. Relative deprivation and the likelihood-feasibility effect. Unpublished manuscript, Southern Methodist University, 1980. (Available from R. Folger, Psychology Department, Southern Methodist University, Dallas, Texas, 75275.)

3. Hennigan, K. M., and Cook, T. D. A comparison of the prevalence, intensity, and distribution of feelings of personal, fraternal, and double unfairness. Unpublished manuscript, Northwestern University, 1977. (Available from T. D. Cook, Psychology Department, Northwestern University, Evanston, Illinois, 60202.)

4. Muehrer, P. Testing Crosby's model. Unpublished manuscript, Yale University, 1982. (Available from F. Crosby, Psychology Department, Yale University, Box 11A Yale Station, New Haven, Connecticut, 06520.)

5. Major, B., and Konar, E. An investigation of sex differences in pay expectations and their possible causes. (Available from B. Major, Psychology Department, State University of New York at Buffalo, 4230 Ridge Lea Road, Amherst, New York, 14226.)

References

Abeles, R. P. *Subjective deprivation and Black militancy.* Unpublished doctoral dissertation, Harvard University, 1972.

———. Relative deprivation, rising expectation, and Black militancy. *Journal of Social Issues,* 1976, *32*(2), 119–138.

Aberle, D. F. A note on relative deprivation theory. In S. L. Thrupp (Ed.), *Millenial dreams in action: Essays in comparative study.* The Hague: Mouton, 1962.

Adams, J. S. Inequity in social exchange. In L. Berkowitz (Ed.), *Advances in experimental social psychology* (Vol. 2). New York: Academic Press, 1965.

Allport, G. *The nature of prejudice.* Reading, Mass.: Addison-Wesley, 1954.

Anderson, B., Berger, J., Zelditch, M., & Cohen, B. P. Reactions to inequity. *Acta Sociologica,* 1969, *12*, 1–12.

Anderson, B., & Zelditch, M. Rank equilibrium and political behaviour. *European Journal of Sociology,* 1964, *5*, 112–124.

Andrews, F., & Withey, S. *Social indicators of well-being.* New York: Plenum, 1976.

Araji, S. K. Husbands' and wives' attitude-behavior congruence on family roles. *Journal of Marriage and the Family,* 1977, *39*, 309–322.

Astin, H. S., Suniewick, N., & Dweck, S. Women: *A bibliography of their education and careers.* Washington, D.C.: Human Services Press, 1971.

Axelson, L. Marital adjustment and marital role definitions of husbands of working and non-working wives. *Marriage and Family Living,* 1963, *25*, 189–195.

Bailyn, L. Career and family orientations of husbands and wives in relation to marital happiness. *Human Relations,* 1970, *23,* 97–113.

Bane, M. J. *Here to stay. American families in the twentieth century.* New York: Basic Books, 1976.

Bass, B. M., Krusell, J., & Alexander, R. A. Male managers' attitudes toward working women. *American Behavioral Scientist,* 1971, *15,* 221–236.

Bateson, G. *Steps to an ecology of mind.* London: Paladin, 1973.

Benoit-Smullyan, E. Status and status-types and status relationships. *American Sociological Review,* 1944, *9,* 151–161.

Berger, J., Zelditch, M., Anderson, B., & Cohen, B. P. Structural aspects of distributive justice: A status value formulation. In J. Berger, M. Zelditch, and B. Anderson (Eds.), *Sociological theories in progress* (Vol. 2). Boston: Houghton Mifflin, 1972.

Berk, S. F., & Berheide, C. W. Going backstage: Gaining access to observe household work. *Sociology of Work and Occupations,* 1977, *4,* 27–48.

Berkowitz, L. *Aggression: A social psychological analysis.* New York: McGraw-Hill, 1962.

———. Social motivation. In G. Lindzey & E. Aronson (Eds.), *Handbook of Social Psychology* (Vol. 3). Reading, Mass.: Addison-Wesley, 1968. (a)

———. The study of urban violence: Some implications of laboratory studies of frustration and aggression. *American Behavioral Scientist,* 1968, *11*(4), 14–17. (b)

———. Frustration, comparisons, and other sources of emotional arousal as contributors to social unrest. *Journal of Social Issues,* 1972, *28,* 77–91.

Berkowitz, L., & Walster, E. (Eds.), *Advances in experimental social psychology* (Vol. 9). New York: Academic Press, 1976.

Bernard, J. *The future of marriage.* London: Souvenir Press, 1973.

———. *The future of motherhood.* New York: Penguin, 1975.

Bernstein, M., & Crosby, F. Relative deprivation: Testing the models. Paper presented at the American Psychological Association annual meeting. Toronto, 1978.

———. An empirical examination of relative deprivation theory. *Journal of Experimental Social Psychology,* 1980, *16,* 442–456.

Biddle, B. J., & Thomas, E. J. *Role theory: Concepts and research.* New York: Wiley and Sons, 1966.

Blasier, C. Studies of social revolution: Origins in Mexico, Bolivia and Cuba. *Latin American Review,* 1967, *2,* 28–64.

Blauner, R. *Alienation and freedom*. Chicago: University of Chicago Press, 1970.

Blood, R. O., Jr. Long-range causes and consequences of the employment of married women. *Journal of Marriage and the Family*, 1965, *27*, 43–47.

Blood, R. O., Jr., & Wolfe, D. *Husbands and wives. The dynamics of married living*. New York: The Free Press, 1960.

Bradburn, N. *The structure of psychological well-being*. Chicago: Aldine, 1969.

Bradburn, N., & Caplovitz, D. *Reports on happiness*. Chicago: Aldine, 1965.

Bradley, G. W. Self-serving biases in the attribution process: A reexamination of the fact or fiction question. *Journal of Personality and Social Psychology*, 1978, *36*, 56–71.

Brickman, P. Adaptation level determinants of satisfaction with equal and unequal outcome distributions in skill and chance situations. *Journal of Personality and Social Psychology*, 1975, *32*, 191–198.

Brickman, P., & Campbell, D. T. Hedonic relativism and planning in the good society. In M. H. Appley (Ed.), *Adaptation level theory: A symposium*. New York: Academic Press, 1971.

Brickman, P., Coates, D., & Janoff-Bulman, R. Lottery winners and accident victims: Is happiness relative? *Journal of Personality and Social Psychology*, 1978, *36*, 917–927.

Brickman, P., Folger, R., Goode, E., & Schul, Y. Micro and macro justice. In M. J. Lerner & S. C. Lerner (Eds.), *The justice motive in social behavior: Adapting to times of scarcity and change*. New York: Plenum, 1981.

Brief, A. P., & Aldag, R. J. Male-female differences in occupational values within majority groups. *Journal of Vocational Behavior*, 1975, *6*, 305–314.

Brief, A. P., & Oliver, R. L. Male-female differences in work attitudes among retail sales managers. *Journal of Applied Psychology*, 1976, *61*, 526–528.

Brief, A. P., Rose, G. L., & Aldag, R. J. Sex differences in preferences for job attributes revisited. *Journal of Applied Psychology*, 1977, *62*, 645–646.

Bronfenbrenner, U. Socialization and social class through time and space. In E. E. Maccoby, T. M. Newcomb, & E. Hartley (Eds.), *Readings in social psychology*. New York: Holt, Rinehart, and Winston, 1958.

Bunge, M. *Causality. The place of the causal principle in modern science*. Cambridge, Mass.: Harvard University Press, 1959.

Burke, R. J., & Weir, T. Relationship of wives' employment status to husband, wife, and pair satisfaction and performance. *Journal of Marriage and the Family*, 1976, *38*, 279–288.

Butler, R. J. Relative deprivation and power: A switched replication design using time series data of strike rates in American and British coal mining. *Human Relations*, 1976, *29*, 623–642.

Campbell, A., Converse, P., & Rodgers, W. *The quality of American life.* New York: Russell Sage, 1976.

Campbell, D., & Fiske, D. Convergent and discriminant validation by the multi-trait multi-method matrix. *Psychological Bulletin*, 1959, *56*, 81–105.

Caplan, N. The new ghetto man: A review of recent empirical studies. *Journal of Social Issues*, 1970, *26*, 59–73.

Caplan, N., & Paige, J. M. A study of ghetto rioters. *Scientific American*, 1968, *219*(2), 15–22.

Cartwright, L. K. Conscious factors entering into decisions of women to study medicine. *Journal of Social Issues*, 1972, *28*(2), 201–215.

Cecil, E. A., Paul, R. J., & Olins, R. A. Perceived importance of selected variables used to evaluate male and female job applicants. *Personnel Psychology*, 1973, *26*, 397–404.

Center for Political Studies. *Codebook.* Ann Arbor: University of Michigan, Institute of Social Research, 1977.

Clark, R. A., Nye, F. I., & Gecas, V. Work involvement and marital role performance. *Journal of Marriage and the Family*, 1978, *40*, 9–22.

Clemente, F., & Sauer, W. J. Life satisfaction in the United States. *Social Forces*, 1976, *54*, 621–631.

Cohen, R. L. On the distinction between individual deserving and distributive justice. *Journal for the Theory of Social Behaviour*, 1979, *9*, 167–185.

Cohen, S. L., & Bunker, K. A. Subtle effects of sex role stereotypes in recruiters' hiring decisions. *Journal of Applied Psychology*, 1975, *60*, 566–572.

Cook, T. D., Crosby, F., & Hennigan, K. M. The construct validity of relative deprivation. In J. M. Suls & R. L. Miller (Eds.), *Social comparison processes: Theoretical and empirical perspectives.* New York: Hemisphere Press, 1977.

Coser, R. L., & Rokoff, G. Women in the occupational world: Social disruption and conflicts. *Social Problems*, 1971, *18*, 535–554.

Crandall, V. D., Katkovsky, W., & Crandall, V. J. Children's beliefs in their own control of reinforcement in intellectual-academic achievement situations. *Child Development*, 1965, *36*, 91–109.

Crosby, F. A model of egoistical relative deprivation. *Psychological Review*, 1976, *83*, 85–113.

———. Relative deprivation and working women: Causes of their discontents. Paper presented at the International Society for Political Psychology, New York, 1978.

———. Deprivation and deservingness: Distributive justice at home and at work. Paper presented at the American Psychological Association, New York, 1979.

Crosby, F., & Gonzalez-Intal, M. Relative deprivation and equity theories: Felt injustice and the undeserved benefits of others. In R. Folger (Ed.), *The sense of injustice: Social psychological perspectives.* New York: Plenum Press, 1982.

Darley, S. A. Big-time careers for the little woman: A dual-role dilemma. *Journal of Social Issues*, 1976, *32*(3), 85–94.

Darling, J. *The role of women in the economy.* Paris: Organization for Economic Development, 1975.

Davies, J. C. Toward a theory of revolution. *American Sociological Review*, 1962, *27*, 5–19.

———. The J-curve of rising and declining satisfactions as a cause of some great revolutions and a contained rebellion. In H. D. Graham & T. R. Gurr (Eds.), *Violence in America*. New York: Signet Books, 1969.

———. The J-curve and power-struggle theories of collective violence. *American Sociological Review*, 1974, *39*, 607–610.

———. The J-curve theory. *American Political Science Review*, 1978, *72*, 1357–1358.

———. Comment. *American Political Science Review*, 1979, *73*, 825–830.

Davis, J. A. A formal interpretation of the theory of relative deprivation. *Sociometry*, 1959, *22*, 280–296.

Deaux, K. Sex: A perspective in the attribution process. In J. H. Harvey, W. J. Ickes, & R. F. Kidd (Eds.), *New directions in attribution research.* Hillsdale, N.J.: Erlbaum, 1976.

———. Self evaluations of male and female managers. *Sex Roles*, 1979, *5*, 571–580.

Deaux, K., & Farris, E. Attributing causes for one's own performance: The effects of sex, norms, and outcome. *Journal of Research in Personality*, 1977, *11*, 59–72.

DeLamater, J., & Fidell, L. S. On the status of women. An assessment and introduction. *American Behavioral Scientist*, 1971, *15*, 163–171.

Deutsch, M. Equity, equality and need: What determines which value will be used as the basis of distributive justice? *Journal of Social Issues*, 1975, *31*(3), 137–149.

————. Education and distributive justice. *American Psychologist*, 1979, *34*, 391–401.

Dipboye, R. L., Fromkin, H. L., & Wiback, K. Relative importance of applicant sex, attractiveness and scholastic standing in evaluation of job applicant résumés. *Journal of Applied Psychology*, 1975, *60*, 39–43.

Dollard, J., Doob, L., Miller, N., Mowrer, O., & Sears, R. *Frustration and aggression*. New Haven: Yale University Press, 1939.

Duncan, O. D. A socioeconomic index for all occupations. In A. J. Reiss, Jr., (Ed.), *Occupations and social status*. New York: Free Press, 1961.

Duncan, R. P., & Perrucci, C. C. Dual occupation families and migration. *American Sociological Review*, 1976, *41*, 252–261.

Dyer, L., & Theriault, R. The determinants of pay satisfaction. *Journal of Applied Psychology*, 1976, *61*, 596–609.

Dweck, C. S., & Reppucci, N. D. Learned helplessness and reinforcement responsibility in children. *Journal of Personality and Social Psychology*, 1973, *25*, 109–116.

Ebeling, J., King, M., & Rogers, M. Hierarchical position in the work organization and job satisfaction: Findings in national survey data. *Human Relations*, 1977, *32*, 387–394.

Een, J. D., & Rosenberg-Dishman, M. B. *Women and society*. Beverly Hills: Sage Publications, 1978, 2 vols.

Epstein, C. F. *Woman's place: Options and limits in professional careers*. Berkeley: University of California Press, 1970.

————. Law partners and marital partners. *Human Relations*, 1971, *24*, 549–564. (a)

————. Women lawyers and their professions: Inconsistency of social controls and their consequences for professional performance. In A. Theodore (Ed.), *The professional woman*. Cambridge, Mass.: Schenkman Publishing Co., 1971. (b)

Ericksen, J. A., Yancey, W. L., & Erickson, E. P. The division of family roles. *Journal of Marriage and the Family*, 1979, *41*, 301–314.

Etzioni, A. (Ed.), *The semi-professions and their organizations: Teachers, nurses, and social workers*. New York: Free Press, 1969.

Featherman, D. L., & Hauser, R. M. Sexual inequalities and socioeconomic achievement in the U.S., 1962–1973. *American Sociological Review,* 1976, *41,* 462–483.

——. The measurement of occupation arrays of prestige and socioeconomic status. In R. M. Hauser & D. L. Featherman (Eds.), *The process of stratification. Trends and analyses.* New York: Academic Press, 1977.

Fiedel, L. Empirical verification of sex discrimination in hiring practices in psychology. *American Psychologist,* 1970, *25,* 1094–1098.

Feierabend, I. K., and Feierabend, R. L. Aggressive behaviors within polities, 1948–1962: A cross-national study. *Journal of Conflict Resolution,* 1966, *10,* 249–271.

Feierabend, I. K., Feierabend, R. L., & Nesvold, B. A. Social and political violence: Cross-national patterns. In H. D. Graham & T. R. Gurr (Eds.), *Violence in America.* New York: Signet Books, 1969.

Feldman, S. D. Impediment or stimulant? Marital status and graduate education. *American Journal of Sociology,* 1973, *78,* 982–994.

Ferber, M. A., & Loeb, J. W. Performance, rewards, and perceptions of sex discrimination among male and female faculty. *American Journal of Sociology,* 1973, *78,* 995–1002.

Fogarty, M., Allen, A. J., Allen, J., & Walters, P. *Women in top jobs.* London: George Allen & Unwin, 1971.

Fogarty, M. P., Rapoport, R., & Rapoport, R. N. *Sex, career, and family.* London: George Allen and Unwin, 1971.

Frank, F. D., & Drucker, J. The influence of evaluatee's sex on evaluation of a response on a managerial selection instrument. *Sex Roles,* 1977, *3,* 59–64.

Freud, S. Feminity. In *New Introductory Lectures,* New York: W. W. Norton, 1965. (tr. James Strachey). [Originally published in 1933].

Friedan, B. *The feminine mystique.* New York: Dell Books, 1963.

Fullerton, H. N., Jr., & Flaim, P. O. *New labor force projections to 1990.* Washington, D.C.: U.S. Dept. of Labor, Bureau of Labor Statistics, Special Labor Force Report 197, 1976.

Geschwender, B. N., & Geschwender, J. A. Relative deprivation and participation in the civil rights movement. *Social Science Quarterly,* 1973, *54,* 403–411.

Geschwender, J. A. Social structure and the Negro revolt: An examination of some hypotheses. *Social Forces,* 1964, *43,* 248–256.

——. Continuities in theories of status consistency and cognitive dissonance. *Social Forces,* 1967, *46,* 160–171.

Geschwender, J. A., & Singer, B. D. Deprivation and the Detroit riot. *Social Problems,* 1970, *17,* 457–463.

Ginzberg, E. *Life styles of educated women.* New York: Columbia University Press, 1966.

Glenn, N. D. The contribution of marriage to the psychological well-being of males and females. *Journal of Marriage and the Family,* 1975, *37,* 594–600.

Glenn, N. D., Alston, J. P., & Weiner, D. (Eds.), *Social stratification: A research bibliography.* Berkeley: The Glendessay Press, 1970.

Glenn, N. D., Taylor, P. A., & Weaver, C. N. Age and job satisfaction among males and females: A multivariate, multisurvey study. *Journal of Applied Psychology,* 1977, *62,* 189–193.

Goodman, L. A. A general model for the analysis of surveys. *American Journal of Sociology,* 1972, *77,* 1035–1086.

————. Causal analysis of data from panel studies and other kinds of surveys. *American Journal of Sociology,* 1973, *78,* 1135–1191.

Greer, G. *The female eunuch.* New York: McGraw-Hill, 1970.

Gross, E. Plus ça change . . . ? The sexual structure of occupations over time. *Social Problems,* 1968, *16,* 198–208.

Grossman, A. S. The labor force patterns of divorced and separated women. *Monthly Labor Review,* 1977, *100*(1), 48–53.

————. Divorced and separated women in the labor force—an update. *Monthly Labor Review,* 1978, *101*(10), 43–45.

Gruneberg, M. M. *Understanding job satisfaction.* New York: Halsted Press, 1979.

Gurin, G., Veroff, J., & Feld, S. *Americans view their mental health.* New York: Basic Books, 1960.

Gurin, P. The role of worker expectancies in the study of employment discrimination. In P. A. Wallace & A. M. LeMond (Eds.), *Women, minorities, and employment discrimination.* Lexington: D. C. Heath and Co., 1977.

Gurr, T. R. A causal model of civil strife: A comparative analysis using new indices. *American Political Science Review,* 1968, *62,* 1104–1124. (a)

————. Psychological factors in civil violence. *World Politics,* 1968, *20,* 245–278. (b)

————. Urban disorder, perspectives from the comparative study of civil strife. In L. H. Masotti & D. R. Bowen (Eds.), *Riots and rebellion: Civil violence in the urban community.* Beverly Hills, Calif.: Sage, 1968. (c)

————. A comparative study of civil strife. In H. D. Graham & T. R. Gurr (Eds.), *Violence in America.* New York: Signet Books, 1969.

————. *Why men rebel.* Princeton, N.J.: Princeton University Press, 1970.

Haavio-Mannila, E. Sex differentiation in role expectations and performance. *Journal of Marriage and the Family,* 1967, *29,* 568–578.

————. Satisfaction with family, work, leisure and life among men and women. *Human Relations,* 1971, *24,* 585–601.

Hacker, H. M. Women as a minority group. *Social Forces,* 1951, *30,* 60–69.

Haefner, J. E. Race, age, sex and competence as factors in employer selection of the disadvantaged. *Journal of Applied Psychology,* 1977, *62,* 199–202. (a)

————. Sources of discrimination among employees: A survey investigation. *Journal of Applied Psychology,* 1977, *62,* 265–270. (b)

Hall, F. S., & Hall, D. T. Effects of job incumbents' race and sex on evaluations of managerial performance. *Academy of Management Journal,* 1976, *19,* 476–481.

Hall, R. H. *Occupations and the social structure.* Englewood Cliffs, N.J.: Prentice-Hall, 1975.

Hart, H. L. A. *The concept of law.* Oxford: The Clarendon Press, 1961.

Havens, E. M. Women, work, and wedlock: A note on female marital patterns in the United States. *American Journal of Sociology,* 1973, *78,* 975–981.

Hayghe, H. Families and the rise of working wives: An overview. *Monthly Labor Review,* May, 1976, 12–19.

Hedges, J. N. Absence from work—measuring hours lost. *Monthly Labor Review,* 1977, *100*(10), 16–23.

Hennigan, K. M. *The construct validity of relative deprivation: Conceptual and empirical analyses.* Unpublished doctoral dissertation, Northwestern University, 1979.

Herman, J. B., & Gyllstrom, K. K. Working men and women: Inter- and intra-role conflict. *Psychology of Women Quarterly,* 1977, *1,* 319–333.

Herzberg, F., Mausner, B., Peterson, R. A., & Capwell, D. F. *Job attitudes: Review of research and opinion.* Pittsburgh: Psychological Service of Pittsburgh, 1957.

Herzberg, F., Mausner, B., & Snyderman, B. *The motivation to work.* New York: Wiley, 1967.

Hesselbart, S. Sex role and occupational stereotypes: Three studies of impression formation. *Sex Roles,* 1977, *3,* 409–422. (a)

————. Women doctors win and male nurses lose: A study of sex role and occupational stereotypes. *Sociology of Work and Occupations,* 1977, *4,* 44–62. (b)

Hicks, M. W., & Platt, M. Marital happiness and stability: A review of research in the sixties. *Journal of Marriage and the Family,* 1970, *32,* 553–574.

Hodge, R. W., Siegel, P. M., & Rossi, P. H. Occupational prestige in the United States, 1925–1963. *American Journal of Sociology,* 1964, *70,* 286–302.

Hoffman, C., & Reed, J. S. Sex discrimination?—The XYZ affair. *The Public Interest,* 1981, *62* (winter), 21–39.

Hoffman, L. W. Psychological factors. In L. W. Hoffman & F. I. Nye (Eds.), *Working mothers.* San Francisco: Jossey-Bass, 1975.

Hoffman, L. W., & Nye, F. I. (Eds.), *Working mothers.* San Francisco: Jossey-Bass, 1975.

Holahan, C. K., & Gilbert, L. A. Conflict between major life roles: Women and men in dual career couples. *Human Relations,* 1979, *32,* 451–468. (a)

——. Inter-role conflict for working women: Careers versus jobs. *Journal of Applied Psychology,* 1979, *64,* 86–90. (b)

Homans, G. C. *Social behavior: Its elementary forms.* New York: Harcourt Brace Jovanovich, 1974.

——. Commentary. In L. Berkowitz & E. Walster (Eds.), *Advances in experimental social psychology* (Vol. 9). New York: Academic Press, 1976.

Hopper, E., & Weyman, A. Modes of conformity and forms of instrumental adjustment to feelings of relative deprivation. *British Journal of Sociology,* 1975, *27,* 66–77.

Howe, L. K. *Pink collar workers.* New York: G. P. Putnam's Sons, 1977.

Huber, J. (Ed.), Changing women in a changing society. Special edition of *American Journal of Sociology,* 1973, *78* (4, entire issue).

Hulin, C. L. Sources of variation in job and life satisfaction: The role of community and job-related variables. *Journal of Applied Psychology,* 1969, *53,* 279–291.

Hunt, A. *A survey of women's employment.* London: Her majesty's stationery office, 1968.

Hunt, J. W., & Saul, P. N. The relationship of age, tenure, and job satisfaction in males and females. *Academy of Management Journal,* 1975, *18,* 690–702.

Hurley, J. R., & Palonin, D. P. Marital satisfaction and child density among university student parents. *Journal of Marriage and the Family,* 1967, *29,* 483–484.

Hyman, H. H., & Singer, E. (Eds.), *Readings in reference group theory and research.* New York: Free Press, 1968.

Iglehart, A. P. *Married women and work, 1957 and 1976.* Lexington, Mass.: D.C. Heath and Co., 1979.

Jacobson, D. Rejection of the retirée role: A study of female industrial workers in their 50's. *Human Relations*, 1974, *27*, 477–492.

Jacobson, M. B., & Koch, W. Women as leaders: Performance evaluation as a function of method of leader selection. *Organizational Behavior and Human Performance*, 1977, *20*, 149–157.

Jasso, G., & Rossi, P. H. Distributive justice and earned income. *American Sociological Review*, 1977, *42*, 639–651.

Johnson, B. L., & Hayghe, H. *Labor force participation of married women, March, 1976*. U.S. Department of Labor, Bureau of Labor Statistics, Special Labor Force Report 206, 1977.

Jones, E. E., & Davis, K. E. From acts to dispositions. The attribution process in person perception. In L. Berkowitz (Ed.), *Advances in experimental Social Psychology*. (vol. 2). New York: Academic Press, 1965.

Joreskog, K. G. Analyzing psychological data by structural analysis of covariance matrices. In R. C. Atkinson, D. H. Krantz, & R. D. Suppes (Eds.), *Contemporary developments in mathematical psychology* (Vol. 2). San Francisco: W.H. Freeman & Co., 1974.

Jorgensen, S. R. Socioeconomic rewards and perceived marital quality: A reexamination. *Journal of Marriage and the Family*, 1979, *41*, 825–836.

Kahne, H. Economic perspectives on the role of women in the American economy. *Journal of Economic Literature*, 1975, *13*, 1249–1292.

———. Economic research on work and families. *Signs*, 1978, *3*, 652–665.

Kahne, H., & Hybels, J. *Work and family issues: A bibliography of economic and related social science research*. Wellesley: Center for research on women, 1978.

Kanter, R. M. The impact of hierarchical structures on the work behavior of women and men. *Social Problems*, 1976, *23*, 415–430.

———. *Men and women of the corporation*. New York: Basic Books, 1977. (a)

———. *Work and family in the United States: A critical review and agenda for research and policy*. New York: Russell Sage Foundation, 1977. (b)

Kavanagh, M. J., & Halpern, M. The impact of job level and sex differences on the relationship between life and job satisfaction. *Academy of Management Journal*, 1977, *20*, 66–73.

Kidder, L. H., Fagan, M. A., & Cohn, E. S. Giving and receiving:

References   185

Social justice in close relationships. In M. J. Lerner & S. Lerner
(Eds.), *The justice motive in social behavior: Adapting to times of scarcity
and change*. New York: Plenum Press, 1981.

Kinder, D. R., & Kiewiet, D. R. Economic grievances and political behavior: The role of personal discontents and collective judgments in Congressional voting. *American Journal of Political Science*, 1979, *23*, 495–527.

Kinder, D. R., & Sears, D. O. Prejudice and politics: Symbolic racism
versus racial threats to the good life. *Journal of Personality and
Social Psychology*, 1981, *40*, 414–431.

Kramnick, I. Reflections on revolution: Definition and explanation in
recent scholarship. *History and Theory*, 1972, *11*, 26–63.

Kreps, J. *Sex in the marketplace. American women at work*. Baltimore: The
Johns Hopkins Press, 1971.

Kresge, P. The human dimensions of sex discrimination. *Journal of the
American Association of University Women*, 1970, 64(2), 6–9.

Kuhlen, R. G. Needs, perceived need satisfaction, opportunities, and
satisfaction with occupation. *Journal of Applied Psychology*, 1963,
47, 56–64.

Lakoff, R. *Language and woman's place*. New York: Harper & Row, 1975.

Lane, R. E. *Political ideology: Why the American common man believes what
he does*. New York: The Free Press, 1962.

Langer, E. Inside the New York Telephone Company. In W. L. O'Neill
(Ed.), *Women at work*. Chicago: Quadrangle Books, 1972.

Latané, B. (Ed.), Studies in social comparison. *Journal of Experimental
Social Psychology*, 1966, Supplement I.

Laurence, M. W. Sources of satisfaction in the lives of working women.
Journal of Gerontology, 1961, 163–167.

Lawler, E. E. Equity theory as a predictor of productivity and work
quality. *Psychological Bulletin*, 1968, *70*, 596–610.

———. *Pay and organizational effectiveness. A psychological view*. New York:
McGraw-Hill, 1971.

Lemasters, E. E. Parenthood as crisis. *Marriage and Family Living*, 1957,
19, 352–355.

Lein, L. Male participation in home life: Impact of social supports and
breadwinner responsibility on the allocation of tasks. *The Family
Coordinator*, 1979, *28*, 489–495.

Lenski, G. Status crystallization: A non-vertical dimension of social status. *American Sociological Review*, 1954, *19*, 405–413.

Lerner, M. J. The justice motive in social behavior: Introduction. *Journal of Social Issues*, 1975, *31*(3), 1–19.

———. The justice motive: Some hypotheses as to its origins and forms. *Journal of Personality*, 1977, *45*, 1–52.

———. *The belief in a just world*. New York: Plenum Press, 1981.

———. The justice motive in human relations and the economic model of man: A radical analysis of facts and fictions. In V. Derlega & J. Grzelak (Eds.), *Living with other people: Theories and research on cooperative and helping behavior*. New York: Academic Press, 1982.

Lerner, M. J., & Lerner, S. C. (Eds.). *The justice motive in social behavior: Adapting to times of scarcity and change*. New York: Plenum Press, 1981.

Lerner, M. J., & Miller, D. J. Just world research and the attribution process: Looking back and ahead. *Psychological Bulletin*, 1978, *85*, 1030–1151.

Lerner, M. J., Miller, D. T., & Holmes, J. G. Deserving and the emergence of forms of justice. In L. Berkowitz & E. Walster (Eds.), *Advances in experimental social psychology* (Vol. 9). New York: Academic Press, 1976.

Leventhal, G. S. The distribution of rewards and resources in groups and organizations. In L. Berkowitz & E. Walster (Eds.), *Advances in experimental social psychology* (Vol. 9). New York: Academic Press, 1976.

Levinson, R. M. Sex discrimination and employment practices: An experiment with unconventional job inquiries. *Social Problems*, 1975, *22*, 533–542.

Levitin, T., Quinn, R. P., & Staines, G. L. Sex discrimination against the American working woman. *American Behavioral Scientist*, 1971, *15*(2), 237–254.

Lewis, H. B. *Psychic war in men and women*. New York: New York University Press, 1976.

Linn, E. L. Women dentists: Career and family. *Social Problems*, 1971, *18*, 393–404.

Liss, L. Why academic women don't revolt. *Sex Roles*, 1975, *1*, 209–233.

Lloyd, C. B. (Ed.), *Sex discrimination and the division of labor*. New York: Columbia University Press, 1975.

London, M., Crandall, R., & Seals, G. W. The contribution of job leisure satisfaction to quality of life. *Journal of Applied Psychology*, 1977, *62*, 328–334.

Maccoby, E. E., & Jacklin, C. N. *The psychology of sex differences*. Stanford, Calif.: Stanford University Press, 1974.

Madden, J. F. *The economics of sex discrimination.* Lexington, Mass.: Lexington Books, 1973.

Manhardt, P. J. Job orientations of male and female college graduates on business. *Personnel Psychology,* 1972, *25,* 361–368.

Martin, J. *When prosperity fails: Distributional determinants of the perception of justice.* Unpublished doctoral dissertation, Harvard University, 1979.

Mason, K. O., & Bumpass, L. L. U.S. Women's sex-role ideology, 1970. *American Journal of Sociology,* 1975, *80,* 1212–1219.

Mason, K. O., Czajka, J. L., & Arber, S. Change in U.S. women's sex-role attitudes, 1964–1974. *American Sociological Review,* 1976, *41,* 573–596.

McClendon, M. J. The occupational status attainment process of males and females. *American Sociological Review,* 1976, *41,* 52–64.

McCune, S. Thousands reply to opinionnaire: Many document cases of sex discrimination. *Journal of the American Association of University Women.* May, 1970, 202–206.

McLaughlin, S. D. Occupational sex identification and the assessment of male and female earnings inequality. *American Sociological Review,* 1978, *43,* 909–921.

Mennerick, L. A. Organizational structuring of sex roles in a non-stereotyped industry. *Administrative Science Quarterly,* 1975, *20,* 570–586.

Merton, R., & Rossi, A. S. Contributions to the theory of reference group behavior. In R. Merton (Ed.), *Social theory and social structure.* New York: Free Press, 1957.

Messick, D. M., & Sentis, K. P. Fairness and preference. *Journal of Experimental Social Psychology,* 1979, *15,* 418–434.

Milgram, S. *Obedience to authority: An experimental view.* New York: Harper & Row, 1974.

Miller, A. H., Bolce, L. H., & Halligan, M. The J-curve theory and the black urban riots. *American Political Science Review,* 1977, *71,* 964–982.

Miller, B. C. A multivariate developmental model of marital satisfaction. *Journal of Marriage and the Family,* 1976, *38,* 643–658.

Miller, D. T. Ego-involvement and attributions for success and failure. *Journal of Personality and Social Psychology,* 1976, *34,* 901–906.

Miller, D. T., & Ross, M. Self-serving biases in the attribution of causality: Fact or fiction? *Psychological Bulletin,* 1975, *82,* 213–225.

Miller, F. S. *Biographical variables, racism, sexism and the personality development of black female undergraduates: An exploratory investigation.* Unpublished doctoral dissertation, Texas Christian University, 1981.

Miller, J., Labovitz, S., & Fry, L. Inequities in the organizational experiences of women and men. *Social Forces,* 1975, *54,* 365–381.

Miner, J. B. Motivational potential for upgrading among minority and female managers. *Journal of Applied Psychology,* 1977, *62,* 691–697.

Mizruchi, E. H. *Success and opportunity.* New York: Free Press, 1964.

Molm, L. D. Sex role attitudes and the employment of married women: The direction of causality. *The Sociological Quarterly,* 1978, *19,* 522–533.

Morrison, D. Some notes toward theory on relative deprivation. Social movements and social change. *American Behavioral Scientist,* 1971, *14,* 675–690.

Morse, S. J., Gruzen, J., & Reis, H. T. The nature of equity-restoration: Some approval-seeking considerations. *Journal of Experimental Social Psychology,* 1976, *12,* 1–8.

Mueller, C. W., & Campbell, B. G. Female occupational achievement and marital status: A research note. *Journal of Marriage and the Family,* 1977, *39,* 587–599.

Myrdal, G. *An American dilemma.* New York: Harper, 1944.

Nagel, E. *The structure of science. Problems in the logic of scientific explanation.* New York: Harcourt, Brace and World, 1961.

———. Types of causal explanations in science. In D. Lerner (Ed.), *Cause and effect.* New York: Free Press, 1965.

Near, J. R., Rice, R. W., & Hunt, R. G. Work and extra-work correlates of life and job satisfaction. *Academy of Management Journal,* 1978, *21,* 248–264.

Nicholls, J. C. Causal attributions and other achievement related cognitions: Effects of test outcome, attainment value, and sex. *Journal of Personality and Social Psychology,* 1975, *31,* 379–389.

Nisbett, R., & Ross, L. *Human inference: Strategies and shortcomings of social judgment.* Englewood Cliffs: Prentice-Hall, 1980.

Notman, M., & Nadelson, C. C. Medicine: A career conflict for women. *American Journal of Psychiatry,* 1973, *130,* 1123–1127.

Orden, S. R., & Bradburn, N. M. Working wives and marriage happiness. *American Journal of Sociology,* 1969, *74,* 392–407.

Orvis, B. R., Kelley, H. H., & Butler, D. Attributional conflict in young couples. In J. H. Harvey, W. J. Ickes, & R. F. Kidd (Eds.), *New directions in attribution research* (Vol. 1). Hillsdale, N.J.: Erlbaum, 1976.

Parducci, A. The relativism of absolute judgments. *Scientific American,* 1968, *219*(6), 84–90.

Parrish, J. B. Are there women in engineering's future? *Journal of the American Association of University Women,* 1965, *59,* 29–31.

Parelius, A. P. Change and stability in college women's orientations toward education, family and work. *Social Problems,* 1975, *22,* 420–431.

Parsons, T., & Bales, R. F. (Eds.), *Family, socialization and interaction process.* Glencoe, Ill.: Free Press, 1955.

Parvin, M. Economic determinants of political unrest: An econometric approach. *Journal of Conflict Resolution,* 1973, *17,* 271–296.

Patchen, M. *The choice of wage comparisons.* Englewood Cliffs, N.J.: Prentice-Hall, 1961. (a)

————. A conceptual framework and some empirical data regarding comparisons of social rewards. *Sociometry,* 1961, *24,* 136–156. (b)

Peck, T. When women evaluate women, nothing succeeds like success: The differential effects of status upon evaluations of male and female professional ability. *Sex Roles,* 1978, *4,* 205–214.

Perelman, C. *The idea of justice and the problem of argument.* London: Routledge and Kegan Paul, 1963.

Pettigrew, T. *A profile of the Negro American.* Princeton, N.J.: Van Nostrand, 1964.

————. Social evaluation theory. In D. Levine (Ed.), *Nebraska symposium on motivation* (Vol. 15). Lincoln: University of Nebraska Press, 1967.

————. Three issues in ethnicity: Boundaries, deprivations, and perceptions. In J. M. Yinger & S. J. Cutler (Eds.), *Major social issues: A multidisciplinary view.* New York: Free Press, 1978.

Piotrkowski, C. S. *Work and the family system.* New York: Free Press, 1979.

Pleck, J. H. The work-family role system. *Social Problems,* 1977, *24,* 417–427.

————. Men's family work: Three perspectives and some new data. *The Family Coordinator,* 1979, *28,* 481–488.

Pleck, J. H., & Lang, L. *Men's family role: Its nature and consequences.* Wellesley, Mass.: Center for Research on Women, Wellesley College, Working paper number 10, 1978.

Pleck, J. H., Staines, G. L., & Lang, L. Conflicts between work and family life. *Monthly Labor Review,* 1980, *103*(3), 29–32.

Poloma, M. M., & Garland, T. N. The myth of the equalitarian family: Familial roles and the professionally employed wife. In A. Theodore (Ed.), *The professional woman.* Cambridge, Mass.: Schenckman Pub. Co., 1971.

Porter, L. W., & Steers, R. M. Organizational work, and personal fac-
    tors in employee turnover and absenteeism. *Psychological Bulle-
    tin,* 1973, *80,* 151–176.

Quadagno, J. Occupational sex-typing and internal labor market dis-
    tributions: An assessment of medical specialities. *Social Problems,*
    1976, *23,* 442–453.
Quinn, R., & Staines, G. *The 1977 quality of employment survey.* Ann
    Arbor, Michigan: Institute for Social Research, 1978.

Radloff, L. Sex differences in depression: The effects of occupation
    and marital status. *Sex Roles,* 1975, *1,* 249–269.
Rapoport, R., & Rapoport, R. N. *Dual career families.* Harmondsworth:
    Penguin Books, 1971. (a)
———. Further considerations on the dual career family. *Human Re-
    lations,* 1971, *24,* 519–534. (b)
———. *Dual career families re-examined.* New York: Harper & Row, 1976.
Reagan, B. B., & Blaxall, M. Introduction: Occupational segregation
    in international women's year. In M. Blaxall & B. B. Reagan
    (Eds.), *Women and the marketplace.* Chicago: University of Chi-
    cago, Press, 1976.
Reif, W. E., Newstrom, J. W., & St. Louis, R. D., Jr. Sex as a discrim-
    inating variable in organizational reward decisions. *Academy of
    Management Journal,* 1976, *19,* 469–475.
Renne, K. S. Correlates of dissatisfaction in marriage. *Journal of Mar-
    riage and the Family,* 1970, *32,* 54–67.
Rhodebeck, L. Group deprivation: An alternative model for explain-
    ing collective political action. *Micropolitics,* 1981, *1,* 239–267.
Rice, R. W., Near, J. P., & Hunt, R. G. Unique variance in job and life
    satisfaction associated with work-related and extra-work place
    variables. *Human Relations,* 1979, *32,* 605–624.
Riess, M., Rosenfeld, P., Melburg, V., & Tedeschi, J. T. Self-serving
    attributions: Biased private perceptions and distorted public de-
    scriptions. *Journal of Personality and Social Psychology,* 1981, *41,*
    224–231.
Robinson, J. P., Yerby, J., Fieweger, M., & Somerick, N. Sex-role dif-
    ferences in time use. *Sex Roles,* 1977, *3,* 443–458.
Rollins, B. C., & Feldman, H. Marital satisfaction over the family life
    cycle. *Journal of Marriage and the Family,* 1970, *32,* 20–28.
Roseman, I. Cognitive aspects of emotions and emotional behavior.

Paper presented at the American Psychological Association. New York, 1979.

Rosen, B., & Jerdee, T. H. Sex stereotyping in the executive suite. *Harvard Business Review*, 1974, *52*, 45–48.

Rosen, B., Jerdee, T. H., & Prestwich, T. L. Dual-career marital adjustment: Potential effects of discriminatory managerial attitudes. *Journal of Marriage and the Family*, 1975, *37*, 565–572.

Rosenbach, W., Dailey, R. C., & Morgan, C. P. Perceptions of job characteristics and affective work outcomes for women and men. *Sex Roles*, 1979, *5*, 267–278.

Ross, L. The intuitive psychologist and his shortcomings: Distortions in the attribution process. In L. Berkowitz (Ed.), *Advances in experimental social psychology* (Vol. 10). New York: Academic Press, 1977.

Rubin, Z., & Peplau, A. Who believes in a just world? *Journal of Social Issues*, 1975, *31*(3), 65–89.

Runciman, W. G. *Relative deprivation and social justice*. Berkeley: University of California Press, 1966.

Russo, N. F. The motherhood mandate. *Journal of Social Issues*, 1976, *32*(3), 143–153.

Ryan, W. *Blaming the victim*. New York: Random House, 1971.

Saleh, S., & Lalljee, M. Sex and job orientation. *Personnel Psychology*, 1969, *32*, 465–471.

Sampson, E. E. Justice and social character. In G. Mikula (Ed.), *Justice and social interaction. Experimental and theoretical contributions from psychological research*. New York: Springer-Verlag, 1980.

Scanzoni, J. *Sexual bargaining: Power politics in the American marriage*. Englewood Cliffs, N.J.: Prentice-Hall, 1972.

———. *Sex roles, women's work and marital conflict*. Lexington, Mass.: D. C. Heath, 1978.

Scase, R. Relative deprivation: A comparison of English and Swedish manual workers. In D. Wedderburn (Ed.), *Poverty, inequality, and class structure*. Cambridge, England: Cambridge University Press, 1974.

Schein, V. E. Relationships between sex role stereotypes and requisite management characteristics among female managers. *Journal of Applied Psychology*, 1975, *60*, 340–344.

Schmitt, N., Coyle, B. W., White, J. K., & Rauschenberger, J. Background needs, job perceptions, and job satisfaction: A causal model. *Personnel Psychology*, 1978, *31*, 889–900.

Schreiber, C. T. *Changing places: Men and women in transitional occupations.* Cambridge, Mass.: Massachusetts Institute of Technology Press, 1979.

Schwab, D. P., & Wallace, M. J. Correlates of employee satisfaction with pay. *Industrial Relations,* 1974, *13,* 78–89.

Schwinger, T. Just allocations of goods: Decisions among three principles. In G. Mikula (Ed.), *Justice and social interaction. Experimental and theoretical contributions from psychological research.* New York: Springer-Verlag, 1980.

Sears, D. O., Hensler, C. P., & Speer, L. K. White opposition to busing: Self interest or symbolic politics. *American Political Science Review,* 1979, *73,* 369–384.

Sears, D. O., & Kinder, D. R. Racial tension and voting in Los Angeles. In W. Z. Hirsch (Ed.), *Los Angeles: Viability and prospects for metropolitan leadership.* New York: Praeger, 1971.

Sears, D. O., & McConahay, J. S. *The politics of violence: The new urban blacks and the Watts riots.* Boston: Houghton Mifflin, 1973.

Seeman, M. Alienation studies. *Annual Review of Sociology,* 1975, *1,* 91–123.

———. Some real and imaginary consequences of social mobility: A French-American comparison. *American Journal of Sociology,* 1977, *82,* 757–782.

Simon, P. J., Clark, S. M., & Tifft, L. L. Of nepotism, marriage, and the pursuit of an academic career. *Sociology of Education,* 1966, *39,* 344–358.

Smith, C. B. Influence of internal opportunity structure and sex of worker on turnover patterns. *Administrative Science Quarterly,* 1979, *24,* 362–381.

Smith, P. C., Kendall, L. M., & Hulin, C. L. *The measurement of satisfaction in work and retirement.* Chicago: Rand McNally, 1969.

Snyder, D., & Kelly, W. R. Industrial violence in Italy, 1878–1903. *American Journal of Sociology,* 1976, *82,* 131–162.

Spanier, G. B., Lewis, R. A., & Cole, C. L. Marital adjustment over the family life cycle: The issue of curvilinearity. *Journal of Marriage and the Family,* 1975, *37,* 263–276.

Spence, J. T., & Helmreich, R. Who likes competent women? *Journal of Applied Social Psychology,* 1972, *2,* 197–213.

Spilerman, S. The causes of racial disturbances: A comparison of alternate explanations. *American Sociological Review,* 1970, *35,* 627–649.

———. The causes of racial disturbances: Tests of explanations. *American Sociological Review,* 1971, *36,* 427–442.

Spreitzer, E., Snyder, E. E., & Larson, D. L. Multiple roles and psychological well being. *Sociological Focus*, 1979, *12*, 141–148.

Staines, G. L., Pleck, J. H., Shepard, L. J., & O'Connor, P. Wives' employment status and mental adjustment: Yet another look. *Psychology of Women Quarterly*, 1978, *3*, 90–119.

Stevens, L., & Jones, E. E. Defensive attribution and the Kelley cube. *Journal of Personality and Social Psychology*, 1976, *34*, 809–820.

Stone, L. Theories of revolution. *World Politics*, 1966, *18*, 159–176.

Stouffer, S. A., Suchman, E. A., DeVinney, L. C., Star, S. A., & Williams, R. M., Jr. *The American soldier: Adjustment during Army life* (Vol. 1). Princeton, N.J.: Princeton University Press, 1949.

Suls, J. M., & Miller, R. L. (Eds.), *Social comparison processes: Theoretical and empirical perspectives.* New York: Wiley, 1977.

Suter, L. E., & Miller, H. P. Income differences between men and career women. *American Journal of Sociology*, 1973, *78*, 962–974.

Szasz, T. *The myth of mental illness.* New York: Harper, 1961.

Szinovacz, M. Role allocation, family structure and female employment. *Journal of Marriage and the Family*, 1977, *39*, 781–792.

Taveggia, T. C., & Ziemba, T. Linkages to work. A study of the "central life interests" and "work attachments" of male and female workers. *Journal of Vocational Behavior*, 1978, *12*, 305–320.

Taylor, D. M., & Simard-Dubé, L. *Les relations intergroups au Québec et la loi 101.* Québec: Gouvernement du Québec, 1981.

Terborg, J. R., & Ilgen, D. R. A theoretical approach to sex discrimination in traditionally masculine occupations. *Organizational Behavior and Human Performance*, 1975, *13*, 352–376.

Tetlock, P. E., & Levi, A. Attribution bias: On the inconclusiveness of the cognition-motivation debate. *Journal of Experimental Social Psychology*, 1982, *18*, 68–88.

Thibaut, J., & Kelley, H. H. *Social psychology of groups.* New York: Wiley, 1959.

Thornton, A., & Freedman, D. Changes in the sex role attitudes of women, 1962–1977: Evidence from a panel study. *American Sociological Review*, 1979, *44*, 831–842.

Thrall, C. A. Who does what: Role stereotyping, children's work, and continuity between generations in the household division of labor. *Human Relations*, 1978, *31*, 249–265.

Tinker, I. Nonacademic professional scientists. *American Behavioral Scientist*, 1971, *15*, 206–212.

Treiman, D. J. *Occupational prestige in comparative perspective.* New York: Academic Press, 1977.

Treiman, D. J., & Terrell, K. Sex and the process of status attainment: A comparison of working women and men. *American Sociological Review,* 1975, *40,* 174–200.

U. S. Bureau of Census. *Alphabetical index of occupations and industries.* Washington, D.C.: USGPO, 1960.

U. S. Department of Labor. Bureau of Labor statistics. *News.* Oct. 12, 1978. (a)

———. *Employment in perspective: Working women.* No. 3, Third quarter, 1978. Report 547. (b)

———. *Employment in perspective: Working women.* No. 1, First quarter, 1979. (a)

———. *News.* October 31, 1979. (b)

———. *Employment in perspective: Working women.* 1979 Summary. February, 1980. (a)

———. *News.* August 29, 1980. (b)

Vanek, J. Time spent in housework. *Scientific American,* 1974, *231*(5), 116–120.

Vanneman, R. D., & Pettigrew, T. F. Race and relative deprivation in the urban United States. *Race,* 1972, *13,* 461–486.

Veroff, J., Douvan, E., & Kalka, R. *The inner American: A self portrait from 1957 to 1976.* New York: Basic Books, 1981.

Vetter, B. M. Women scientists and engineers: Trends in participation. *Science,* 1981, *214,* 1313–1321.

Vroom, V. H. *Work and motivation.* New York: Wiley, 1964.

———. Industrial psychology. In G. Lindzey & E. Aronson (Eds.), *The handbook of social psychology* (Vol. 5). Reading, Mass.: Addison-Wesley, 1969.

Waite, L. J. Working wives: 1940–1960. *American Sociological Review,* 1976, *41,* 65–80.

Walker, K., and Woods, M. *Time use: A measure of household production of family goods and services.* Washington: American Home Economics Association, 1976.

Walker, N. *Morale in the civil service.* Edinburgh: Edinburgh University Press, 1961.

Wallis, R. Relative deprivation and social movements: A cautionary note. *British Journal of Sociology*, 1975, *26*, 360–365.

Walsh, M. R. Coping strategies of professional women: A comparison of two generations of women physicians. Paper presented at Research Conference of Association of Women in Psychology, St. Louis, Feb. 6, 1977.

Walsh, M. R., & Stewart, A. The professional woman: Coping with being outnumbered. Paper presented at Conference on Women in Mid-life Crisis. Cornell University, October, 1976.

Walster, E., Berscheid, E., & Walster, G. W. New directions in equity research. *Journal of Personality and Social Psychology*, 1973, *25*, 151–176.

Walster, E., & Paté, M. A. Why are women so hard on women? *Forum on Public Affairs*, 1974, *7*, 1–31.

Walster, E., Walster, G. W., & Berscheid, E. *Equity, theory and research.* Boston: Allyn and Bacon, 1978.

Weaver, C. N. Job satisfaction as a component of happiness among males and females. *Personnel Psychology*, 1978, *31*, 831–840. (a)

———. Sex differences in the determinants of job satisfaction. *Academy of Management Journal*, 1978, *21*, 265–274. (b)

Weingarten, K. The employment patterns of professional couples and their distribution of involvement in the family. *Psychology of Women Quarterly*, 1978, *3*, 43–52.

Weiss, R. L., & Aved, B. M. Marital satisfaction and depression as predictors of physical health status. *Journal of Consulting and Clinical Psychology*, 1978, *46*, 1379–1384.

Weitzel, W., Harpaz, I., & Weiner, N. Predicting pay satisfaction from nonpay work variables. *Industrial Relations*, 1977, *16*, 323–334.

Wheeler, L., & Zuckerman, M. Commentary. In J. M. Suls & R. L. Miller (Eds.), *Social comparison processes. Theoretical and empirical perspectives.* New York: Wiley, 1977.

White, J. J. Women in the law. *Michigan Law Review*, 1967, *65*, 1084–1095.

Widom, C. S., & Burke, B. N. Performance, attitudes, and professional socialization of women in academia. *Sex Roles*, 1978, *4*, 549–562.

Williams, G. Trends in occupational differentiation by sex. *Sociology of Work and Occupations*, 1976, *3*, 38–62.

Williams, R. M., Jr. Relative deprivation. In L. A. Coser (Ed.), *The idea of social structure: Papers in honor of Robert K. Merton.* New York: Harcourt Brace Jovanovich, 1975.

Wilson, W. Correlates of avowed happiness. *Psychological Bulletin*, 1967, *67*, 294–306.

Wolf, W. C., & Fligstein, N. D. Sex and authority in the work-place: The causes of sexual inequality. *American Sociological Review,* 1979, *44,* 235–252.

Young, C. J., MacKenzie, D. L., & Sherif, C. W. In search of token women in academia. *Psychology of Women Quarterly,* 1980, *4,* 508–525.

Young, M., & Willmott, P. *The symmetrical family.* New York: Pantheon Books, 1973.

Appendix I

The Logic of ANOVAs

In an analysis of variance (ANOVA), we look at the clustering of scores within any one group *relative* to the differentiation between groups. Imagine the simple case: a group of 10 men and a group of 10 women. Imagine that both groups answered the X Scale and that the average score among men was 3 and among women, 6. Are women more X-like than men? To answer the question, we need to see how much the scores vary within each group as well as how much they vary between groups. Imagine this array of scores:

women: 5,6,6,6,6,6,6,6,6,7

men: 2,3,3,3,3,3,3,3,3,4.

Intuitively, we would say the two groups look different. But consider this array:

women: 1,3,4,4,4,5,9,10,10,10

men: 1,1,1,2,2,2,4,4,5,8.

The men and women no longer look so different from each other. Yet in the second example, as in the first, the mean (or average) score among women is 6 and the mean score among men is 3. What's the critical factor? Dispersion of the scores within the two groups is greater in the second example than in the first.

In an analysis of variance, the F-statistic is a strict and systematic rendering of the intuitively obvious example we have considered. The F is a numerical summary of the variance between groups relative to the variation of scores within groups. The greater the F-value, the more substantial the difference between groups. Then, using probability tables, we can say how likely it is that we might obtain any given F-value for any given number of groups of given sizes. If there are only 5 chances in 100 that the F-value of a given magnitude could be obtained by fluke, we consider the results to be "significant." We denote the fact thus: $p = .05$.

The simple example of 10 men and 10 women shows a case in which there is one independent variable, sex. The same principle can extend to several independent variables simultaneously. In a two-way ANOVA, we look at two independent variables. If each of these variables is represented at "two levels," we speak of a 2 by 2 ANOVA. Here is a diagram of a 2 by 2 ANOVA design:

Sex

Job level high		
low		

Here is an example of a 3 by 2 by 2 ANOVA design:

Sex and job level

		men		women	
		high	low	high	low
family single					
status married					
parents					

In the example above, one of the independent variables, family status, has three "levels" (single, married, parents). The second independent variable, sex, has two: male and female. The third, job level, also has two.

When there is more than one independent variable in an ANOVA design, we refer to main effects and to interaction effects. A main effect means that one of the independent variables makes a difference in the "dependent variable" under study. A main effect for sex, for example, means that men and women—in our examples—are different in their X-ness. A main effect for job level means that high and low job levels differ from each other. A main effect for family status means that X-ness is different for people who are single, married, or parents. Another way to say that there is a main effect for any of the independent variables is to say that the dependent variable "varies as a function of" the independent variable.

An interaction effect can occur between any two or more independent variables. An interaction effect between, say, sex and job level means that job level mediates the effects of sex on X-ness. Here is one example of an interaction: males with high-level jobs are X-like, but males with low-level jobs are not; while females with low-level jobs are X-like, and females with high-level jobs are not. Here is another example of an interaction: among males, job level makes a difference; among females, it does not.

The terms used in the text, such as main effect and inter-action effect, are not intended to imply causality. We use them as part of the language conventions of social scientists. They are a shorthand way of indicating which group differences are reliable (i.e., are probably not flukes) and which might be due to chance.

An analysis of covariance (ANCOVA) resembles an ANOVA. It is appropriate when the groups under study differ systematically in terms of one or more factors that are considered irrelevant to the study. Because the single respondents are younger than the married and parental respondents in the study, we use analyses of covariance for some of the analyses reported in Chapters 4, 5, and 6.

Appendix II A

Creating the Scales

For each theoretical variable listed, there was a scale created from the questions shown. For the raw score scales, a respondent's score was the sum of his score on each question making up the scale. For the standard score scales, a respondent's score was the average of his standardized score on each question making up the scale.

Theoretical variables	Questions	Special coding instructions
Variables concerning one's job		
Dissatisfaction	22	obtain average
	23	
Deprivation	14	Sum options: angry (2), annoyed (1), bitter (2), deprived (3), grateful (−2), infuriated (2), resentful (3)
	17	
	43	obtain average
	46b	
Wanting	19	
	20	
	21	
Comparison other	33c	obtain average
	34	obtain average
	35	obtain average
	36	

Theoretical variables	*Questions*	*Special coding instructions*
Deserving	24	
	25	
	26	obtain average
Past expectations	27	
	28	obtain average
Future expectations	29	
	30	obtain average
	31	
(No) self-blame	37	
	41	

Variables concerning the position of women

Dissatisfaction	73	
Deprivation	72	obtain average
Wanting	51	
	53	obtain average
	54	
Comparison other	64	
	65	obtain average
	70	
Deserving	55	obtain average
	56	
Past expectations	57	
	58	obtain average
Future expectations	59	
	60	obtain average
	61	
(No) blame	67	
	68	
	69	

Theoretical variables	Questions	Special coding instructions
Variables concerning one's home life		
Dissatisfaction	81	obtain average
	82	
Deprivation	77	Sum options: angry (2), annoyed (1), bitter (2), deprived (3), grateful (-2), infuriated (2), resentful (3)
	80	
	83	obtain average
	97	
	118	
Wanting	86	
	89	
Comparison other	95	
	95c	obtain average
Deserving	90	
	91	
	92	
Past expectations	87	Coding depends on answer to Q. 85. If answer to Q. 85 is *more*, then 1 is given to "much more" and "a little more." If answer to Q. 85 is *less*, then 1 is given to "a little less" and "a lot less." Otherwise, a zero is scored.
Future expectations	88	Coding depends on answer to Q. 86. If answer to Q. 86 is *more*, then 3 is given to "probably decrease" and 2 is given to "probably remain about the same." If answer to Q. 86 is *less*, then

Theoretical variables	*Questions*	*Special coding instructions*
		3 is given to "certainly increase" and "probably increase" and 2 is given to "probably remain about the same." If answer to Q. 86 is *right,* 2 is given to "certainly increase" and "probably increase." Everything else is scored as 1.
(No) self-blame	93a	

Appendix II B

Dichotomizing the Variables

Theoretical variables	*Scored* ON *if any of these is true*
Variables concerning one's job	
Wanting	Q. 19 equals 3 or 4
	Q. 20 equals 4, 5, or 6
	Q. 21 equals 0, 10, or 11
Comparison other	Q. 33c (1) equals 3
	Q. 33c (2) equals 3
	Q. 33c (3) equals 3
	Q. 34 (pay) equals 4 or 5
	any other aspect in Q. 34 equals 5
	Q. 35 (pay) equals 4 or 5
	any other aspect in Q. 35 equals 5
	Q. 36 equals 4 or 5
Deserving	Q. 24 equals 4 or 5
	Q. 25 equals 4
	Q. 26 equals 5 (any aspect)
Past expectations	Q. 27 equals 4 or 5
	Q. 28 (pay) equals 4 or 5
	any other aspect in Q. 28 equals 5
Future expectations	Q. 29 equals 4 or 5
	Q. 30 equals 5 (any aspect)

Theoretical variables	*Scored* ON *if any of these is true*
(No) self-blame	Q. 37 equals 2
	Q. 41 equals 3 or 4

Variables concerning the position of women

Wanting	Q. 51 equals 2
	Q. 53 (pay) equals 4 or 5
	any other aspect in Q. 53 equals 5
	Q. 54 equals 4 or 5
Comparison other	Q. 64 equals 4 or 5
	Q. 65 (pay) equals 4 or 5
	any other aspect in Q. 65 equals 5
	Q. 70 equals 3
Deserving	Q. 55 (pay) equals 4 or 5
	any other aspect in Q. 55 equals 5
	Q. 56 equals 4 or 5
Past expectations	Q. 57 equals 3
	Q. 58 (pay) equals 4 or 5
	any other aspect in Q. 58 equals 5
Future expectations	Q. 59 equals 4 or 5
	Q. 60 equals 5
	Q. 61 equals 3
(No) blame	Q. 67 equals 2
	Q. 68 equals 2
	Q. 69 equals 2

Variables concerning one's home life

Wanting	Q. 86 equals 1
Comparison other	Q. 95c (1) equals 3
	Q. 95c (2) equals 3
	Q. 95c (3) equals 3
Deserving	Q. 91 equals 4 or 5

Theoretical variables	*Scored* ON *if any of these is true*
Past expectations	Q. 87 equals 1
Future expectations	Q. 88 equals 2 or 3
(No) self-blame	Q. 93a equals 1 Q. 94 equals 3 or 4

Appendix III A

Telephone Screening Interview

ID#

"Hello. This is _____ calling from Abt Associates in Cambridge.

May I speak with _____ (ASK FOR   PERSON NAMED ABOVE)?"

ONCE YOU ARE SPEAKING WITH THE CORRECT PERSON, RE-INTRODUCE YOURSELF. THEN, CONTINUE:

"Recently you may have received a letter from Yale University explaining the study I'm calling about. This study is currently being conducted with people who live in Newton, to find out how they feel about their jobs and family lives. We'd like you to participate in the study. Of course, all information will be completely confidential. First, I'd like to ask a few questions just to check our facts."

IF RESPONDENT ASKS FOR MORE INFORMATION:

"We're calling people who have been randomly selected from the Newton Street Directory. Our study has been designed to reach a variety of people, and I will be asking certain people if I can come to their homes for a longer interview. Before I know whether you belong to a group I need to interview, let me ask you a few questions just to check my facts."

Q.1a Could you please tell me your marital status:

                                         SINGLE............1
                                         MARRIED...........2
                                         SEPARATED 3
                                         DIVORCED..........4
                                         WIDOWED...........5

```
IF SINGLE, CHECK QUOTA CONTROL SHEET.   IF QUOTA IS FILLED,
TERMINATE AND SAVE SCREENER.   IF QUOTA IS OPEN, SKIP TO
Q.2a.                                                        TERMINATE

     ALL OTHERS, ASK Q.1b.
```

208

Q.1b Do you have any children living at home under 18 years of age?

                                                    Yes ... 1

                                                    No 2

> CHECK QUOTA CONTROL SHEET. IF QUOTA IS FILLED, TERMINATE AND SAVE
> SCREENER. IF QUOTA IS OPEN, CONTINUE.

Q.2a I want to be sure I'm speaking to the right person. Could you please
      spell your name for me?

                    Spelling agrees with above 1
                    Spelling is different 2
                    CORRECT SPELLING: _____

Q.2b What is your current street address? Is it (READ ABOVE ADDRESS)?

                    Address is correct 1
                    Address is different 2
                    CORRECT ADDRESS:_____

> IF ADDRESS IS DIFFERENT, CONFIRM THAT RESPONDENT STILL LIVES IN
> NEWTON. IF OUTSIDE OF NEWTON, TERMINATE.

Q.2c What year were you born?

                    Same year 1
                    Different 2
                    RECORD YEAR: _____

> IF YEAR IS NOT BETWEEN 1938 AND 1953, TERMINATE. OTHERWISE, CONTINUE.

Q.2d   What is your occupation?

Occupation is correct 1

Occupation is different 2

INTERVIEWER INSTRUCTIONS

If occupation is different:

o   If changed to "umemployed" or "student", terminate.

o   If changed to "housewife", ask for her husband's occupation.
    Record where indicated in the Newton Street List Information
    Box on Page 1. Then, continue to Q.2e.

o   If changed from "housewife", record respondent's new
    occupation in the Newton Stret List Information Box on Page 1.
    Then, skip to Q.2g.

o   If changed from one job title to another, record respondent's
    new occupation in the Newton Street List Information Box on
    Page 1. Then, skp to Q.2g.

For those respondents whose occupation has changed to "housewife"
or an occupation (other than "student" or "unemployed") you must
continue to interview and if the respondent is otherwise eligible,
set up an appointment. You must then notify your supervisor of the
change, and she will confirm the respondent's status group.

Q.2e   (ASK "HOUSEWIVES" ONLY.)   What is your husband's occupation?

Occupation is correct...............1

Occupation is different 2

RECORD OCCUPATION:_____

IF OCCUPATION IS DIFFERENT, RECORD HUSBAND'S NEW OCCUPATION
IN THE NEWTON STREET LIST INFORMATION BOX ON PAGE 1. AFTER
COMPLETING SCREENER, BE SURE TO NOTIFY YOUR SUPERVISOR SO SHE
MAY CONFIRM RESPONDENT'S STATUS GROUP.

210

Q.2f (<u>ASK "HOUSEWIVES" ONLY</u>:) Do <u>you</u> have any paid employment outside the home?

> Yes (<u>SKIP TO Q.2h</u>)........ 1
>
> No (<u>SKIP TO Q.3</u>) 2

Q.2g (<u>ASK ALL, EXCEPT "HOUSEWIVES"</u>:) Are you currently employed full-time or part-time in your occupation?

> Full-time 1
>
> Part-time 2
>
> Not currently employed (<u>TERMINATE</u>) ... 3

Q.2h Approximately how many hours per week do you work?

> _____
> (hours per week)

> ● IF "HOUSEWIFE," MUST BE LESS THAN 10 HOURS. OTHERWISE, TERMINATE.
> ● ALL OTHERS, MUST BE AT LEAST 35 HOURS. OTHERWISE, TERMINATE.

Q.3 Which of these best describes your ethnic affiliation (<u>READ LIST</u>):

> Caucasian-American 1
>
> Afro-American .... 2 ⎫
>
> Hispanic American .... 3 ⎬ <u>TERMINATE</u>
>
> Oriental American .... 4 ⎭
>
> Other (<u>SPECIFY</u>) _____

> IF "OTHER" IS MENTIONED, ANY EUROPEAN-AMERICAN IDENTITY IS ACCEPTABLE,
> E.G., IRISH-AMERICAN, ITALIAN-AMERICAN, ETC. PLEASE RECORD THESE AS
> CAUCASIAN-AMERICANS.
> OTHERWISE, TERMINATE AND SAVE SCREENER.

Well, that completes the information that I need to obtain over the telephone.
I wonder if you would be willing to participate further in our research. More
specifically, I wonder if I might come and interview you for about [45 MINUTES
FOR HOUSEWIVES; 1½ HOURS FOR EMPLOYED PEOPLE) in your home and
at your convenience. I'd be asking some questions about your general lifestyle,
and about your work. What we're most interested in finding out is how people
with different life patterns feel about various things such as their work, their
home lives, and some issues of more general concern. If it's okay with you,
could we set up an appointment?

APPOINTMENT DATE: _____

TIME: _____

REFUSED APPOINTMENT ☐

Thank you very much!

Interviewer Name:_____

Time Ended: _____

Total Time: _____

FOR OFFICE USE ONLY :

		Single	Married-No Children	Married With Children
I.	MALE - Low Stat.	1	2	3
II.	MALE - High Stat.	1	2	3
III.	WORKING FEMALE - Low Stat.	1	2	3
IV.	WORKING FEMALE - High Stat.	1	2	3
V.	HOUSEWIFE - Low Stat.	-	-	3
VI.	HOUSEWIFE - High Stat.	-	-	3

212

Appendix III B

The Interview Schedule

(Note: Coding of the close-ended questions is shown. When a response category was scored as a missing value, an M is written.)

This interview is part of a Yale University study investigating
various patterns of life among men and women in all walks of
life. Your participation in the interview or any part of it is
completely voluntary. If you have any questions concerning this
interview, please feel free to contact Ms. Linda DeSimone at
Abt Associates in Cambridge, 492-7100.

No identifying information will be used in the presentation of
data. After completion of the study, all identifying
information will be destroyed.

I have read and understood the above form and agree to participate
in this study.

_____   _____
Name   Date

214

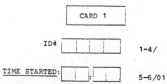

CARD 1

ID# ☐☐☐☐   1-4/

TIME STARTED: ☐☐ : ☐☐   5-6/01

1. First, I'd like to get some information about the people who live in your household. Could you please tell me the first name of each person, including children, and tell me their relationship to you:

	Sex				Relationship				
First Name	M	F	Age	Spouse	Own Child	Parent/ In-law	Rela- tive	Room- mate	Other (SPECIFY)
_____ 7/	1	2	8-9/ ___	1	2	3	4	5	_____ 6 10/
_____ 11/	1	2	12-13/ ___	1	2	3	4	5	_____ 6 14/
_____ 15/	1	2	16-17/ ___	1	2	3	4	5	_____ 6 18/
_____ 19/	1	2	20-21/ ___	1	2	3	4	5	_____ 6 22/
_____ 23/	1	2	24-25/ ___	1	2	3	4	5	_____ 6 26/
_____ 27/	1	2	28-29/ ___	1	2	3	4	5	_____ 6 30/
_____ 31/	1	2	32-33/ ___	1	2	3	4	5	_____ 6 34/

2. What was the last year of schooling you completed?

Some high school 1   35/

Finished high school 2

Some college 3

Finished college 4

Graduate (SPECIFY):

_____ 5   36/37

IF RESPONDENT IS SINGLE, SKIP TO Q. 4.

3. What was the last year of schooling your spouse completed?

Some high school 1   38/

Finished high school 2

Some college 3

Finished college 4

Graduate (SPECIFY):

_____ 5   39-40/

4. My notes from our telephone conversation indicate that you are currently employed as a (REFER TO FRONT OF QUESTIONNAIRE.) Are my notes correct?

Yes. 1   41/

No 2

IF "NO", FIND OUT PRESENT OCCUPATION, CONTINUE WITH INTERVIEW BUT REPORT CHANGE TO SUPERVISOR. NOTE OCCUPATION ON FRONT PAGE.

IF RESPONDENT IS SINGLE, SKIP TO Q. 6

5. What is your spouse's occupation?

_____ 42-43/
(Spouse's Occupation)

IF RESPONDENT IS A HOUSEWIFE, CHECK HUSBAND'S OCCUPATION LISTED ON THE FRONT PAGE. IF DIFFERENT, CONTINUE WITH INTERVIEW BUT REPORT CHANGE TO SUPERVISOR.

---

6. What is or was your father's occupation?

_____ 44-45/
(Father's Occupation)

---

7. What is or was your mother's occupation?

_____ 46-47/
(Mother's occupation)

IF RESPONDENT IS A HOUSEWIFE, SKIP TO Q. 48.

8. Now I'd like to ask you some questions about your job. How long have you held your present job?

_____ 48-49/
(Time in Months/Years) 50-51/

---

9. What job did you have before this one?

_____ 52-53/
(Job Title)

---

10. How long did you have that job?

_____ 54-55/
(Time in Months/Years) 56-57/

216

11. Since your marriage, have you always worked?

                              Yes (SKIP TO Q. 12) 1   58/
                              No (ASK Q. 11a) 2

    11a. When did you interrupt working?

         From 19__ 59-60/   From 19__ 63-64/   From 19 __ 67-68/
         To   19__ 61/62/   To   19__ 65-66/   To   19 __ 69-70/

CARD 2

12. If you won the lottery next year, would you continue working?   5-6/02
     (READ LIST.)

                              Definitely 1
                                                                  7/
                              Probably 2
                              Might or might not 3
                              Probably not 4
                              Definitely not 5

---

13. Would you be working now if you did not need the money? (READ LIST.)

                              Definitely 1
                                                                  8/
                              Probably 2
                              Might or might not 3
                              Probably not 4
                              Definitely not 5

---

14. Think for a second about the last two days at work (yesterday and today).
    Which of the following emotions did you feel at any time during the last
    two days while at work? Please look at this card and tell me the number
    beside each word that applies.

1.	Angry	2	19.	Guilty	1
2.	Annoyed	1	20.	Happy	1
3.	Anxious	1	21.	Hating	1
4.	Ashamed	1	22.	Hopeful.	1
5.	Bitter	2	23.	Indignant.	1
6.	Bored	1	24.	Infuriated	2
7.	Depressed	1	25.	Joyous	1
8.	Deprived	3	26.	Lonely	1
9.	Discouraged	1	27.	Loving	1
10.	Disgusted	1	28.	Proud	1
11.	Dislike	1	29.	Relieved	1
12.	Dissatisfied	1	30.	Remorseful	1
13.	Distressed	1	31.	Resentful	3
14.	Elated	1	32.	Sad	1
15.	Excited	1	33.	Satisfied.	1
16.	Fearful	1	34.	Self-Confident	1
17.	Frustrated	1	35.	Trusting	1
18.	Grateful	-2	36.	Unhappy	1
			37.	Upset	1
			38.	Worried	1

15. What are the things about your work that you find especially gratifying
    or rewarding? (<u>PROBE</u>: What makes you feel really good?)

_____ 47-48/

_____ 49-50/

_____ 51-52/

_____ 53-54/

_____ 55-56/

16. What are the things about your work that you find especially bothersome or distressing? (PROBE: What makes you feel really bad?)

_____ 57-58/

_____ 59-60/

_____ 61-62/

_____ 63-64/

_____ 65-66/

17. Within the last year, how often have you felt that work is a gratifying experience? (READ LIST.)

Almost never or never 7   67/
Only once or twice 6
About once a month 5
About once a week 4
A couple of times a week 3
Every day 2
Almost all the time 1

18. Ideally, what are the one or two things you want most from a job?

_____ 68-69/

_____ 70-71/

19. How close does your present job come to actually giving you these things? (READ LIST.)

Very close 1   72/
Somewhat close 2
Not very close 3
Not at all close 4

219

20. During the last month, how often have you felt that you wanted more from your job than you are getting from it now? (READ LIST.)   5-6/03

                    Constantly 6   7/

                    At least once each day 5

                    A couple of times a week 4

                    Once a week 3

                    Not very often 2

                    Never 1

---

21. Thinking about your job right now, and taking everything into account, how much does your job fulfill your wants? Give the job a score between zero (if it fails totally) and 10 (if it succeeds absolutely).

                                                              8-9/

    [For coding, reverse the scores] $\overline{}$ (Score)

HAND CARD B

ASK THIS QUESTION FOR EACH LISTED ASPECT.

22. Could you tell me how satisfied you feel with various aspects of your job? Which statement on this card best describes how satisfied you are with (ASPECT)?

Aspect	Very Satisfied	Somewhat Satisfied	Neither	Somewhat Dissatisfied	Very Dissatisfied	(DOES NOT APPLY)
Pay and fringe benefits	1	2	3	4	5	M 10/
Number of hours	1	2	3	4	5	M 11/
Co-workers	1	2	3	4	5	M 12/
Chances for advancement	1	2	3	4	5	M 13/
Challenge	1	2	3	4	5	M 14/
Respect and prestige. .	1	2	3	4	5	M 15/
Job security	1	2	3	4	5	M 16/
General working conditions	1	2	3	4	5	M 17/

220

23. Now, taking everything into account, how satisfied would you say you are with your present job?

        Very satisfied 1   18/
        Somewhat satisfied 2
        Neither satisfied nor dissatisfied . . 3
        Somewhat dissatisfied 4
        Very dissatisfied 5

TAKE BACK CARD B

24. In view of your training and abilities, is your present job as good as it ought to be? (READ LIST)

        Definitely 1   19/
        Probably 2
        I'm not sure 3
        Probably not 4
        Definitely not 5

HAND CARD C

25. Would you say that your pay and fringe benefits are (READ LIST):

        Better than you deserve 1   20/
        What you deserve 2
        Slightly less than you deserve . . . 3
        Much less than you deserve 4

ASK THIS QUESTION FOR EACH LISTED ASPECT.

26. How about these other aspects of your job? Which statement on this card best describes your (ASPECT)?

Aspect	Better Than I Deserve	What I Deserve	Slightly Less Than I Deserve	Much Less Than I Deserve	(DOES NOT APPLY)	
Number of hours	1	2	3	4	M	21/
Chances for advancement . .	1	2	3	4	M	22/
Challenge	1	2	3	4	M	23/
Respect and prestige. . . .	1	2	3	4	M	24/
Job security.	1	2	3	4	M	25/
General working conditions.	1	2	3	4	M	26/

221

TAKE BACK CARD C

HAND CARD D

27. Most of us have dreams and hopes about our jobs and some more realistic expectations. Could you think back now for a minute to the expectations you had when you first started working. How does your present job compare with those expectations?

(READ:) It's much better than I expected 1   27/

It's slightly better than I expected 2

It's about what I expected 3

It's slightly worse than I expected 4

It's much worse than I expected 5

(DO NOT READ:) Didn't know/don't remember 3

STILL USING CARD D, ASK THIS QUESTION FOR EACH LISTED ASPECT.

28. What about these particular aspects of your job? Which statement on this card best describes your (ASPECT)?

Aspect	Much Better	Slightly Better	About the Same	Slightly Worse	Much Worse	(DON'T KNOW)	
Pay and fringe benefits . .	1	2	3	4	5	3	28/
Number of hours	1	2	3	4	5	3	29/
Chances for advance	1	2	3	4	5	3	30/
Challenge	1	2	3	4	5	3	31/
Respect and prestige . . .	1	2	3	4	5	3	32/
Job security	1	2	3	4	5	3	33/
General working conditions.	1	2	3	4	5	3	34/

TAKE BACK CARD D

222

29. How do you feel about the kind of salary you'll be earning in the next five or so years?

Very optimistic 1	35/
Fairly optimistic 2	
Uncertain 3	
Fairly pessimistic. 4	
Very pessimistic 5	

STILL USING CARD E, ASK THIS QUESTION FOR EACH LISTED ASPECT.

30. What about these other aspects of your job? Which statement on this card best describes how you feel about the next five years in terms of your (ASPECT)?

Aspect	Very Optimistic	Fairly Optimistic	Uncertain	Fairly Pessimistic	Very Pessimistic	(DOES NOT APPLY)	
Number of hours .	1	2	3	4	5	M	36/
Chances for advancement . . .	1	2	3	4	5	M	37/
Challenge	1	2	3	4	5	M	38/
Respect and prestige.	1	2	3	4	5	M	39/
Job security. . .	1	2	3	4	5	M	40/
General working conditions. . . .	1	2	3	4	5	M	41/

223

31. Are there any things you really want from your present job that you feel you will never get?

$$\text{Yes (\underline{ASK Q. 31a \& 32})} \cdot \cdot \cdot \cdot 2$$
$$\text{No (\underline{SKIP TO Q. 33})} \cdot \cdot \cdot \cdot \cdot 1$$

42/

    31a. What specifically?

    _____ 43-44/

    _____ 45-46/

    _____ 47-48/

32. How does that make you feel?

    _____ 49-50/

    _____ 51-52/

    _____ 53-54/

33. In trying to decide how good your own job is, do you ever compare yourself with anyone else?

$$\text{Yes (\underline{ASK Q. 33a})} \cdot \cdot \cdot \cdot \cdot 2$$
$$\text{No (\underline{SKIP TO Q. 33b})} \cdot \cdot \cdot \cdot 1$$

55/

ASK EITHER Q. 33a OR Q. 33b, ACCORDING TO RESPONSE IN Q. 33 ABOVE. RECORD ANSWER IN GRID BELOW Q. 33e.

    33a. (IF 'YES' IN Q. 33): Could you name three people you compare yourself to? (SKIP TO Q. 33c):

    33b. (IF 'NO' IN Q. 33): Could you right now think of three people who work at the same place as you?

    33c. Would you say that you are better off, worse off, or about the same as (NAME)? (READ AND RECORD FOR EACH NAME GIVEN)

    33d. (IF YES IN Q. 33): Does (NAME) work at the same place you do? (READ AND RECORD FOR EACH NAME GIVEN).

    33e. (READ IF NECESSARY): Is (NAME) a man or woman? (READ AND RECORD FOR EACH NAME GIVEN)

Q. 33a/33b	Q. 33c			Q. 33d Work at Same Place		Q. 33e	
Name	Better Off	Worse Off	Same	Yes	No	M	F
1. _____	1	3	2	1	2	1	2
2. _____	1	3	2	1	2	1	2
3. _____	1	3	2	1	2	1	2

LIST NO MORE THAN 3

ASK Q. 34 AN Q. 35 IN ORDER FOR EACH LISTED ASPECT.

34. Think for a minute about the average lawyer's job. How does your job compare with that kind of job? Using the statements on Card F, how does your job compare in terms of (ASPECT)?

35. Now think about the average factory worker's job. How does your job compare with that kind of job in terms of (ASPECT)?

Aspect	Question 34 - Professional						Question 35 - Blue Collar					
	Much Better	Slightly Better	Same	Slightly Worse	Much Worse	(DOES NOT APPLY)	Much Better	Slightly Better	Same	Slightly Worse	Much Worse	(DOES NOT APPLY)
Pay and fringe benefits	1	2	3	4	5	M	1	2	3	4	5	M
Number of hours	1	2	3	4	5	M	1	2	3	4	5	M
Chances for advancement	1	2	3	4	5	M	1	2	3	4	5	M
Challenge	1	2	3	4	5	M	1	2	3	4	5	M
Respect and prestige	1	2	3	4	5	M	1	2	3	4	5	M
Job security	1	2	3	4	5	M	1	2	3	4	5	M
General working conditions	1	2	3	4	5	M	1	2	3	4	5	M

225

SELF-ADMINISTERED SECTION A   5-6/04

(PLEASE READ ALONG WITH THE RESPONDENT): Now we have a few questions about
your work which we would like you to answer for us. Please read each question carefully, and read through all of the alternative answers before
selecting one which you feel comes closest. Please choose only one best
answer for each question, and circle the code number next to that statement.
(HAND THE QUESTIONNAIRE AND PENCIL TO THE RESPONDENT.)

36. For a person with your experience and your type of job, what would you
     say about your earnings?

             I am paid far above average 1   7/

             I am paid somewhat above average 2

             My pay is average 3

             I am paid somewhat below average 4

             I am paid far below average 5

37. If your present job is not ideal, why is this? Pick the one statement
     that comes closest to the truth.

             There are no ideal jobs 2   8-9/

             Generally, economic conditions are poor 2

             It takes time to get a good job 2

             I've been unlucky 2

             I lack the right training 1

             I lack the right connections 2

             I have not tried to get an ideal job 1

             My employer makes my job difficult 2

             My co-workers make my job difficult 2

             Doesn't apply to me: My job is ideal 2

38. Please think of the little things that have gone wrong within the last
     week. Why did these things go wrong? Was it because of mistakes you
     made or because of things beyond your control?

             Entirely due to things beyond my control 5   10/

             Almost always due to things beyond my control . . . 4

             Usually due to things beyond my control 3

             Hardly ever due to things beyond my control 2

             Never due to things beyond my control 1

             Doesn't apply to me: Nothing went wrong . . . . . M

39. What about the big things that go wrong, during the course of a month
    or a year? To what extent are you responsible for big problems at work?

      I am almost never responsible 6   11/

      I am hardly ever responsible 5

      I am sometimes responsible 4

      I am responsible about half the time 3

      I am usually responsible 2

      I am always responsible 1

      Doesn't apply to me: Nothing went wrong . . . . . . M

40. When something does go wrong at work, no matter who is to blame, is it
    generally within your control to fix things?

      Almost always within my control 1   12/

      Sometimes within my control 2

      Rarely within my control 3

      Usually beyond my control 4

      Almost always beyond my control 5

41. Did you select your present job as a matter of choice or not?

      It was entirely my own choice 1   13/

      It was mostly my own choice 2

      It was not really my own choice 3

      It was not at all my own choice 4

PLEASE HAND THE QUESTIONNAIRE BACK TO THE INTERVIEWER AFTER THESE QUESTIONS
ARE COMPLETED.

227

ASK THIS QUESTION FOR EACH AREA (a - d) LISTED BELOW.

42. Frustrating incidents happen more or less frequently in people's jobs. Please tell me how often you feel angry, frustrated or bitter about the way things go at work. Think about things involving: (READ EACH AREA.)

AREA

How often:	a) Your Own Immediate Work Group		b) Your Organization		c) Outside Organizations or Individuals	
At least 2-3 times a <u>day</u>	8	14/	8	15/	8	16/
Once a <u>day</u>	7		7		7	
At least 2-3 times a <u>week</u>.	6		6		6	
Once a <u>week</u>	5		5		5	
At least 2-3 times a <u>month</u>	4		4		4	
Once a <u>month</u>	3		3		3	
At least 2-3 times a <u>year</u>	2		2		2	
Once a <u>year</u> or less	1		1		1	
(DOES NOT APPLY)	M		M		M	

228

43. Within this last year, how often have you felt some sense of grievance
    concerning each of these aspects of your job: (READ EACH LISTED ASPECT)

Aspect	Always	Frequently	Occa-sionally	Seldom	Never	(DOES NOT APPLY)	
Pay and fringe benefits	5	4	3	2	1	M	17/
Number of hours . . .	5	4	3	2	1	M	18/
Chances for advancement	5	4	3	2	1	M	19/
Challenge	5	4	3	2	1	M	20/
Respect and prestige.	5	4	3	2	1	M	21/
Job security.	5	4	3	2	1	M	22/
General working conditions	5	4	3	2	1	M	23/

HAND CARD H

(PLEASE READ ALONG WITH THE RESPONDENT.) Once again, I would like you to
read each question and select the one best answer for each as you did before.
Please remember to circle the code number next to each answer you select.
(HAND QUESTIONNAIRE TO RESPONDENT.)

44. When you think of things that are wrong with your job, do you get
   angry, resentful, or bitter toward anyone in particular or do you get
   mad at things in general?

   It's always just things in general 1   24/

   Usually things in general. 2

   Half and half .3

   Usually some person or people 4

   Always some person or people 5

45. Within the last month, how often has your boss let you down?

   Very frequently 5   25/

   Fairly often .4

   Sometimes 3

   Hardly ever 2

   Never 1

46a. How about your co-workers? Within the last month have any co-workers
   let you down?

   Very frequently 5   26/

   Fairly often .4

   Sometimes 3

   Hardly ever 2

   Never 1

   Doesn't apply
   I work alone. . . . .   M

46b. How about other people who you come in contact with on your job?
   Within the last month have other people let you down?

   Very frequently 5   27/

   Fairly often .4

   Sometimes 3

   Hardly ever 2

   Never 1

47a. Do you see others around you who are getting things from their jobs
   that they didn't deserve?

   Yes (CONTINUE TO Q. 47b). 1   28/

   No   (SKIP TO Q. 48) 2

47b. If you said 'Yes' to the last question, please indicate how you feel about this?

                    I resent them 1   29/

                    I resent the situation 2

                    I am glad for them 3

                    I feel indifferent (nothing) 4

                    I don't think about it 5

PLEASE HAND THE QUESTIONNAIRE BACK TO THE INTERVIEWER.

TO HOUSEWIVES: "First, I'd like to ask you ... "

TO ALL OTHERS: "I've asked you a lot of questions about your own job.
Now I'd like to ask you ... "

Your opinions about women in the paid labor force. What I'm
really interested in are your own thoughts and feelings, not
factual information.

48. First, I'd like to ask: Have you ever thought about the employment
situation of women in general? (READ LIST)

Often 1   30/

Sometimes 2

Once or twice 3

Never. 4

---

49. How much interest would you say that you have in how women as a whole
are getting along in this country? (READ LIST)

A great deal of interest 1   31/

Some interest. 2

A little interest. 3

Not too much 4

None 5

ASK THIS QUESTION FOR EACH LISTED ASPECT

50. Thinking of women's employment situation right now, which of the statements on this card to you feel indicates how your situation compares with that of women in general, in terms of (ASPECT)?

Aspect	Much Better	Slightly Better	Same	Slightly Worse	Much Worse	(DOES NOT APPLY)	
Pay and fringe benefits . .	1	2	3	4	5	M	32/
Number of hours . .	1	2	3	4	5	M	33/
Chances for advancement	1	2	3	4	5	M	34/
Challenge	1	2	3	4	5	M	35/
Respect and prestige	1	2	3	4	5	M	36/
Job security. . . .	1	2	3	4	5	M	37/
General working conditions.	1	2	3	4	5	M	38/

TAKE BACK CARD I

---

51. Which of the following two statements do you agree with more: (READ)

Only a few women today have the kinds of jobs they want. . . 2   39/

Most women today have the kinds of jobs they want. 1

---

52. In your opinion, what proportion of full time housewives would like to have a paying job? (READ LIST)

Most of them 1   40/

A good number. 2

Some of them 3

A few. 4

None 5

ASK THIS QUESTION FOR EACH LISTED ASPECT.

53. In your opinion, does the "average" American working woman get what she wants from a job, in terms of (ASPECT)?

Aspect	Definitely	Probably	Probably Not	Definitely Not	(DON'T KNOW)	
Pay and fringe benefits . . .	1	2	4	5	3	41/
Number of hours . . .	1	2	4	5	3	42/
Chances for advancement	1	2	4	5	3	43/
Challenge	1	2	4	5	3	44/
Respect and prestige	1	2	4	5	3	45/
Job security.	1	2	4	5	3	46/
General working conditions.	1	2	4	5	3	47/

54. Taking everything into account, what proportion of American women get what they want from a job (READ LIST)?

```
                          Almost all . . . . . . . . .  1      48/
                          Most . . . . . . . . . . . .  2
                          Some . . . . . . . . . . . .  3
                          A few. . . . . . . . . . . .  4
                          None . . . . . . . . . . . .  5
```

234

ASK THIS QUESTION FOR EACH LISTED ASPECT.

55. What about deserving? Using the statements on this card, tell me which one best describes whether or not working women in general get what they deserve in terms of (ASPECT)?

Aspect	Much More	Slightly More	About Right	Slightly Less	Much Less	(DON'T KNOW)	
Pay and fringe benefits . . .	1	2	3	4	5	3	49/
Number of hours . . .	1	2	3	4	5	3	50/
Chances for advancement	1	2	3	4	5	3	51/
Challenge	1	2	3	4	5	3	52/
Respect and prestige	1	2	3	4	5	3	53/
Job security.	1	2	3	4	5	3	54/
General working conditions.	1	2	3	4	5	3	55/

TAKE BACK CARD K

56. All in all, do you think that the employment situation of women in America is as good as it ought to be? (READ LIST)

Definitely yes 1   56/

Probably yes 2

Probably not 4

Definitely not 5

(DO NOT READ:) DON'T KNOW 3

57. Now, think back to 1970 or 1971. At that time, did you think that women would make as many gains as they have made, or did you think more gains, or fewer gains would be made?

READS:	As many as they have 2	57/
	Fewer gains 1	
	More gains. 3	
DO NOT READ:	I DON'T REMEMBER WHAT I THOUGHT 2	
	I NEVER THOUGHT ABOUT IT IN 1970. . . . 2	

HAND CARD L

ASK THIS QUESTION FOR EACH LISTED ASPECT

58. What about these specific aspects of working? Which statement on this card best describes (ASPECT) for women today, compared to what you expected in 1970?

Aspect	Much Better	Slightly Better	About Right	Slightly Worse	Much Worse	(DON'T KNOW)	
Pay and fringe benefits . . . 1		2	3	4	5	3	58/
Number of hours . . . 1		2	3	4	5	3	59/
Chances for advancement 1		2	3	4	5	3	60/
Challenge 1		2	3	4	5	3	61/
Respect and prestige. 1		2	3	4	5	3	62/
Job security. 1		2	3	4	5	3	63/
General working conditions. 1		2	3	4	5	3	64/

TAKE BACK CARD L

59. What do you feel about the kinds of salaries that women will be earning
    in the next five or so years?

                        I'm very optimistic 1   65/
                        I'm fairly optimistic 2
                        I'm uncertain 3
                        I'm fairly pessimistic. 4
                        I'm very pessimistic. 5

STILL USING CARD M, ASK THIS QUESTION FOR EACH LISTED ASPECT

60. What about these specific aspects of working? Which statement on this
    card best describes (ASPECT) for women in the next five or so years?

Aspect	Very Optimistic	Fairly Optimistic	Uncertain	Fairly Pessimistic	Very Pessimistic	
Number of hours . . .	1	2	3	4	5	66/
Chances for advancement	1	2	3	4	5	67/
Challenge	1	2	3	4	5	68/
Respect and prestige.	1	2	3	4	5	69/
Job security.	1	2	3	4	5	70/
General working conditions.	1	2	3	4	5	71/

61. In general, then which one statement seems <u>most</u> true: (READ ALL FOUR
CHOICES)

The employment situation for women will be good by 1985 . . . 1   7/

Things probably won't improve much by 1985 3

Things will probably improve slightly by 1985 2

Things are already good today 1

62. Would you say that men and women want the same or different things
from a job?

Same (<u>SKIP TO Q. 63</u>) 1   8/

Different (<u>ASK Q. 62a</u>) 2

62a. What's the difference?

_____   9-10/

_____   11-12/

<u>IF RESPONDENT IS A HOUSEWIFE, SKIP TO Q. 64</u>

63. Which statement do you think best describes how men and women are
generally paid in your line of work (<u>READ LIST</u>).

Men are much better paid. 5   13/

Men are slightly better paid. 4

They are paid the same. 3

Women are slightly better paid. 2

Women are much better paid. 1

There are no men (women) in my line of work . M

238

64. Generally speaking, which statement do you think describes how women are paid in comparison to men (in other lines of work)? (READ LIST).

Men are much better paid. 5   14/

Men are slightly better paid. 4

They are paid the same. 3

Women are slightly better paid. 2

Women are much better paid. 1

| HAND CARD N |

ASK THIS QUESTION FOR EACH LISTED ASPECT

65. Imagine a woman and a man with equal job training and experience. Which one would you expect to be better off in terms of (ASPECT)?

Aspect	Woman Much Better Off	Woman Slightly Better Off	Same	Man Slightly Better Off	Man Much Better Off	(DON'T KNOW)	
Pay and fringe benefits. .	1	2	3	4	5	3	15/
Number of hours. .	1	2	3	4	5	3	16/
Chances for advancement. . . .	1	2	3	4	5	3	17/
Challenge	1	2	3	4˙	5	3	18/
Respect and prestige.	1	2	3	4	5	3	19/
Job security . . .	1	2	3	4	5	3	20/
General working conditions	1	2	3	4	5	3	21/

| TAKE BACK CARD N |

239

66. I wonder if you could make a guess about the salaries women earn. What
    would you say is the average yearly salary of white collar women who
    work full time? What about blue collar women? White collar men? Blue
    collar men? (RECORD ESTIMATED SALARY FOR EACH)

                                    White collar women: $_____   22-27/

                                    Blue collar women: $_____   28-33/

                                    White collar men: $_____   34-39/

                                    Blue collar men: $_____   40-45/

---

67. Which of the following statements do you agree with more? (READ
    STATEMENTS

    a. If a woman can't get a good job, it's
       almost always her own fault. 1   46/

    b. Many women can't get good jobs through
       no fault of their own. 2

---

68. Which of these? (READ STATEMENTS)

    a. If a woman doesn't get the pay she deserves it's
       usually because she is too timid to ask for a raise. 1   47/

    b. Many women are underpaid because of the system 2

---

69. Which of these? (READ STATEMENTS)

    a. When a woman does not advance in her job,
       she is usually the one to blame. 1   48/

    b. When a woman does not advance in her job,
       some man is usually to blame 2

    c. Many women do not advance, but no one person
       is to blame. 2

---

70. Which of these? (READ STATEMENTS)

    a. Women today are given economic advantages
       over men (ASK Q. 71) 1   49/

    b. Men today are given economic advantages
       over women (ASK Q. 71) 3

    c. Neither men nor women are given economic
       advantages (SKIP TO Q. 72) 2

240

IF STATEMENT a. OR b.SELECTED IN Q. 70, ASK:

71. Does this make you feel resentful? (READ LIST)

Definitely 1   50/

Probably 2

Uncertain. 3

Probably not 4

Definitely not 5

HAND CARD O

ASK THIS QUESTION FOR EACH LISTED ASPECT.

72. Would you say that you feel bitter or resentful about any of the following aspects of women's employment situation? In particular, are you bitter or resentful about (ASPECT)?

Aspect	Very	Somewhat	A little	Not Certain	Not Really	Not At All	
Pay and fringe benefits. . .	6	5	4	3	2	1	51/
Number of hours. . .	6	5	4	3	2	1	52/
Chances for Advancement.	6	5	4	3	2	1	53/
Challenge	6	5	4	3	2	1	54/
Respect and prestige.	6	5	4	3	2	1	55/
Job security	6	5	4	3	2	1	56/
General working conditions	6	5	4	3	2	1	57/

TAKE BACK CARD O

241

73. All in all, how satisfied do you feel about the work situation for women in America today? (READ LIST)

Very satisfied (SKIP TO Q. 75)   1   58/
Somewhat satisfied   2
Somewhat dissatisfied.   3
Very dissatisfied.   4

74. How much do you think you--alone or with others--can do to change things for the better? (READ LIST)

A very great deal.   1   59/
A great deal   2
A bit.   3
Not too much   4
Nothing.   5

75. When you do think of things that are wrong for women, do you get angry, resentful, or bitter toward anyone in particular or do you get mad at things in general? (READ LIST)

It's always things in general . . .   2   60/
Half and half   2
Usually, some person or people. . .   2
Always some person or people. . . .   2
I don't get angry   1

ASK WOMEN ONLY. IF MALE, SKIP TO Q. 77

76. Comparing yourself with women who have jobs outside the home, would you say that you are better off than they are, worse off than they are, or about the same?

I'm better off   1   61/
I'm worse off.   2
In some ways better, in
   some way worse   3
We're about the same   4
(DO NOT READ) Don't know   5

242

76a. Comparing yourself with women who <u>don't have</u> jobs outside
the home, would you say that you are better off than they
are, worse off than they are, or about the same?

I'm better off 1

I'm worse off. 2

In some ways better, in
some ways worse. 3

We're about the same 4

(<u>DO NOT READ</u>) Don't know . . . . M

Now, I'd like to ask you some questions about your family life.

HAND CARD P

77. Think for a second about the last two days at home. Which of these
    emotions did you feel at any time during the last two days while at
    home? Please look at this card and tell me the number beside each
    word that applies.

1. Angry	2		20. Happy	1
2. Annoyed	1		21. Hating	1
3. Anxious	1		22. Hopeful	1
4. Ashamed	1		23. Indignant	1
5. Bitter	2		24. Infuriated	2
6. Bored	1		25. Joyous	1
7. Depressed	1		26. Lonely	1
8. Deprived	3		27. Loving	1
9. Discouraged	1		28. Proud	1
10. Disgusted	1		29. Relieved	1
11. Dislike	1		30. Remorseful	1
12. Dissatisfied	1		31. Resentful	3
13. Distressed	1		32. Sad	1
14. Elated	1		33. Satisfied	1
15. Excited	1		34. Self-Confident	1
16. Fearful	1		35. Trusting	1
17. Frustrated	1		36. Unhappy	1
18. Grateful	-2		37. Upset	1
19. Guilty	1		38. Worried	1

TAKE BACK CARD P

---

78. What are the aspects of your home life that you find especially gratifying or rewarding?

_____   45-46/
                                                     47-48/

_____   49-50/
                                                     51-52/

_____   53-54/

79. What are the things about your home life that you find especially
bothersome or distressing?

_____   55-56/
                                                     57-58/

_____   59-60
                                                     61-62/

_____   63-64/

80. Within the last year, how often have you felt really good about the
way things are going at home? (READ LIST)

                    Almost never or never. 6   65/
                    Only once or twice 5
                    About once a month 4
                    About once a week. 3
                    Every day. 2
                    Almost all the time. 1

245

IF RESPONDENT LIVES ALONE, SKIP TO Q. 82

HAND CARD Q

ASK THIS QUESTION FOR EACH LISTED ASPECT.

81. Could you tell me how satisfied you feel with various aspects of your home life? What about (ASPECTS)?

Aspect	Very Satisfied	Somewhat Saftisfied	Neither	Somewhat Dissatisfied	Very Dissatisfied	(Does Not Apply)	
Amount of work around the house	1	2	3	4	5	M	66/
Way tasks get divided . . .	1	2	3	4	5	M	67/
Way decisions get made.	1	2	3	4	5	M	68/
Relations with spouse . . .	1	2	3	4	5	M	69/
Relations with children . .	1	2	3	4	5	M	70/
Relations with other family members. .	1	2	3	4	5	M	71/
Free time for yourself. . .	1	2	3	4	5	M	72/
General level of comfort. . . .	1	2	3	4	5	M	73/

STILL USING CARD Q

82. Now, taking everything into account how would you say you feel about your family life?

Very satisfied 1   74/

Somewhat satisfied 2

Neither satisfied
nor dissatisfied 3

Somewhat dissatisfied. 4

Very dissatisfied. 5

TAKE BACK CARD Q

246

ASK THIS QUESTION FOR EACH LISTED ASPECT.

83. Frustrating incidents happen more or less frequently in the course of family life. How many times within the last week did something happen which made you feel angry, resentful, or bothered? Please think about things which have to do with (ASPECT)

Aspect	Rarely	Sometimes	Occasionally	Most of the Time	Does Not Apply
Work inside the house (e.g. cleaning)	1	2	3	4	M 7/
Work outside the house (e.g. shopping)	1	2	3	4	M 8/
Dealings with service people (e.g. repairmen).	1	2	3	4	M 9/
Financial issues. . . .	1	2	3	4	M 10/

IF RESPONDENT LIVES ALONE, SKIP TO Q. 84

Aspect	Rarely	Sometimes	Occasionally	Most of the Time	Does Not Apply
Relations with spouse	1	2	3	4	M 11/
Relations with children.	1	2	3	4	M 12/
Relations with other family members	1	2	3	4	M 13/

84. Could you tell me please how many hours a month, on average, you spend on:

Political activities: _____   14-16/
(hours per month)

Religious activities: _____   17-19/
(hours per month)

Other volunteer
activities: _____   20-22/
(hours per month)

247

Now I'd like to ask you about some specific parts of your family life. I'll be asking you about housework [about child care] [and about your marriage.] Let's consider that housework includes general household maintenance, cleaning, washing, cooking, marketing, laundry, and yard work. [Housework does not include child care.]

85. Approximately how many hours do you spend each week on housework?

_____ 23-24/
(hours per week)

86. Would you like to spend less, more or is this just about right?

More 1 25/

Less L

About right 0

87. When you finished your schooling, did you expect to spend (Q. 85) hours a week on housework?

READ

Yes I did. . . . .

I thought I would spend much more. . . . . .

I thought I would spend a little more . . .

I thought I would spend a little less. . . .

I thought that I would spend a lot less. . .

DO NOT READ
I DON'T REMEMBER . . . .

I NEVER THOUGHT ABOUT IT . . . .

[Coding depends on answer to Q 86]

88. What do you expect for the next 5 or so years? Do you think that the amount of time you spend on household chores will? (READ LIST)

Certainly increase. . . . .

Probably increase . . . .

Probably remain about the same. . . . .

Probably decrease . . . .

Certainly decrease. . . . .

(DO NOT READ) Don't know. . . . .

[Coding depends on answer to Q 86]

89. Here is a list of chores. Please tell me each chore that you now do but dislike doing. (RECORD ALL THAT APPLY IN COL. Q. 89 BELOW).

IF RESPONDENT LIVES ALONE, SKIP TO Q. 92

90. Now, please look at all the chores on this list again, and tell me each chore where you do more than your fair share, that is, where you do the chore more ofter than you should. (RECORD ALL THAT APPLY IN COL. Q. 90 BELOW).

		Column Q. 89 Do and Dislike		Column Q. 90 Do Too Much	
1.	Shop for food	1	28/	1	50/
2.	Shop for clothing	1	29/	1	51/
3.	Everyday cooking	1	30/	1	52/
4.	Special cooking	1	31/	1	53/
5.	Dishwashing	1	32/	1	54/
6.	Empty garbage	1	33/	1	55/
7.	Laundry	1	34/	1	56/
8.	Wash windows	1	35/	1	57/
9.	Straighten up	1	36/	1	58/
10.	Clean floors	1	37/	1	59/
11.	Make beds	1	38/	1	60/
12.	Budget	1	39/	1	61/
13.	Pay bills	1	40/	1	62/
14.	Minor repairs	1	41/	1	63/
15.	Major repairs	1	42/	1	64/
16.	Wash car	1	43/	1	65/
17.	Cut lawn	1	44/	1	66/
18.	Take care of pets	1	45/	1	67/
(ASK FOR PARENTS ONLY)					
19.	Bathe children	1	46/	1	68/
20.	Feed children	1	47/	1	69/
21.	Discipline children	1	48/	1	70/
22.	Take care of sick children	1	49	1	71/

249

91. Taking all things into account, would you say that you do more or less work around the house than you deserve to do? (READ LIST)

Much more. 5   7/

Little more. 4

Don't know 3

Little less. 2

Much less. 1

About right. 3

92. Does housework take more time than it ought? (IF NO, SKIP TO Q. 94.)

Yes. 2   8/

No 1

93. Why is this? (READ LIST. CIRCLE ALL THAT APPLY UNDER COL. Q. 93a)

ASK Q. 93b ONLY IF TWO OR MORE REASONS CIRCLED IN Q. 93a.

93b. Which is the single most important reason? (RECORD IN COL. Q. 93)

	Column Q. 93a		Column Q. 93b	
Too many demands	o	9/	0	16/
Not enough paid help	1	10/	1	
Not enough help from other family members	1	11/	1	
Lack of organization	0	12/	0	
Other_____	1	13	1	
		14-15		

IF RESPONDENT LIVES ALONE, SKIP TO Q. 95

94. Would you say that you or someone else is mostly responsible for the way the house chores get divided? (READ LIST)

I am totally responsible . . . 1 17/

I am mostly responsible. . . . 2

I am not really responsible. . 3

I am not at all responsible. . 4

250

95. When thinking about the amount of work you do around the house, do you ever compare your situation with that of anyone else?

Yes (ASK Q. 95a) 2 18/
No (SKIP TO Q. 95b). 1

95a. (IF 'YES' IN Q. 95): Could you name three people you compare yourself to?

95b. (IF 'NO' IN Q. 95): Could you right now think of three friends or neighbors?

95c. Would you say that you are better off, worse off, or about the same as (NAME)? (READ AND RECORD FOR EACH PERSON NAMED)

95d. Is (NAME) a relative, friend, or neighbor of yours? (READ AND RECORD FOR EACH PERSON NAMED. CIRCLE ALL THAT APPLY)

95e. (ASK IF NECESSARY): Is (NAME) a man or a woman? (READ AND RECORD FOR EACH PERSON NAMED.)

| Q. 95a/95b | Q. 95c | | | Q. 95d | | | Q. 95e | |
Name	Better Off	Worse Off	Same	Rela-tive	Friend	Neigh-bor	Sex M	F
1. _____	1	3	2	1	2	3	1	2
2. _____	1	3	2	1	2	3	1	2
3. _____	1	3	2	1	2	3	1	2

(LIST UP TO 3 PEOPLE)

---

96. How many hours do all other people in your household spend on housework?

_____ 28-29/
(hours per week)

---

97. Within the last year, how often have you felt resentful about the amount of housework that you have had to do? (READ LIST)

Most of the time 6 30/
Very frequently. 5
Fairly often 4
Sometimes. 3
Rarely 2
Never. 1

REFER TO Q. 1
IF RESPONDENT DOES NOT HAVE CHILDREN LIVING AT HOME, SKIP TO Q. 108 ON
PAGE 30.

Now I'd like to ask you some questions on child care.

98.   Approximately how many hours each week do you spend on child care?

                                    _____   31/33
                                    (hours per week)

_____

99.   Would you like to spend less, more, or is this just about right?
      (READ LIST)

                          I'd like to spend a lot less 3 34/
                          I'd like to spend a little less. . . 2
                          It's just about right. 1
                          I'd like to spend a little more. . . 2
                          I'd like to spend a lot more 3

_____

IF RESPONDENT IS NOT MARRIED, SKIP TO Q. 120

100. Before you had your first child, did you expect to spend (Q. 98)
      hours a week on child care?

                    READ

                    Yes I did. . . . .
                    I thought I would spend much more. . . . . .
                    I thought I would spend a little more. . . .
                    I thought I would spend a little less. . . .
                    I thought that I would spend a lot less. . .
                    DO NOT READ
                    I DON'T REMEMBER . . . .
                    I NEVER THOUGHT ABOUT IT . . . .
      [Coding depends on answer to Q 99]

_____

101. What do you expect for the next five or so years? Will child care
      (READ LIST)?

                          Definitely increase . . . .
                          Probably increase. . . . .
                          Probably remain about the same .
                          Probably decrease. . . . .
                          Definitely decrease . . . .
                  (DO NOT READ):   DON'T KNOW . . . .
      [Coding depends on answer to Q 99]

252

102. How many hours a week does your spouse spend on child care?

_____   37-39/
(hours per week)

---

103. Do you think that you spend more or less time on child care than most of your friends do? (READ LIST)

I spend much more. 5   40/

I spend a little more. 4

It's equal 3

I spend a little less. 2

I spend much less. 1

(DO NOT READ):   DON'T KNOW 3

---

104. Would you say that the way you and your spouse divide up the child care is fair? (READ LIST)

No, my spouse does much more than (s)he ought to. . . 1   41/

No, my spouse does a little more than (s)he ought to.   2

Yes, it's fair.   3

No, I do a little more than I ought to.   4

No, I do a lot more than I ought to   5

---

105. Taking all things into account, would you say that you do more or less child care than you deserve to do? (READ LIST)

Much more. 5   42/

A little more. 4

Just the right amount. . . . 3

A little less. 2

Much less. 1

106a. Does child care take more time than it ought? (IF NO, SKIP TO Q.107.)

Yes. 2   43/

No 1

253

106b. If child care takes more time than it ought, why is this? (<u>READ</u>
<u>LIST</u>.   CIRCLE ALL THAT APPLY.)

Too many demands 0   **44/**

Not enough paid help 1

Not enough help from other
family members 1

Lack of organization 0

---

107. Within the last month, how often have you felt resentful about the
amount of child care that you have had to do? (<u>READ LIST</u>)

Most of the time 6   **45/**

Very frequently. 5

Fairly often 4

Sometimes. 3

Rarely 2

Never. 1

IF RESPONDENT IS NOT MARRIED, SKIP TO Q. 120.

254

(<u>PLEASE READ ALONG WITH THE RESPONDENT</u>): Here are some questions about
your marriage. Please read each question and all the possible answers
for that question. Then circle the code number next to the <u>one</u> answer
you feel is most appropriate. (<u>GIVE QUESTIONNAIRE AND PENCIL TO THE</u>
<u>RESPONDENT</u>.)

108. Which statement comes closest to your feelings? (<u>READ LIST</u>)

My marriage fulfills all of my wants.	1	46/
My marriage fulfills most of my wants	2	
My marriage fulfills some of my wants	3	
My marriage fulfills a few of my wants.	4	
My marriage fulfills none of my wants	5	

109. Everything considered, how happy has your marriage been for you?

Nearly perfect	1	47/
Extremely happy.	2	
Fairly happy	3	
Average in happiness	4	
Fairly unhappy	5	
Extremely unhappy	6	

110. Taking everything into account, how does your own marriage compare
with that of your friends?

Mine is much better.	1	48/
Mine is slightly better. . . .	2	
Equal.	3	
Theirs are slightly better . .	4	
Theirs are much better	5	

111. Considering the amount of effort you put into your marriage, does
it work as well as it should?

Definitely yes	1	49/
Probably yes	2	
I'm not sure	3	
Probably not	4	
Definitely not	5	

112. Does your spouse treat you as well as you deserve?

Definitely yes 1   50/

Probably yes 2

I'm not sure 3

Probably not 4

Definitely not 5

113. Before you got married, you probably had expectations about how it would be. How does your marriage compare with those expectations?

It's much better than I expected. 1   51/

It's slightly better than I expected. 2

It's what I expected. 3

It's slightly worse than I expected 4

It's much worse than I expected 5

I had no expectations 6

I don't remember what I expected. 7

114. What does the next five or so years hold in store for your marriage?

I'm very optmistic. 1   52/

I'm fairly optimistic 2

I'm uncertain 3

I'm fairly pessimistic. 4

I'm very pessimistic. 5

115. If your marriage is not perfect now, why is this?

Mostly my fault 1   53/

Mostly my spouse's fault. 2

The fault of both of us 3

Nobody's fault. 4

Doesn't apply to me--my marriage is perfect 5

256

116. When something goes wrong in your home life, no matter whose fault it is, is it generally within your control to fix things?

Almost always within my control. . 1   54/

Sometimes within my control. . . . 2

Rarely within my control 3

Usually beyond my control. 4

Almost always beyond my control. . 5

117. When things go wrong at home, do you get angry, resentful, or bitter toward anyone in particular or do you get mad at things in general?

It's always things in general. . . 1   55/

Usually things in general. 2

Half and half. 3

Usually someone or some people . . 4

Always some person or people . . . 5

118. Within the last month, how often has your spouse let you down?

Very frequently. 5   56/

Fairly often 4

Sometimes. 3

Hardly ever. 2

Never. 1

119. How about others in your household (parents, children, etc.)?

Very frequently. 5   57/

Fairly often 4

Sometimes. 3

Hardly ever. 2

Never. 1

No one else in household . . . . . M

257

Now we have just a few general questions.

120.   Some people feel that it is possible to control most of the things
        that happen to them. Others feel the opposite. Please indicate how
        much control you feel that you have. Zero means that you have abso-
        lutely no control; ten means that you have full control. Now, please
        rate how much you can influence things when these have to do with:

Your life opportunities: _____   58-59/

Your job: _____   60-61/

Your home life: _____   62-63/

National affairs: _____   64-65/

Your love life: _____   66-67/

The development of your
children: _____   68-69

Financial advancement: _____   70-71

120a.   For people who grew up when you did, how much would you say a per-
        son's chances for getting ahead in life depended on him or herself and
        how much on things beyond his or her control?

Almost entirely on the person . . . 1   72/
Mostly on the person. 2

Somewhat on the person. 3

Very little on the person 4

Not at all on the person. 5

IF YOU ARE A HOUSEWIFE, PLEASE SKIP TO Q. 121
IF YOU ARE NOT A HOUSEWIFE, PLEASE CONTINUE

120b. Thinking about your place of work, how much would you say advancement usually depends on how well a person can do a job and how much on other things?

             Almost entirely on how well a person can do a job . . 1   73/

             Mostly on how well a person can do a job. 2

             Somewhat on how well a person can do a job. 3

             Very little on how well a person can do a job 4

             Not at all on how well a person can do a job. 5

```
                                              CARD 9
                                              5-6/09
```

121. Suppose that you were in a job where you were discriminated against because of your sex.

    a. How would you feel?

    _____   . 7-9/

    _____   10-12/

    _____   13-15/

    b. What would you do?

    _____   16-18/

    _____   19-21/

    _____   22-24/

259

122. Now, below is a list of ways you might have felt or behaved. Please record how often you have felt this way during the past week, by circling the number of days you felt each of the following ways:

During the past week	Rarely (less than 1 day)	Some (1 - 2 days)	Occasionally (3 - 4 days)	Most of the Time (5 - 7 days)	
1. I was bothered by things that usually don't bother me.	1	2	3	4	25/
2. I did not feel like eating; my appetite was poor.	1	2	3	4	26/
3. I felt that I could not shake off the blues even with help from my family or friends.	1	2	3	4	27/
4. I felt that I was just as good as other people.	4	3	2	1	28/
5. I had trouble keeping my mind on what I was doing.	1	2	3	4	29/
6. I felt depressed.	1	2	3	4	30/
7. I felt that everything I did was an effort.	1	2	3	4	31/
8. I felt hopeful about the future.	4	3	2	1	32/
9. I thought my life had been a failure.	1	2	3	4	33/
10. I felt fearful.	1	2	3	4	34/
11. My sleep was restless.	1	2	3	4	35/
12. I was happy.	4	3	2	1	36/
13. I talked less than usual.	1	2	3	4	37/
14. I felt lonely.	1	2	3	4	38/
15. People were unfriendly.	1	2	3	4	39/
16. I enjoyed life.	4	3	2	1	40/
17. I had crying spells.	1	2	3	4	41/
18. I felt sad.	1	2	3	4	42/
19. I felt that people dislike me.	1	2	3	4	43/
20. I could not get "going."	1	2	3	4	44/

260

123. Approximately how much do you earn yearly?

Nothing	01	45-46/
Under 6,000	02	
6-10,000	03	
11-15,000	04	
16-20,000	05	
21-25,000	06	
26-30,000	07	
31-35,000	08	
36-40,000	09	
41-45,000	10	
46-50,000	11	
Over 50,000	12	

124. What is the approximate yearly income of your household?

Nothing	01	47-48/
Under 6,000	02	
6-10,000	03	
11-15,000	04	
16-20,000	05	
21-25,000	06	
26-30,000	07	
31-35,000	08	
36-40,000	09	
41-45,000	10	
46-50,000	11	
Over 50,000	12	

THANK YOU. PLEASE HAND THE QUESTIONNAIRE BACK TO THE INTERVIEWER NOW.

Index

Index